WIN Your Social Security Disability Case

Advance Your SSD Claim and Receive the Benefits You Deserve

WIN Your Social Security Disability Case

Advance Your SSD Claim and Receive the Benefits You Deserve

BENJAMIN H. BERKLEY
Attorney at Law

SPHINX® PUBLISHING
AN IMPRINT OF SOURCEBOOKS, INC.®
NAPERVILLE, ILLINOIS
www.SphinxLegal.com

First Edition: 2008

Published by: Sphinx® Publishing, An Imprint of Sourcebooks, Inc.®

Naperville Office
P.O. Box 4410
Naperville, Illinois 60567-4410
630-961-3900
Fax: 630-961-2168
www.sourcebooks.com
www.SphinxLegal.com

This publication is designed to provide accurate and authoritative information in regard to the subject matter covered. It is sold with the understanding that the publisher is not engaged in rendering legal, accounting, or other professional service. If legal advice or other expert assistance is required, the services of a competent professional person should be sought.
From a Declaration of Principles Jointly Adopted by a Committee of the American Bar Association and a Committee of Publishers and Associations

This product is not a substitute for legal advice.
Disclaimer required by Texas statutes.

Library of Congress Cataloging-in-Publication Data

Berkley, Benjamin.
  Win your social security disability case : advance your SSD claim and receive the benefits you deserve / by Benjamin H. Berkley.
     p. cm.
  Includes index.
  ISBN 978-1-57248-641-6 (pbk. : alk. paper) 1. Insurance, Disability--Law and legislation--United States. 2. Disability evaluation--Law and legislation--United States. 3. Social security--Law and legislation--United States. I. Title.

KF3650.B47 2008
344.7302'3--dc22
                                        2007048104

Printed and bound in the United State of America.
SB — 10 9 8 7 6 5 4 3 2 1

Dedication

To my godson Jeffrey Preston.
You have proven that the challenges that life presents are just another
road to get to your destination.

PREFACE

While writing this book, I was constantly reminded of why I chose a career in law. It was not for the fancy car that I might someday drive. Nor did I see using law as a political stepping stone. Instead, I envisioned a career in which I would be truly helping people.

When asked, most attorneys are dissatisfied with their profession. Part of this may have been a result of the long hours required. More often, it is due to the fact that an attorney is retained to unravel a problem that someone has created, and at the end of the day, although the case may be won, there is little satisfaction; the client begrudgingly pays for services of which he or she cannot see the real value.

However, in the world of Social Security Disability law, it is quite a different picture. Each day, people who are ill, sick, confused, and frustrated contact me. They do not want to be calling my office and would much prefer to be leading productive lives, but too often they have been dealt a bad hand of cards and are now facing what seems like an insurmountable battle against a system that they believed was designed to help and not hurt them.

If you are sick and disabled, you are tired of being asked how you feel. Likewise, if you had to stop working because of an injury or illness, or attempted to return to work but could not, there is nothing more frustrating than to be told to try a little harder because "there is some work out there that you can do."

As a Social Security Disability attorney, I am very proud of the work that I do. In assisting my clients in their claims for benefits, I am helping people navigate through a system that broke many years ago and whose future prognosis is very poor.

Win Your Social Security Disability Case was written to guide you through this very difficult period in your life. It will provide all the information needed to apply for benefits. If you are initially denied, it will explain the appeal process, including a hearing before a judge. In addition, it will provide all the tools necessary to develop your medical evidence, as well as strategies you can use in countering the government's argument that you are not disabled.

Win Your Social Security Disability Case provides a logical step-by-step approach to getting the benefits that you deserve. However, if your medical issues are too complex, or if you do not have the strength or stamina to continue pursuing the claim on your own, the book provides referral and resource information if you wish to consult with an attorney. Regardless, even if you do seek representation, this book will assist you in understanding the legal process. Furthermore, the book will provide hand-holding at a time when you may need a hand to hold.

Finally, *Win Your Social Security Disability Case* is a reference book. Depending on where your claim may be in the evaluation and appeal process, some of the material may not be relevant. Accordingly, the book does not have to be read cover to cover, but I am confident that you will find what you need within the pages of this book.

—Ben Berkley

CONTENTS

Assets that Have Been Invested for Your Child
Calculating the Amount of Benefits
The Representative Payee

INTRODUCTION

As a disabled person, no one needs to remind you how difficult it is to be able to perform daily activities. When you have your health, you take for granted that when you wake up in the morning you will be able to bathe, dress and feed yourself, and enjoy life. You can open the door to the refrigerator, throw a ball with your son or daughter, and rock your grandchild in your arms. Your world is pain free. But when you are disabled, what you know of daily life turns upside down. Regardless of your disability, doing the simple things is not so simple anymore.

Most claimants who apply for benefits share the following scenario.

When you were working, life was great. You felt productive. However, you stopped working because your impairment interfered with your ability to do your job, and when you tried to find less demanding work, no one would hire you with a preexisting condition because employers want people who will show up for work on time and be productive on the job.

Eventually you learned that the government has a program where people can get benefits if they are unable to work. Since your doctor said you were disabled and your employer told you that you cannot return to your previous work because of your disability, you filed an application for Social Security Disability benefits, assuming that within a few weeks you would get a check.

Stop the presses! Your first sign that this was not going to be as easy as you thought was when you were faced with filling out the initial forms. This was followed by more forms and more questions. During this process, you started talking to other people who shared their war stories with you of how difficult their experiences were in applying for benefits.

Finally, the mail arrived and there was a letter from the Social Security Administration. It was a thick envelope, which is usually an ominous indication of something not good, as good news usually is reported in thin envelopes. As you read the letter the words became blurred as your eyes focused on the paragraph that explained why the government says you are not disabled.

The following are excerpts from actual denial letters received by my clients.

"Though you complain about tightness in your chest, difficulty breathing, **and are on a waiting list for a heart transplant**, it does not appear that your condition will last for twelve months and therefore you are not disabled."

"Though you have a compression fracture of your back and had surgery, and had rods and plates inserted, and are depressed, and have pain . . . **you can still do sedentary work**."

"Though you have been **diagnosed with leukemia and are receiving chemotherapy**, your condition does not appear disabling."

"Though you have mental problems, **have attempted suicide multiple times**, and are receiving psychiatric care, you are able to follow simple directions and can perform your past work as a child care provider."

If you have received such a letter, it would be normal for you to react with anger and frustration. In fact, many clients walk into my office waving their letters, saying:

"I have paid into this system since I was 18. How can they deny me? It's my money!"

"My doctor said I can never go back to work. This can't be right!"

"No one will ever hire me!"

Or even worse:

"I am dying. I have a terminal illness. Do I have to actually die for Social Security to be convinced that I am disabled?"

Does this all seem absurd? Welcome to the world of Social Security Disability appeals. It is the land where everything is out of focus and no matter how many times you clean your glasses and rub your eyes, the picture is blurred.

How do you juggle between treating your disability and managing to get the benefits you believe you are qualified for? Even worse, if you have a terminal illness, how do you fight the biggest battle of your life and still have the energy to contend with the government? You already have enough to worry about with seeing your doctors, going for tests, and taking your prescribed medication. You also know from your doctor that stress aggravates a physical condition.

Win Your Social Security Disability Case was written to guide you through this very difficult period in your life. It will provide all the information needed, from filing your claim to effectively representing yourself at a Social Security hearing. If it becomes too difficult to navigate solo through the sea of Social Security, this book provides resource material as well as referral information in finding an attorney who specializes in Social Security Disability law. (This book is not a substitute for legal representation.) Regardless, even if you do seek representation, this book will assist you in understanding the legal process.

Finally, you cannot allow the Social Security Administration to get in your way of obtaining the benefits you deserve. Aside from all the information that is provided, the best advice I can offer is to never give up!

Part One: An Overview of Social Security Disability

Chapter 1 provides an overview of the Social Security Disability program, including why it was created, how it works, and what its goal is.

Chapter 2 explains the Social Security Administration's complicated and often confusing definition of *disability*.

Chapter 3 explains the two disability programs—*Social Security Disability Income* and *Supplemental Security Income*—and the eligibility requirements for each program.

The Social Security Administration reviews all medical impairments by applying a multistep sequential evaluation process. Chapter 4 provides an overview of the five-step evaluation for adult disabilities.

Chapter 5 provides an in-depth analysis of the third step of the sequential evaluation—does your impairment meet or equal the medical listings?

To be found disabled, it is not enough to prove that you cannot return to your last job—it must be proven that you are incapable of doing any of the work you have performed in the last fifteen years before becoming disabled. Chapter 6 analyzes this step of the sequential evaluation.

If you cannot perform any of your past work, you must still prove that there is no work that you can perform with your impairments that are a result of your disability. Chapter 7 discusses the grids and the fifth step of the sequential evaluation.

Even if you can perform some type of work, you may still have physical exertional or mental limitations that affect your ability to be productive on the job. Chapter 8 discusses when the grids do not apply.

Part Two: The Application Process and Strategies for Winning Benefits

Chapter 9 discusses how to file an initial application.

The Social Security Administration, at its expense, may decide to have you examined by its doctor. Chapter 10 explains consultative examinations.

Chapter 11 provides the informational tools necessary to develop the medical evidence of your disability.

Over 75% of cases that are filed are denied. Chapter 12 discusses the first appeal, called the Request for Reconsideration.

Unless there has been a major change in your condition, most claims are denied again at the Request for Reconsideration stage. Chapter 13 discusses the second appeal, called the Request for a Hearing.

After you request a hearing, the court will send you a letter explaining the hearing process, including whether the government will present experts to testify at your hearing. Chapter 14 explains the hearing letter and provides tips for preparation.

Chapter 15 explains how to request an on-the-record decision when you believe that the evidence is overwhelmingly in your favor.

Chapter 16 provides detailed information on how a hearing is conducted, how to answer the judge's questions, and how to question the experts who may appear at the hearing.

In most cases, it may take two years or longer before a claim is decided. Meanwhile, you may be without any income to pay your bills. Chapter 17 provides some solutions while you wait for a decision.

If you are awarded benefits, the Social Security Administration will issue an awards letter explaining your benefits and how they are calculated. Chapter 18 discusses favorable decisions and the benefits letter.

If you lose at the hearing stage, you still have further options. Chapter 19 discusses Appeals Council reviews and filing a complaint in federal court.

For most complaints, the Social Security process is very lengthy, and often you will encounter surprises along the way. Chapter 20 provides a chronology and timeline of a typical Social Security claim.

Chapter 21 illustrates four claims and provides strategies for turning an initial denial of a claim into a favorable decision.

Chapter 22 explains the process for obtaining benefits for children as well as adults with childhood disabilities.

If your case is very complicated, or you no longer wish to represent yourself, Chapter 23 provides resource information about attorney's fees and how to find an experienced attorney.

After Chapter 23 is a glossary of the acronyms most commonly used by the Social Security Administration, and a list of some commonly asked questions and answers in Social Security Disability claims.

Appendix A includes medical questionnaires to be answered by your treating doctors. These questionnaires aid in documenting and developing your medical evidence and assist the Social Security Administration in evaluating your disability.

Appendix B includes the complete listing of the grids, and Appendix C includes listings of support groups you can contact.

MEET THE SOCIAL SECURITY ADMINISTRATION

Some of you may remember the comedy team of Abbott and Costello. One of their funniest skits was called "Who's On First." It was an exchange of information where two people were talking to each other though neither knew what the other was saying. After practicing law for twenty-nine years, whenever I call a Social Security Administration (SSA) office I am reminded of this routine, as it is typical for the person I am speaking with to have no knowledge or information about the paperwork I have submitted about my client, and I often want to shout "Who's On First!" To add to the frustration, in order to communicate effectively with the SSA, you must be able to understand its language. Unfortunately, the move to speaking in plain English has not been embraced by the SSA. Granted, every profession has its own terminology, and the legal field is no exception. (Perhaps that is why the phrase *in layman's terms* was born, so that the non-attorney could understand the legal process.) However, the government has adopted and continues to reinvent a system that is filled with acronyms and form numbers, and it makes the assumption that everyone speaks that language.

To illustrate, the child of a person receiving benefits is known as an *auxiliary*. When I first came across this term, I thought auxiliary had something to do with a backup for electricity. Another example is that the place where hearings are held is known as ODAR. Why not call it the court? People applying for benefits are often confronted with acronyms that are difficult to understand and translate.

Along with a mountain of paperwork to be filled out and more hurdles to jump over than an Olympic runner would face, over 75% of those who initially apply for benefits are denied. There are several reasons for this alarmingly high rate.

- Social Security was not originally intended to insure the disabled.

When President Roosevelt originally proposed the Social Security system, its intended purpose was to provide income to persons when they retired upon reaching a certain age. It was designed to allow a worker who paid into the retirement system during his or her working years to receive income that would attempt to replace his or her income when he or she was no longer working. It was not, however, designed to provide income to persons of any age who could not work.

When the Social Security program was extended to allow benefits to workers who became disabled yet had not reached retirement age, the SSA wanted to ensure that benefits would be awarded to only those claimants who could not do any type of work as a result of their disability. Accordingly, the SSA developed a very restrictive definition of disability.

- Some claimants abuse the system.

Unfortunately, there are claimants who file for benefits who are not disabled and just do not want to work. When a client contacts my office seeking representation, we ask that client many questions before we schedule an appointment. We need to know:

- the nature of the disability;

- his or her age;

- how the disability limits his or her activities;

- why he or she believes he or she cannot work; and,

- whether he or she is seeing a doctor and whether the doctor supports the claim that the client cannot work.

Most importantly, we are evaluating how the client answers the questions so that we can judge his or her sincerity. We then decide whether to schedule a consultation. If we do, it is very rare that we will decline representation, as we know what it takes to win a case.

- Anyone can file a claim.

The SSA is keenly aware of this problem. Unfortunately, the SSA application process does not allow for those who are trying to take advantage of the system to be weeded out early on, and every case is evaluated the same way. As a result of the great numbers of claimants who file but are not qualified, the SSA is somewhat jaded (though a disability evaluator would never admit this), and takes a very conservative approach in awarding benefits.

- Depending on where you live, there is a built-in bias.

One of the factors in denying claimants is based on the state in which they live. Yes, Social Security Disability is a federal program. However, despite this, denial rates differ dramatically between the various states. In general, the southern states of the United States tend to have rates of denial that are significantly higher than the rates of denial in the northeast. No one has ever been able to put a finger on the reason why. However, few would argue with the fact that a *culture of denial* exists in many of the state agencies that perform disability determinations for the Social Security Administration (each state has at least one such agency, and usually these are called *disability determination services*).

- The SSA does not meet the claimant until the end of the process.

Time after time, when I try to reassure my clients that they will get benefits even though they have already been denied twice, I am asked, *"How can the SSA get it wrong 75% of the time only to be proven their first conclusion was incorrect?"*

The answer lies in the way cases are evaluated. From the time you make your initial application up to your Request for a Hearing before an administrative law judge, your testimony is limited to what you state on paper. The SSA has developed form after form that asks for information but does not always allow you to paint the true picture of your disability.

JOE'S STORY

Joe was 45 years old when he was brought by his brother into my office for representation. Joe had applied for benefits and was denied twice. He had never married and lived with his parents. Upon first glance, he seemed healthy and was very pleasant. Upon review, I learned that Joe graduated high school but was in the "slower classes" (his school did not have special education). He never was able to hold a job for more than a few weeks, as he had difficulty with memory. He could read but his retention was poor. Joe had no health issues and was not under medical care. When he applied, his brother stated on the application that Joe had memory problems. The SSA scheduled Joe for a consultative examination with their doctor but the examination was to determine if Joe had any physical problems and did not test his mental abilities. When we appeared at the hearing, the judge was able to question Joe about his limitations. We also had his brother and mother testify that Joe dresses slowly and does not bathe unless told to do so, and that he cannot read a newspaper and then tell you what the article said. Finally, for the first time after eighteen months of applying, the judge saw with his eyes and heard with his ears Joe's plight. Joe was awarded benefits.

In the previous example, Joe's case was hampered because the forms are limiting and ask about doctors and treatment. There is a presumption that if you are not seeking medical care, you are not disabled.

- The SSA is not a private company and does not have to answer to its shareholders.

The SSA is an agency of the federal government. Unlike a private company that needs to show a profit, the SSA does not have to answer to shareholders. Unlike General Electric, which would be out of business if every refrigerator it manufactured broke within thirty days, the SSA can continue to turn out broken products and not worry about the consequences. As a result, in the twenty-nine years that I have practiced this area of the law, I have seen the system only worsen with no foreseeable recovery in the future.

Practical Point

Aside from the reasons cited, there is light at the end of the tunnel. As discouraging as the statistic of the percentage of people who are initially denied is, the pendulum swings in the opposite direction for people who continue to apply and appeal their cases. In fact, as of 2006, more than 75% of persons who appeal and who are represented or have obtained legal assistance are approved for benefits. The message is simple: Do not give up!

Defining Disability

2

The Social Security Administration awards *disability* benefits to people who cannot work due to physical and mental problems. To qualify, you must meet a very strict definition, which includes finding that:

- you have a severe physical or mental impairment;

- the impairment results in *marked limitations*;

- these limitations prevent you from doing any substantial gainful work; and,

- the disability is expected to last or has lasted at least twelve months, or is expected to result in death.

Legally Speaking

Whether you have been made to retire by an employer based on a disability or are receiving benefits from a long-term disability insurance carrier, you are not automatically qualified to receive Social Security Disability benefits. It must still be proven that you cannot perform any other type of work, as discussed in Chapter 7.

In addition, you must also satisfy the nonmedical requirements to obtain benefits, as discussed in Chapter 3.

The SSA Definition of Disability

Part of the reason why obtaining benefits is difficult is that the Social Security Administration's definition of *disability* differs from what is often used by doctors and other fact finders to determine if you are disabled. For example, suppose that you were injured on the job and you filed a claim for workers' compensation benefits. After a hearing, a workers' compensation court rules that you can no longer work as a carpenter and finds that you are 100% disabled. With such a finding, if logic was to prevail, it would conclude that you are disabled. However, such a finding does not automatically mean that you qualify, because you may still be able to work at a desk job doing inside phone sales. As a result, if there is still work available that you can perform with your limitations, you may not be disabled according to the Social Security regulations.

Do Not Presume You Are Disabled

In preparation for their appointments, many clients bring what they presume is the information necessary to evaluate their cases. Often that includes *decisions or conclusions* of disability by other fact finders, including:

- state disability medical evaluators;

- workers' compensation judges;

- long-term disability insurance carriers;

- Veterans Administration benefits administrators;

- agreed and independent medical experts; and,

- treating doctors.

In all of these examples, although there has been a finding that you are disabled, it does not guarantee that you will be awarded Social Security Disability benefits.

SUE'S STORY

Sue had worked for a large utility company as a programmer for over twenty years. She developed severe headaches. After submitting to weeks of testing, she was diagnosed with a slow-growing but malignant brain tumor that was not operable because of its position. Other than medication to reduce the intensity of her headaches, there are not other treatments. She immediately applied for benefits through her long-term disability insurance, for which she was quickly approved. The insurance carrier required her, however, to also apply for Social Security Disability benefits. To her surprise, she was initially denied. Her denial letter stated, "Though you have been diagnosed with cancer, your condition may improve and therefore will not last for twelve months or longer or result in death."

Upon appealing her denial, we were able to prove that her diagnosis, though it might not result in death in twelve months, causes her to be fatigued and therefore does not permit her to be gainfully employed.

Whose Word Counts?

In determining whether you meet the strict definition of disability, the medical aspect of your claim is initially evaluated by your state's Department of Disability Services (DDS). (The SSA contracts with each state's office of disability services.) However, the SSA's definition of disability is not black and white. Specifically, part of the definition includes a finding that "the disability is severe, and results in marked limitations." What is severe as opposed to not severe, and how can you quantify marked limitations? Arguably, no two people have the same threshold of pain, and what is tolerable to you may be completely disabling to your

---

LEGALLY SPEAKING

The SSA has developed a five-step sequential evaluation to determine if you are disabled. This evaluation is fully discussed in Chapters 4 through 8.

---

neighbor. As a result, *many* claimants are initially denied only to have their claims approved when they are heard by a judge. Unfortunately for most, the time between filing the initial claim for benefits and having the case scheduled for a hearing may take as long as two years. Meanwhile, you may be without adequate financial resources to pay your obligations while you wait for a hearing.

Your Doctor Says You Are Disabled

When asked if his or her patient is disabled, a doctor's answer will be based on the medical symptoms that the patient exhibits. If those symptoms fit a diagnosis, and working would aggravate the condition, most doctors would conclude that the patient is disabled. However, most doctors are unfamiliar with Social Security's definition of disability. Therefore, you cannot solely rely on what your doctor says as to whether you are disabled and qualify for benefits.

Proving to the SSA that You Are Disabled

As a result of the SSA's strict definition, getting disability benefits is a challenge but not an impossibility. In fact, over 75% of cases that are initially denied benefits are approved on appeal. Proving that you are disabled requires that you:

- analyze the definition of Social Security Disability and apply that definition to your disability;

- understand how the SSA application and appeal processes work;

- learn how to develop your medical evidence;

- prove that you cannot work at your previous job nor at any other job;

- learn how to present your case before an administrative law judge; and, most importantly,

- remain calm and not give up.

WHO IS ELIGIBLE TO FILE? | 3

The federal government provides disability benefits through two programs collectively referred to as *Social Security Disability benefits*.

The *Social Security Disability Insurance* (SSDI) benefits program, authorized under Title II of the *Social Security Act*, provides benefits to disabled workers, dependents, and surviving spouses.

The *Supplemental Security Income* (SSI) program, authorized under Title XVI of the *Social Security Act*, provides benefits to disabled individuals whose income and assets fall below a specified level.

If you are disabled and cannot work, you may apply for Social Security Disability benefits under either program. The criteria for determining whether you meet the medical requirements is the same for either program. Under both programs, a person is disabled if he or she cannot "engage in any substantial gainful activity by reason of a medically determinable physical or mental impairment which can be expected to result in death or has lasted or can be expected to last for a continuous period of not less than 12 months."

To meet this definition, SSDI or SSI applicants must have a "physical or mental impairment[s] of such severity that they are not only unable to do their previous work but cannot, considering their age, education, and work experience, engage in any other type of substantial gainful work existing in the national economy."

Social Security Disability Income (SSDI)

To be eligible for Social Security Disability Income (SSDI) (sometimes called Title 2 claims), you must have worked and had wages withheld that were paid into the Social Security system. In addition, in order to receive SSDI, you must have earned enough work credits prior to becoming disabled.

Social Security Disability–Worker's Insured Status

The Social Security program for workers functions like an insurance plan. There are requirements that a claimant for disability insurance must meet. The claimant must have:

- contributed to the program (paid Social Security taxes) over a sufficiently long period to be *fully insured;* and,

- contributed to the program recently enough to have *disability insured status.*

In short, a worker must have paid Social Security taxes in order to be "insured," just like he or she would have to pay the premiums for a private insurance policy. After the claimant stops working (and stops paying Social Security taxes), there will come a time when his or her insured status will lapse, just like with a private insurance policy.

Contributions are counted in *quarters of coverage* (QC), with minimum earnings requirements that go up every year since 1978. Before 1978 a worker generally could earn only one QC if he or she worked in only one *calendar quarter* of the year. (A calendar quarter is one of the following three-month periods: January through March, April through June, July through September, or October through December.) Before 1978 a worker needed to earn only $50 in wages in a calendar quarter to count as a quarter of coverage. Thus, to evaluate how many QCs a worker earned prior to 1978, you need to know how much a worker earned and during what months of the year he or she earned it.

Beginning in 1978, an individual with sufficient earnings in one calendar quarter could earn QCs for the entire year, up to a total of four QCs for a calendar year. Thus, beginning in 1978, you only need to consider the total annual earnings and compare them to the minimum earnings for a quarter of coverage. For example, in 1990 minimum earnings for a QC were $520. A claimant who earned $2,080 or more in wages in 1990 was credited with four QCs, no matter when he or she earned the money during 1990.

To be fully insured, as a rule, a claimant must have one QC for every calendar year after the year in which he or she turned 21, up to the calendar year before he or she became disabled. Those claimants who turned 21 in 1950 or earlier only need to have one QC for every year after 1950.

The rule for disability insured status for those over 31 years old is that they must have twenty quarters of coverage out of the forty calendar quarters before they become disabled. Significant work in five years out of the last ten years usually satisfies this requirement. For a claimant with a steady work record, insured status will lapse about five years after he or she stops working. To receive any Social Security Disability benefits, such a claimant will have to prove that he or she was disabled before his or her *last date insured*.

Calculating Work Credits

In order to qualify to receive SSDI, you must have earned enough work credits prior to the point at which you became disabled. The number of work credits required to qualify depends on your age when you became disabled. For every three months of work, you earn one work credit.

The formula to determine work credits is as follows.

- If you are disabled before age 24:

  At least six credits must have been earned in the three-year period prior to the date that you claim you became disabled.

- If you are disabled between age 24 and 31:

At least one-half of the work credits available to be earned had to be earned between age 21 and the date that you claim you became disabled. For example, if your disability began at age 25, you would need to have earned eight credits, as that represents one-half of a maximum of 16 credits that could have been earned between ages 21 and 25.

- If you are disabled after age 31, the required credits are calculated as follows:

At age 31 through 42: 20 credits

At age 44: 22 credits

At age 46: 24 credits

At age 48: 26 credits

At age 50: 28 credits

At age 52: 30 credits

At age 54: 32 credits

At age 56: 34 credits

At age 58: 36 credits

At age 60: 38 credits

At age 62 or older: 40 credits

Twenty Credits Earned in Last Ten Years

In addition to the total number of credits you must have earned, twenty of the work credits must have been earned within the ten years preceding the date that you became disabled.

As an example, if a claimant was born after 1929 and becomes disabled at age 46, he or she would need 24 quarters. However, even if he or she worked continuously since he or she was 18, but did not work from age 36 to 46, he or she is not qualified to receive SSDI, because even though he or she has seventy-two earned work credits (eighteen years times four quarters in a year equals seventy-two credits), he or she has not earned twenty of those quarters in the last ten years.

Accordingly, regardless of how severe your disability is, you do not qualify for Social Security Disability income. The only other disability program that you may qualify for is Supplemental Security Income (SSI). However, to qualify, you must have assets less than $2,000 ($3,000 for married couples) and not have a monthly income in excess of what your state has determined as the maximum allowable income. For a complete discussion of SSI requirements, see page 21.

RUBIN'S STORY

Rubin was 58 years old when he was diagnosed with Parkinson's disease. He had been a house painter for the past twenty years. On all of his jobs, his customers paid him by check or cash. However, he did not report all of his income. Furthermore, he never withheld Social Security taxes. As a result, though he had earned work credits from the time he began working at age 18 to age 38, there were no credits reported for the past 20 years. Therefore, the SSA was correct in denying him benefits for SSDI. Furthermore, because his wife's income was in excess of their state limit for SSI, he did not qualify for that program either.

Practical Point

You may obtain a form to request a copy of your Social Security statement by contacting the SSA at 800–772–1213 or applying online at **www.socialsecurity. gov**. Form SSA-7004 is reproduced on page 20. Upon completion of this form, mail your request to:

Social Security Administration
Wilkes Barre Data Operations Center
P.O. Box 7004
Wilkes Barre, PA 18767

The Social Security Statement

Once a year, the SSA mails you a Social Security statement, which includes reportable earnings for each year that you have worked. The statement also indicates how much you will receive if you retired from working at age 65 and how much your monthly benefit would be today if you were to become disabled. Prior to filing your initial application for benefits, you should review this statement for accuracy. It is very possible that a tax year of earnings was not reported correctly. If this has occurred, and you do not have enough work credits, you will be denied regardless of your medical condition. Furthermore, the burden is on you to provide the Internal Revenue Service (IRS) with corrected information so that your statement can be updated.

SOCIAL SECURITY ADMINISTRATION

Request for *Social Security Statement*

Within four to six weeks after you return this form, we will send you:

- a record of your earnings history;
- an estimate of how much you have paid in Social Security taxes; and
- estimates of benefits you (and your family) may be eligible for now and in the future.

Please note: If you have been receiving a *Social Security Statement* each year about three months before your birthday, this request will stop your next scheduled mailing. You will not receive a scheduled *Statement* until the following year.

We hope you will find the *Statement* useful in planning your financial future. Remember, Social Security is more than a program for retired people. It helps people of all ages in many ways. For example, it can help support your family in the event of your death and pay you benefits if you become severely disabled.

If you have questions about Social Security or this form, please call our toll-free number, **1-800-772-1213.**

Mail completed form to:
Social Security Administration
Wilkes Barre Data Operations Center
PO Box 7004
Wilkes Barre, PA 18767-7004

About The Privacy Act

Social Security is allowed to collect the facts on this form under section 205 of the Social Security Act. We need them to quickly identify your record and prepare the *Statement* you asked us for. Giving us these facts is voluntary. However, without them we may not be able to give you a *Statement*. Neither the Social Security Administration nor its contractor will use the information for any other purpose.

Paperwork Reduction Act Notice

This information collection meets the requirements of 44 U. S. C. §3507, as amended by Section 2 of the Paperwork Reduction Act of 1995. You do not need to answer these questions unless we display a valid Office of Management and Budget control number. We estimate that it will take about 5 minutes to read the instructions, gather the facts, and answer the questions. *You may send comments on our time estimate above to: SSA, 6401 Security Blvd., Baltimore, MD 21235-6401. Send only comments relating to our time estimate to this address, not the completed form.*

Form Approved
OMB No. 0960-0446

SP

Request for Social Security Statement

☐ Please check this box if you want to get your *Statement* in Spanish instead of English.

Please print or type your answers. When you have completed the form, fold it and mail it to us. If you prefer to send your request using the Internet, contact us at *www.socialsecurity.gov.*

1. Name shown on your Social Security card:

_____   _____
First Name   Middle Initial

_____
Last Name Only

2. Your Social Security number as shown on your card:

☐☐☐ - ☐☐ - ☐☐☐☐

3. Your date of birth (Mo.-Day-Yr.)

☐☐ - ☐☐ - ☐☐☐☐

4. Other Social Security numbers you have used:

☐☐☐ - ☐☐ - ☐☐☐☐
☐☐☐ - ☐☐ - ☐☐☐☐

5. Your Sex: ☐ Male   ☐ Female

For items 6 and 8 show only earnings covered by Social Security. Do NOT include wages from state, local or federal government employment that are NOT covered by Social Security or that are covered ONLY by Medicare.

6. Show your actual earnings (wages and/or net self-employment income) for last year and your estimated earnings for this year.

   A. Last year's actual earnings: *(Dollars Only)*

   $ ☐☐☐,☐☐☐.0 0

   B. This year's estimated earnings: *(Dollars Only)*

   $ ☐☐☐,☐☐☐.0 0

7. Show the age at which you plan to stop working:

   ☐☐   *(Show only one age)*

8. Below, show the average yearly amount (not your total future lifetime earnings) that you think you will earn between now and when you plan to stop working. Include performance or scheduled pay increases or bonuses, but not cost-of-living increases.

   If you expect to earn significantly more or less in the future due to promotions, job changes, part-time work, or an absence from the work force, enter the amount that most closely reflects your future average yearly earnings.

   If you don't expect any significant changes, show the same amount you are earning now (the amount in 6B).

   Future average yearly earnings: *(Dollars Only)*

   $ ☐☐☐,☐☐☐.0 0

9. Do you want us to send the *Statement:*
   • To you? Enter your name and mailing address.
   • To someone else (your accountant, pension plan, etc.)? Enter your name with "c/o" and the name and address of that person or organization.

_____
"C/O" or Street Address (Include Apt. No., P.O. Box, Rural Route)

_____
Street Address

_____
Street Address (If Foreign Address, enter City, Province, Postal Code)

_____
U.S. City, State, ZIP code (If Foreign Address, enter Name of Country only)

NOTICE:
I am asking for information about my own Social Security record or the record of a person I am authorized to represent. I declare under penalty of perjury that I have examined all the information on this form, and on any accompanying statements or forms, and it is true and correct to the best of my knowledge. I authorize you to use a contractor to send the *Social Security Statement* to the person and address in item 9.

▲

Please sign your name (Do Not Print)

_____

_____
Date   (Area Code) Daytime Telephone No.

Form SSA-7004-SM (10-2006) EF (10-2006)   ♲ Printed on recycled paper

Additional Requirements for Applying for SSDI

In addition to having earned enough work credits, you must be a U.S. citizen, permanent resident, or resident alien, and you must be:

- disabled and under age 65 OR

- a disabled widow or widower at least 50 years old but less than 60 years old, and your late spouse was receiving SSDI or retirement benefits at the time of death OR

- the surviving spouse and your late spouse was receiving SSDI or retirement benefits at the time of death, and you had a child with your late spouse and the child has been disabled since before age 22.

Supplemental Security Income (SSI)

Persons who do not have enough work credits and have limited income and assets may be eligible to receive SSI (sometimes called Title 16 claims).

Satisfying the Nonmedical Requirements to Qualify for SSI

Supplemental Security Income was set up between the federal government and state governments to provide welfare assistance to disabled citizens, so a person can be denied SSI benefits regardless of the severity of his or her disability if he or she has too much income or too many assets. Likewise, if your income exceeds what the SSA has determined are welfare limits, or if you have assets that you could sell in order to pay for medical care, you will be denied benefits.

Income Limitations

The federal government has established the *federal benefit rate* (FBR). This benchmark amount is adjusted annually based on the cost of living. In 2006, a single person with a monthly income of $603 or less would satisfy the nonmedical requirements to receive SSI. If the claimant was married, his or her total income could not exceed $904.

The FBR represents the federal threshold limit, but since this is both a federal and state welfare program, each state also supplements the federal limit. For example, in California, the limit is $233. When added to the FBR, if a single claimant earned more than $836 (the FBR of $603 plus the California limit of $233), he or she would not qualify.

In calculating the income level, the following are not added:

- $20 of any income besides wages;

- the first $65 of wages and one-half of wages earned in excess of $65;

- the monthly amount received for food stamps; and,

- government assistance for housing assistance and home energy costs.

CARLOS'S STORY

Carlos earns $400 per month working part-time. He lives with his wife, Juanita, and her children from a previous relationship. Juanita receives food stamps. The family lives in government subsidized housing in California. In calculating benefits, the first $65 of Carlos's benefits is not counted. Also, one-half of the $400 is not counted, nor are the food stamps and governmental housing assistance. Therefore, Carlos has an income of $135, which is less than the federal benefit rate (FBR) of $623 for a single person and $934 for a married couple, and therefore meets the nonmedical requirements for SSI benefits.

Resource Limitations

In addition to income limitations, to receive SSI you cannot have assets that are valued at more than $2,000 if you are single or $3,000 if you are married. However, certain assets are not counted, including:

- a home titled in your or your spouse's name and used as your primary residence;

- personal property found in your home, not to exceed $2,000;

- a wedding ring and an engagement ring, regardless of value;

- necessary health aids and devices, such as a wheelchair;

- an automobile, regardless of value, provided it is used for transportation (if the vehicle is not used for transportation, the vehicle cannot exceed a value of $4,500);

- whole life insurance with a face value of $1,500 or less; and,

- burial plots and money set aside for burial, not to exceed $1,500.

Unlike the FBR, the previously listed exclusions are *not* adjusted annually.

LEGALLY SPEAKING

When you apply for SSI, the SSA will require that you provide an itemization of your assets. If benefits are granted, and later it is determined that you provided false information in order to qualify, the SSA can prosecute you for fraud, which could result in both the termination of future benefits and an order to repay benefits already received. You may also be sentenced to prison. This should be enough of a warning that it does not pay to lie.

Practical Point

Some claimants apply for both SSDI and SSI if they have earned enough work credits but the income they would receive from SSDI alone would fall below the federal benefits rate. When you make your initial application, the SSA will determine which program you are eligible for (or if you are eligible for both), even if you do not choose both programs.

THE SEQUENTIAL EVALUATION OF DISABILITY

4

Providing you meet both the medical and nonmedical requirements of the SSA definition of disability, you will be awarded benefits.

Benefits may be awarded after:

- a favorable evaluation of your initial application as discussed in Chapter 9;

- a favorable review of your Request for Reconsideration as discussed in Chapter 12;

- a favorable review of your Request for a Hearing as discussed in Chapter 13;

- a favorable hearing before an administrative law judge as discussed in Chapter 16; or,

- after a favorable review by the Appeals Council as discussed in Chapter 18.

When a claim is initially filed, the SSA will apply a *sequential evaluation*, which consists of five steps. If, at any point during the evaluation, you are found not to be disabled, the evaluation process terminates and the claim for disability insurance benefits is denied. The burden is then on you to file any appeals that you may be entitled to. The following are the five steps in determining disability. Prior to making your application for benefits, you should ask yourself the following questions.

Step 1: Are You Gainfully Employed?

Step 1 requires proof that you are **not gainfully employed**.

If you earn more than the federal benefit rate (FBR), as discussed in Chapter 3, in any month during the period that you are claiming that you are disabled, you are *gainfully employed* regardless of the severity of your disability. To illustrate, if you are single, in a wheelchair, and your legs are paralyzed as a result of a stroke, but you can write with the use of an arm brace, live in California, and earn more than $836 working part-time as a bookkeeper, then you are gainfully employed and are not disabled. It is irrelevant if it is becoming more and more difficult for you to do your job as a result of your disability.

Step 2: Is Your Medical Impairment Severe?

Step 2 requires a showing that **your impairment is severe**.

This step was incorporated into the evaluation process so that the SSA could distinguish valid claims from those that were filed without any real merit. However, any claim in which the impairment results in a reduction in limitations from what the person could do before the disability is severe. For example, if a person had a stroke that left him or her with weakness on his or her left side, limiting his or her ability to lift more than ten pounds, the disability is severe.

Step 3: Does Your Impairment Meet Or Equal the Medical Listings?

Step 3 requires a showing that the **severity of the impairment meets or equals the medical listings**.

What is a medical impairment? The SSA has issued a disability handbook that lists all medically recognizable disabilities. The listings are discussed in Chapter 5 and can be reviewed on the SSA's website at

www.socialsecurity.gov/disability/professionals/ bluebook/AdultListings.htm.

Note that if your disability does not meet or equal the listings, the evaluation process proceeds to Steps 4 and 5.

Step 4: Can You Perform Your Previous Types of Work?

Step 4 requires a showing that you **cannot perform your past relevant work.**

> **Practical Point**
>
> Remember, claims are initially evaluated based on the written information provided by you. Therefore, if your disability has lasted or will last twelve months or longer, you can no longer do your previous work, and your physical and/or mental complaints prevent you from doing any other work, your impairment satisfies step 2.

Even if your disability does not meet or equal the listings, you may still be found disabled based on *vocational factors*. This is a fancy way of saying that you cannot perform *any* of your previous work; *previous work* means *any* work you did in the last fifteen years that lasted for more than thirty days. As an example, if you have had two back surgeries and your doctor says that you cannot lift more than ten pounds, and your previous work for the last fifteen years was as a dock loader, you satisfy Step 4 because your job requires heavy lifting. However, using the same example, if you have also worked as a car salesperson, you may not be found disabled. This is because the salesperson's job does not require heavy lifting and therefore you are capable of performing your past relevant work.

Step 5: Can You Perform Other Generally Available Work?

Step 5 requires proving that **you have not learned or acquired any transferable skills** to do any other work in the national economy.

Note that it does not matter whether an actual job exists. All the government has to prove is that the claimant can do some job for which he or she has the skills or ability. In considering whether you have transferable skills, the SSA will consider your age, education, and work experience. However, an older claimant (age 55 or older) is generally considered less employable than a 35-year-old.

In analyzing the five steps, you will see that you can be found disabled at either Step 3 because your disability meets or equals the listings or at Step 5 because you cannot do your previous relevant work nor is there any other work available in the national economy that you could perform within the limitations of your disability.

There are two exceptions to the requirement of applying the sequential evaluation:

• a claimant age 55 or older who has a severe medical impairment, has not worked in the past fifteen years, and has an 11th-grade education or less is disabled; and,

- a person who has no more than a 6th-grade education and has thirty-five or more years of experience performing unskilled work is commonly referred to as a *worn-out worker* and is disabled.

Step 3 of the Sequential Evaluation: Meeting or Equaling the Listings

5

Step 3 of the sequential evaluation requires a finding that you have a *determinable medical impairment*. In order to organize medical impairments, the Social Security Administration has developed what is termed the *listings*. For adult disabilities, the listings divide the human body into the following systems:

1.00 Musculoskeletal System

2.00 Special Senses and Speech

3.00 Respiratory System

4.00 Cardiovascular System

5.00 Digestive System

6.00 Genitourinary Disorders

7.00 Hematological Disorders

8.00 Skin Disorders

9.00 Endocrine System

10.00 Impairments that Affect Multiple Body Systems

11.00 Neurological

12.00 Mental Disorders

13.00 Malignant Neoplastic Diseases

14.00 Immune System

The adult medical listings may be found online at the Social Security Administration's website:

www.socialsecurity.gov/disability/professionals/
bluebook/AdultListings.htm

For children, the SSA has developed childhood disability listings. Please see Chapter 22 for a discussion of childhood disabilities, and go online to the SSA website at:

www.socialsecurity.gov/disability/professionals/
bluebook/ChildhoodListings.htm

In addition, the SSA publishes a hardbound edition known as the *Blue Book*, which may be ordered by calling 800–772–1213. It may also be ordered online at **www.ssa.gov**. There is no charge for ordering the book.

Understanding the Listings

To be found medically disabled at Step 3 of the sequential evaluation, the medical impairment must be included in the listings. For example, if your complaint about why you cannot work is related to shortness of breath, the listings under 3.00 concerning respiratory problems pertain. If you are diabetic and arthritic, the listings that are applicable are the endocrine system, 9.00, and musculoskeletal system, 1.00.

Practical Point

Chapter 15 includes several resource books, available in most public libraries, that will assist you in interpreting the listings.

Based on your medical record, a favorable decision requires proof that your disability either *meets or equals the listings*. That is, your impairment squarely fits within the wording of the listing and therefore you *meet* the listing, or your impairment and related symptoms *equals* the listing. Understanding the listings requires that you have some knowledge of medical terminology.

TODD'S STORY

Todd is 50 years old and has worked for more than twenty years as a dishwasher. While helping a friend repair his roof, he fell. The fall resulted in a herniated disk in his lower back, which is documented by an MRI examination. He has constant pain when he walks.

Part 1.04 of the musculoskeletal listings discusses disorders of the spine. The listing requires that there must be a finding of a herniated disk with "nerve root compression . . . pain . . . [and] motor loss . . . accompanied by sensory or reflex loss."

In layman's terms, the listings require that, as a result of the herniated disk, Todd must also experience numbness or a loss of feelings, which is another way of saying that he must have nerve damage.

Todd would not meet or equal the listings, because although he has a herniated disk, there is no evidence that it has resulted in nerve damage. Therefore, he would not be medically disabled.

However, add to the facts that Todd also has constant numbness in his toes. When his doctor tested his reflexes in his lower extremities, they revealed positive signs for *reflex loss*. As a finding of reflex loss is required to meet the listings, Todd may be disabled at Step 3.

Note that even without a reflex loss, Todd may still be found disabled with this impairment if he cannot return to his previous work and he has no transferable skills to do any other work. This is Step 5 of the sequential evaluation and is discussed in Chapter 7.

To assist you in winning your case, Appendix A includes both a physical residual functional capacity questionnaire and a mental residual functional capacity questionnaire. Depending upon whether your claim for disability is based on a physical or mental impairment, or both, it is essential that your treating doctor completes the appropriate questionnaire. The questionnaires are based in part on the medical listings—part of the task of winning benefits is being able to prove that you meet or equal the listings. When applying for disability benefits, you are not expected to have the knowledge of your treating doctor to determine which listing you may meet or equal, and reading and understanding the listings can be very challenging for anyone without a medical background. However, having your doctor complete the appropriate questionnaire will go a long way in assisting both your doctor and the SSA in making a proper evaluation of your claim.

LEGALLY SPEAKING

The medical listings are always being reviewed and revised by the SSA. For example, at one time, obesity was a recognized medical impairment. Under the current listings, a person who is obese must also have some other severe medical impairment, such as a heart problem that may have resulted from his or her obesity. In addition, up until 1996 alcohol and drug addictions were recognized as disabilities. It is important that you check the most current listings for any changes made by the SSA.

Step 4 of the Sequential Evaluation: Can You Do Your Past Relevant Work?

6

As discussed in Chapter 5, if you meet or equal the listings, you will be found disabled at Step 3 of the sequential evaluation and therefore qualify for Social Security Disability benefits, providing that you also meet the nonmedical requirements.

If you do not meet or equal the listings, the SSA will then evaluate whether you are able to perform any of your previous work. To be considered by the SSA, past relevant work must:

- have been performed in the last 15 years;

- have been performed for more than 30 days; and,

- result in substantially gainful employment.

Note that work performed for less than 30 days is not relevant and should not be considered by the SSA.

In deciding whether you can perform past relevant work, all that the SSA has to find is that you can do the easiest of all the jobs that you have

> **Practical Point**
>
> If the SSA determines that with your disability you can return to your previous type of work, it will find that you are not disabled at Step 4. It is irrelevant whether or not your employer will take you back or if you can find a similar type of work. Even if the same type of work results in a lower-paying position, so long as the SSA determines that you can do that job, it will deny your claim. As a result, you will need to file a Request for Reconsideration, as discussed in Chapter 12, so that you preserve your appeal options.

done in the last fifteen years. In its reason for denying you at Step 4, the SSA will cite in its letter which job or jobs it has concluded you are able to return to.

It is very important that you read the denial letter carefully to make sure that the SSA did not make a decision based on work that was not relevant.

BLAKE'S STORY

Blake was 49 years old when he applied for disability benefits. He had had two knee replacements, and even with the surgery he was still having difficulty walking and standing. In his employment history, he told the SSA that he had worked as a shoe salesman for the past fifteen years at a store in the mall. He also listed working as a toll-booth collector for two years before he got the job selling shoes.

The SSA denied his case, saying that although he did have a severe impairment that would prevent him from returning to his previous employment as a shoe salesman, he could perform the job as a toll collector, as this job is performed sitting. The SSA would be wrong to consider any work that was done more than 15 years ago. However, for Blake to receive benefits, it must still be proven that there is no other work he is capable of performing, as discussed in the next chapter.

CINDY'S STORY

Cindy, age 47, suffered from multiple sclerosis. She applied for SSI benefits because she did not have enough work credits to apply for SSDI benefits. On her employment history, she said that she worked as an inventory clerk on and off for four years.

Cindy was denied by the SSA because her medical condition did not meet or equal the listings, and she could perform her past work doing inventory. However, Cindy's employment history revealed that she was hired by a temporary agency and each job never lasted more than two weeks. Therefore, though she may have worked more than thirty days, none of her previous jobs lasted more than thirty days at a time, and the SSA would be wrong to include her previous work.

MAURY'S STORY

Maury was 42 and had been on insulin for his diabetes since he was 35. He developed ulcerated sores on his left foot, and eventually had to have two of his toes amputated. Maury could not walk without a walker. His past work for the last fifteen years was as a parking lot attendant collecting parking fees. However, at no time did he work more than fifteen hours per week.

The SSA denied his case, saying he could return to his previous work, which was performed sitting. However, the SSA would be wrong to consider the parking attendant job as past relevant work, because Maury's income never exceeded the federal benefit rate (FBR).

When the SSA reviews your past relevant work, it considers not only the job that you did, but also how you performed the job. As a result, if you had a job title that is normally performed standing but you performed your work sitting and standing, the SSA will view the easiest part of your job and determine if you can do that work.

SAM'S STORY

Sam worked for seventeen years installing air conditioners for his dad's company. However, in the last two years, his father became ill, and Sam handled all the accounting for the company, which included paying bills and payroll. In determining if Sam could do any of his previous work, the SSA would consider the accounting work as the easiest, as it does not require lifting and pulling and can be performed while sitting. As a result, if Sam's disability does not preclude him from sedentary types of work, he would not be found disabled at step 4.

Step 5 of the Sequential Evaluation: Can You Do Any Other Work?

7

After reviewing the five steps of the sequential evaluation, you now know that there are two avenues for a finding of disability with the SSA. One avenue involves a medical determination that the claimant's impairment meets or equals an impairment described in the listing of impairments. The other involves a combination of medical and vocational issues.

Chapter 5 discusses Step 3 of the sequential evaluation. That is, if your disability meets or equals the listings, you are medically disabled. Of course, depending on whether you are applying for SSDI or SSI, you must also meet the nonmedical requirements, which are discussed in Chapter 3.

Chapter 6 discusses Step 4 of the sequential evaluation. That is, to be found disabled, it must be shown that you cannot perform any relevant work from the past fifteen years. Accordingly, it must be demonstrated that, because of your impairments, you cannot even do the easiest work that you have previously performed.

If you cannot, the evaluation moves to Step 5, which is the most complicated step. It is often at this point in the evaluation process that the SSA concludes that there is some work you can do and denies your claim. By its own regulations, all the SSA has to find is that you are "able to do other work which exists in significant numbers in the economy, considering your remaining work capacity, age, education, and work experience."

If you do not qualify for benefits at Step 3, it is because the SSA has determined that your medical impairment may be severe but does not meet all the requirements as set out in the medical listings. Therefore, Step 5 will determine whether, with the impairments that are associated with your disability, you can do any other type of work.

> ### Practical Point
>
> Though the SSA will decline a claim because it concludes that the claimant is capable of performing other work, many cases are reversed after a hearing before an administrative law judge, after the judge takes testimony from the claimant and a vocational expert. Please see Chapter 16, which discusses the hearing process.

Again, it does not matter whether there is an actual job out there or whether someone is willing to hire you with your impairments. All that is necessary to prove is that, with your limitations, there are jobs that you are capable of doing. Sounds unfair? It is. That is why, if you are denied, you must appeal your decision and prove that you cannot do any type of work, as discussed in Part II of this book.

Analysis of Step 5

In Step 5, the SSA evaluates your *residual functional capacity* (RFC) to determine what you are physically or mentally capable of doing with the limitations and restrictions that result from being disabled. This is a fancy way of determining what other type of work you are capable of doing.

If your claim is based on a physical disability, the SSA will evaluate your physical RFC. Likewise, if you have a mental disability, the SSA will assess your mental RFC. If your claim is based on both a mental and physical disability, an RFC will be determined for both. In determining your RFC, the SSA will review all of your medical records as well as the reports from any consultative examinations.

Determining Physical Residual Functional Capacity

The SSA first considers your exertional abilities in determining your physical RFC. *Exertional limitations* are physical limitations involving your ability to lift, stand, and walk as a result of your disability. If you are restricted in your ability to lift or carry, your RFC is classified as follows:

- the ability to do *heavy work*—having the ability to lift or carry one hundred pounds occasionally and fifty pounds frequently, and to stand and walk six to eight hours per day;

- the ability to do *medium work*—having the ability to lift or carry fifty pounds occasionally and twenty-five pounds frequently, and to stand or walk six to eight hours per day;

- the ability to do *light work*—having the ability to lift or carry twenty pounds occasionally and ten pounds frequently, and to stand or walk six to eight hours per day; or,

- the ability to do *sedentary work*—having the ability to lift no more than ten pounds at a time and occasionally lift or carry small articles. Sedentary work usually refers to work that is done while sitting. Therefore, the claimant must also have the ability to sit up to two hours out of an eight-hour day to be able to perform sedentary work.

Note that the definitions include the descriptive words *occasionally* and *frequently*. The SSA defines *occasionally* as the ability to lift or carry less than one-third of the time in an eight-hour period. The ability to lift or carry *frequently* is defined to mean that you have the ability to perform at such an exertional level at least one-third of the time in an eight-hour day.

When evaluating exertion, the SSA may also consider your diagnosis and how such a condition could be aggravated by lifting, carrying, pushing, and pulling.

SAM'S STORY

Sam repaired air conditioners. He injured his back, resulting in two slipped discs. He complained of constant pain running down both his legs. His RFC concluded that he can lift only occasionally. Because his prior work required lifting more than fifty pounds more than 30% of the day, he cannot do heavy work and therefore can no longer perform the job as an air conditioner repairperson. He therefore satisfies Step 4 of the sequential evaluation. However, before Sam can be awarded benefits, it must be determined whether he can do any other type of work.

Once the claimant's physical RFC is determined, the SSA compares the RFC with a set of rules, known as the grids, as discussed in the following section. If, based on the claimant's RFC, he or she squarely fits into the grid rules, the grids will dictate whether or not the claimant is disabled. If, however, the claimant has other limitations, the grids become a framework and are used as a reference for determining whether or not the claimant is disabled.

Understanding the Grid Rules

The SSA has provided an important tool for determining whether a claimant is or is not disabled because of his or her medical impairments and vocational factors. It is called the *Medical-Vocational Guidelines*, popularly known as the *grids*. The grids provide that the older a claimant is, the easier it is to be found disabled.

If your impairment does not meet or equal a listing (see Chapter 5), the grids come into play when an individual has a severe medically determinable physical or mental impairment, is not gainfully employed, and the impairment prevents the individual from performing any past relevant work.

The grids are a series of charts. The Social Security Administration will make a determination on what level of exertion you can perform at in a work environment. The following categories range from the lowest level of exertion to the highest:

- can perform work at the sedentary exertional level;

- can perform work at the light exertional level;

- can perform work at the medium exertional level; and,

- can perform work at the heavy exertional level.

After the Social Security Administration makes a finding on your exertional level, it will then look at the corresponding chart and match your age, education, and past work, which will direct a finding of disabled or not disabled. If you have exertional and nonexertional limitations, the Social Security Administration will first determine if you can be found disabled based on the exertional limitations by themselves. If the grids direct a finding of not disabled, the SSA will then consider any limitations and how much those additional limitations would erode your ability to perform any jobs at that exertional level.

> ### Practical Point
>
> The ability to lift or carry occasionally or frequently are medical judgments often made after a consultative examination, and may be a subjective opinion and not based on any testing. Therefore, if you believe that the consultative examination was not fair and your case reaches the hearing stage, it is most important that you explain this to the administrative law judge so that he or she is not swayed by the conclusion of the consultative examiner. See Chapter 16 for a complete discussion of the hearing process.

Age, Education, and Past Work

Your disability and how it limits you is not the only factor that decides whether you will be approved for SSDI or SSI benefits. In general, the older you are, the better chance you have of getting disability. The theory the SSA goes by is that an older person has a more difficult time adjusting to new work than a younger person.

Age

The SSA classifies age as follows.

- An applicant who is between 18 and 49 is considered to be a younger individual.

- An applicant who is between 50 and 54 is considered closely approaching advanced age.

- An applicant who is between 55 and 59 is considered to be of advanced age.

- An applicant who is between 60 and 64 is considered closely approaching retirement age.

Rounding Up to the Next Age Category. Note that a 50-year-old claimant will be treated the same as a 54-year-old claimant. However, according to the regulations, the SSA has discretion in applying the age categories when a person is close to his or her next birthday if that will place him or her in a different category. Accordingly, a claimant who is within a few months of a birthday that puts him or her into a disabled category in the Medical-Vocational Guidelines is supposed to get the benefit of the doubt.

RENEE'S STORY

Renee was 53 years old when she applied for Social Security Disability benefits. However, after being denied twice, a hearing was finally scheduled two months shy of her 55th birthday. At the hearing, she was found to be disabled at Step 5 of the sequential evaluation, as the vocational expert applied the grid rules for a 55-year-old.

What age category you fall into is very important, especially if you have purely exertional limitations that are keeping you from being defined as disabled. Nonexertional limitations, such as memory loss and issues regarding concentration, are discussed in Chapter 8.

Education

Your education is also an important factor that the SSA uses to decide if you are disabled. The SSA's theory is that the higher your level of education, the easier it is for you to find other work. The SSA has several categories of education. From least educated to most, they are as follows.

- *Illiterate* is defined as the inability to read or write.

- *Marginal* is defined as less than a 6th-grade education.

- *Limited* is defined as less than a high school education.

- A person with a high school education or higher but with no past skills that provide for direct entry into semiskilled or skilled work.

- A person with a high school education or higher where past relevant work does provide for direct entry into skilled work.

The SSA will use the highest grade completed in school in evaluating a person's educational level. However, the regulations provide that a person's actual educational abilities may be higher or lower. Therefore, the SSA will accept evidence that a claimant's actual educational level is lower than the numerical grade completed in school. To illustrate, if a person graduated high school but was always in special education, the SSA will take this into consideration.

Past Work

The SSA classifies work as unskilled, semiskilled, and skilled. *Unskilled* work is work learned in thirty days or less. Everything else is either semiskilled or skilled. For the purposes of the Medical-Vocational Guidelines, semiskilled and skilled work is treated as one category.

In classifying past work, the SSA will consider the following:

- the titles of all your jobs in the past fifteen years, and

- a description of the work you did.

When making your initial application for benefits, it is very important that you accurately describe your job as well as how you performed your job. This is because there are jobs with the same name but very different job duties. Likewise, there are also jobs that have the same job duties but have different names. That is why a job title is not enough to describe your work. In describing your job, make sure to include:

- main responsibilities of your job(s);

- main tasks you performed;

- dates you worked (month and year);

- number of hours a day you worked per week;

- rate of pay you received;

- tools, machinery, and equipment you used;

- knowledge, skills, and abilities your work required;

- extent of supervision you had;

- amount of independent judgment you used;

- objects you had to lift and carry and how much they weighed;

- how much you had to sit, stand, walk, climb, stoop, kneel, crouch, crawl, and balance;

- how you used your hands, arms, and legs;

- speaking, hearing, and vision requirements of your job(s); and,

- environmental conditions of your workplace(s).

Reading the Grids

You read the grids by taking into account your age, education, and previous work experience, and seeing what decision on disability that adds up to, according to the SSA.

Assume the following facts:

- you are 50 years old and graduated high school;

- your previous work was as a heavy laborer nailing drywall, and you did this work for the past twenty years;

- you suffered a serious back injury and had surgery for a ruptured disk;

- as a result of the surgery, you cannot lift or carry more than ten pounds but you have no problem sitting; and,

- you are therefore now limited to doing only sedentary work.

In reading the grids, first look under the column of age. At 50 years old, you are considered closely approaching advanced age. Now look at the column for education. You are a high school graduate, but you have no other formal training that would provide you with skills to allow you direct entry into skilled work. Now look at the column for previous work experience. Your past relevant work was as an unskilled heavy laborer; therefore, your past work is considered unskilled. Now, with these columns lined up, you look at the decision column and it directs a finding of disabled.

What follows is a partial listing of the grids for the purposes of this example. A complete listing of the grids is found in Appendix B.

Rule	Age	Education	Previous Work Experience	Decision
201.01	Advanced Age	Limited or less	Unskilled or none	Disabled
201.02	Advanced Age	Limited or less	Skilled or semiskilled-skills not transferable	Disabled
201.03	Advanced Age	Limited or less	Skilled or semiskilled-skills transferable	Not disabled
201.04	Advanced Age	High school graduate or more-does not provide for direct entry into skilled work	Unskilled or none	Disabled
201.05	Advanced Age	High school graduate or more-provides for direct entry into skilled work	Unskilled or none	Not disabled
201.06	Advanced Age	High school graduate or more-does not provide for direct entry into skilled work	Skilled or semiskilled-skills not transferable	Disabled
201.07	Advanced Age	High school graduate or more-does not provide for direct entry into skilled work	Skilled or semiskilled-skills transferable	Not disabled
201.08	Advanced Age	High school graduate or more-provides for direct entry into skilled work	Skilled or semiskilled-skills not transferable	Not disabled
201.09	Closely approaching advanced age	Limited or less	Unskilled or none	Disabled

201.10	Closely approaching advanced age	Limited or less	Skilled or semiskilled-skills not transferable	Disabled
201.11	Closely approaching advanced age	Limited or less	Skilled or semiskilled-skills transferable	Not disabled
201.12	Closely approaching advanced age	High school graduate or more-does not provide for direct entry into skilled work	Unskilled or none	Disabled
201.13	Closely approaching advanced age	High school graduate or more-provides for direct entry into skilled work	Unskilled or none	Not disabled
201.14	Closely approaching advanced age	High school graduate or more-does not provide for direct entry into skilled work	Skilled or semiskilled-skills not transferable	Disabled
201.15	Closely approaching advanced age	High school graduate or more-does not provide for direct entry into skilled work	Skilled or semiskilled-skills transferable	Not disabled
201.16	Closely approaching advanced age	High school graduate or more-provides for direct entry into skilled work	Skilled or semiskilled-skills not transferable	Not disabled
201.17	Younger individual age 45–49	Illiterate or unable to communicate in English	Unskilled or none	Disabled
201.18	Younger individual age 45–49	Limited or less-at least literate and able to communicate in English	Unskilled or none	Not disabled
201.19	Younger individual age 45–49	Limited or less	Skilled or semiskilled-skills not transferable	Not disabled
201.20	Younger individual age 45–49	Limited or less	Skilled or semiskilled-skills transferable	Not disabled

201.21	Younger individual age 45–49	High school graduate or more	Skilled or semiskilled-skills not transferable	Not disabled
201.22	Younger individual age 45–49	High school graduate or more	Skilled or semiskilled-skills transferable	Not disabled
201.23	Younger individual age 18–44	Illiterate or unable to communicate in English	Unskilled or none	Not disabled
201.24	Younger individual age 18–44	Limited or less-at least literate and able to communicate in English	Unskilled or none	Not disabled
201.25	Younger individual age 18–44	Limited or less	Skilled or semiskilled-skills not transferable	Not disabled
201.26	Younger individual age 18–44	Limited or less	Skilled or semiskilled-skills transferable	Not disabled
201.27	Younger individual age 18–44	High school graduate or more	Unskilled or none	Not disabled
201.28	Younger individual age 18–44	High school graduate or more	Skilled or semiskilled-skills not transferable	Not disabled
201.29	Younger individual age 18–44	High school graduate or more	Skilled or semiskilled-skills transferable	Not disabled

It is extremely important that your treating doctors give an opinion on your residual functional capacity (RFC)—in other words, how much you can lift, how long you can stand, and so on. Also, if you suffer from nonexertional limitations (nonstrength limitations) such as memory difficulties, difficulty concentrating, etc., it is important that your doctor note these as well, because this can further limit the jobs the SSA will be able to find that you can do.

The grids are far from perfect. If a claimant's profile differs in any significant degree from that of a person described in the grids, the rules do not directly answer the question of whether the claimant is or is not disabled. Instead, they must be used as a framework for decision making. This happens when a claimant's exertional limitations fall between those described by the three grids for sedentary, light, and medium work; when a claimant cannot do a full range of sedentary work; in cases involving mental, sensory, or skin impairments, or postural or manipulative limitations; and, when there are environmental limitations.

Practical Point

The grids are applicable in determining whether you can do work that is sedentary, light, medium, or heavy based on your ability to sit, stand, and carry. The grids do not take into account whether you have other exertional limitations, such as difficulty with grasping or holding. The grids also do not consider any mental limitations, such as memory loss. Please see Chapter 8, which discusses when the grids do not apply.

When the Grids Do Not Apply

8

As discussed in Chapter 7, the grids apply when a claimant's physical residual functional capacity classifies him or her as being able to do sedentary, light, or medium work. Thereafter, a determination of whether or not the claimant is disabled is made based on his or her age, education, and skills learned from previous work.

However, not every claimant fits neatly into the grids. A claimant may have vision problems or be unable to be exposed to odors. A claimant may have a mental disability that causes difficulty maintaining concentration. In such cases, the grids serve only as a framework or reference. As a result, the SSA must evaluate the claim further by considering what are called *nonexertional limitations*.

Physical Nonexertional Limitations

Nonexertional limitations are limitations in addition to the ability to walk, sit, and stand. Nonexertional limitations are classified as physical and mental, and each category has its own subcategories.

Posture

In evaluating postural limitations, the SSA considers the ability to bend, stoop, climb, balance, kneel, crouch, and crawl frequently, occasionally, or never. *Frequently* means that, with your postural limitations, you can still perform your work at least one-third of the time out of an eight-hour day. *Occasionally* means that, with your postural limitations, you can perform your work, but less than one-third of the time out of an eight-hour day. *Never* means that, with your postural limitations, you cannot perform your work.

MIKE'S STORY

Mike was a police officer. As a result of a foot chase to apprehend a criminal, he severely injured his back when he jumped over a wall. His doctor stated that he can occasionally climb or balance. Therefore, with an RFC limiting him to occasional climbing and balancing, his postural limitations prevent him from returning to his previous work as a police officer (because in that job he must be able to climb or balance frequently).

Manipulation

All work requires some type of use of your hands, and manipulation includes the ability to reach, handle, finger (use fine manipulation), and feel. Any impairment in the ability to manipulate is categorized as limited. However, unlike exertional and postural limitations, whether someone's ability to manipulate is limited is first evaluated by the type of job that person has, rather than how long that person needs to be able to manipulate in an eight-hour day. For example, a piano teacher's job requires that he or she reach the keyboard all day. Therefore, any impairment to reach would be classified as limited.

Vision

A claimant's vision impairment is categorized as either limited or unlimited. In determining the extent of the impairment, vision is further evaluated by the claimant's ability:

- to see objects up close (acuity);

- to see objects at a distance of more than a few feet away;

- to perceive how far an object is from the claimant (depth perception); and,

- to see objects away from the center of vision (peripheral vision).

In addition, the SSA will evaluate if a person has color blindness and how wearing corrective lenses will improve vision. If the claimant cannot distinguish colors by the use of corrective lenses, his RFC for vision will be limited.

BLAKE'S STORY

Blake worked as a loan officer. His job included reviewing documents. While coaching his son's little league team, he was hit by a softball, resulting in his inability to read up close. Even with glasses, his vision was not improved. His RFC was rated as limited. However, though the SSA concluded that he could no longer work as a loan officer, there were other jobs available and he was therefore not disabled.

Communication

Communication requires the ability to hear and speak. Any inability is categorized as limited or unlimited. Most hearing impairments can be corrected with hearing aids. Likewise, unless your speech is so distorted in sound that it is impossible to understand, the SSA will conclude that there are jobs available to perform even with an RFC as limited.

Environment

Depending on the job description, performing work may include exposure to heat, cold, wetness, humidity, dryness, noise, vibrations, and fumes. Some jobs include work with hazardous machinery or at unprotected heights. Work restrictions based on environmental factors are categorized as follows:

- unlimited;

- avoid concentrated exposure;

- avoid moderate exposure; or,

- avoid all exposure.

RACHEL'S STORY

Rachel worked in a nail salon. She developed aspergillosis, which is a very serious lung disease. When exposed to certain fumes, she developed breathing difficulties. Her RFC was rated as avoid all exposure. Because of the fumes given off by nail polish, she could no longer perform her work as a nail stylist.

Symptoms

In determining a claimant's RFC, the SSA will consider the following symptoms in deciding whether a person can perform his or her work:

- pain;

- numbness;

- nausea; and,

- dizziness.

Note that the severity of the symptom is also a considering factor in determining whether the claimant can perform his or her past work as well as any other work.

SUSAN'S STORY

Susan had a severe bowel obstruction that was surgically removed. Fortunately, it was not cancerous. However, the surgery left Susan with nerve damage, resulting in constant pain. Even with medication, the pain was only lessened when she lay down. Though her condition was not severe, and therefore did not meet or equal the listings, it was determined that she could not return to her previous job as a baker, because the constant pain interfered with her ability to work. Furthermore, because the pain existed even when she sat, there was no work available for her and she was found to be disabled.

Determining Mental Residual Functional Capacity

If a claimant alleges that he or she cannot work due to a mental disability, it must be determined if the disability is severe and whether it meets or equals the listings as discussed in Chapter 5. If the impairment does not meet or equal the listings, the SSA must then evaluate whether the claimant can perform his or her previous work. If the claimant cannot perform previous work, his or her RFC will be determined to evaluate when he or she can perform other types of work with his or her limitations.

Limitations as a result of a mental disability are rated as follows:

- not significantly limited;

- moderately limited;

- markedly limited; or,

- no evidence of limitation.

The purpose of assessing the limitation is to assist a medical consultant at the initial claim or Request for Reconsideration stage, or a vocational expert at the hearing stage, to offer an opinion as to whether the claimant can work at his or her previous job or do any other type of work. More importantly, to be found disabled based on a mental impairment, it must be concluded that the claimant cannot even perform unskilled work.

MARY'S STORY

Mary was a 5th-grade school teacher for over twenty years. While standing on a kitchen chair to reach a platter, a chair leg broke and she fell. She suffered a serious brain injury, which meant she could no longer teach. However, her injury still permitted her to perform unskilled work such as tearing tickets at a movie theater. Whether or not Mary would be hired at such a job, the SSA concluded that she was not entitled to benefits, as she was able to perform unskilled work.

Understanding and Memory

Within the area of understanding and memory, the SSA will evaluate a claimant's ability to remember work-like procedures such as how to:

- understand and remember short and simple instructions, and

- understand and remember detailed instructions.

If a claimant's mental impairment markedly limits his or her ability to understand and remember, he or she cannot perform even unskilled jobs and will therefore be found disabled.

Sustained Concentration and Persistence

In evaluating the ability to concentrate, the SSA will consider whether a claimant can:

- carry out very short and simple instructions;

- carry out detailed instructions;

- maintain attention and concentration for extended periods of time;

- perform activities with a schedule, maintain regular attendance, and be punctual;

- sustain an ordinary routine without special supervision;

- work in coordination with others;

- make simple work-related decisions; and,

- complete a normal workday and workweek without interruptions caused by mental symptoms.

If a claimant's mental impairments markedly limit his or her ability to concentrate, he or she cannot perform even unskilled jobs and is therefore disabled.

Social Interaction

In evaluating the social interaction abilities of a claimant, the SSA must conclude that a claimant's mental impairments markedly limit his or her ability to:

- interact appropriately with the general public;

- ask simple questions or request assistance;

- accept instructions and respond appropriately to criticism from supervisors;

- get along with coworkers or peers without distracting them; and,

- maintain socially appropriate behavior and adhere to basic standards of neatness and cleanliness.

Adaptation

A claimant's mental impairment will be evaluated for the ability to:

- respond appropriately to changes in the work setting;

- be aware of normal hazards and take appropriate precautions;

- be able to travel to unfamiliar places or use public transportation; and,

- set realistic goals or make plans independently of others.

If a claimant is found to be markedly limited in any of these areas, he or she cannot perform even unskilled work and is therefore disabled.

When a mental impairment is alleged, the Disability Determination Service (DDS) must complete a form known as a *Psychiatric Review Technique*, reproduced on page 61. The Administrative Law Judge (ALJ), at a hearing, will review this form and consider your treating doctor's opinion. For this reason, you should have your doctor complete a mental impairment questionnaire found in Appendix A, which covers the same areas of mental assessment evaluation as contained in the Psychiatric Review Technique.

PSYCHIATRIC REVIEW TECHNIQUE

Name   SSN

I. MEDICAL SUMMARY

A. Assessment is from:

_____ to _____

B. Medical Disposition(s):

- □ 1. No Medically Determinable Impairment
- □ 2. Impairment(s) Not Severe
- □ 3. Impairment(s) Severe But Not Expected to Last 12 Months
- □ 4. Meets Listing _____ (Cite Listing)
- □ 5. Equals Listing _____ (Cite Listing)
- □ 6. RFC Assessment Necessary
- □ 7. Coexisting Nonmental Impairment(s) that Requires Referral to Another Medical Specialty
- □ 8. Insufficient Evidence

C. Category(ies) Upon Which the Medical Disposition is Based:

- □ 1. 12.02 Organic Mental Disorders
- □ 2. 12.03 Schizophrenic, Paranoid and Other Psychotic Disorders
- □ 3. 12.04 Affective Disorders
- □ 4. 12.05 Mental Retardation
- □ 5. 12.06 Anxiety-Related Disorders
- □ 6. 12.07 Somatoform Disorders
- □ 7. 12.08 Personality Disorders
- □ 8. 12.09 Substance Addiction Disorders
- □ 9. 12.10 Autism and Other Pervasive Developmental Disorders

DOCUMENTATION OF FACTORS THAT EVIDENCE THE DISORDER

A. 12.02 Organic Mental Disorders

- □ Psychological or behavioral abnormalities associated with a dysfunction of the brain as evidenced by at least one of the following:
  - □ 1. Disorientation to time and place
  - □ 2. Memory impairment
  - □ 3. Perceptual or thinking disturbances
  - □ 4. Change in personality
  - □ 5. Disturbance in mood
  - □ 6. Emotional liability and impairment in impulse control

☐   7. Loss of measured intellectual ability of at least 15 IQ points from premorbid levels or overall impairment index clearly within the severely impaired range on neuropsychological testing, e.g., the Luria-Nebraska, Halstead-Reltan, etc.

☐   A medically determinable impairment is present that does not precisely satisfy the diagnostic criteria above.

Disorder: _____

Pertinent symptoms, signs, and laboratory findings that substantiate the presence of the impairment:

_____

_____

RATING OF FUNCTIONAL LIMITATIONS

A. "B" Criteria of the Listings

Indicate to what degree the following functional limitations (which are found in paragraph B of listings 12.02-12.04, 12.06-12.08 and 12.10 and paragraph D of 12.05) exist as a result of the individual's mental disorder(s).

NOTE: Item 4 below is more than a measure of frequency and duration. See 12.00C4 and also read carefully the instructions for this section.

Specify the listing(s) (i.e., 12.02 through 12.10) under which the items below are being rated

FUNCTIONAL LIMITATION   **DEGREE OF LIMITATION**

Indicate to what degree the following functional limitations exist as a result of your patient's mental impairments. *Note:* **Marked** means more than moderate but less than extreme. A marked limitation may arise when several activities or functions are impaired or even when only one is impaired, so long as the degree of limitation is such as to seriously interfere with the ability to function independently, appropriately, effectively, and on a sustained basis.

1. Restriction of Activities of Daily Living	None	Mild	Moderate	Marked*	Extreme*	Insufficient Evidence
2. Difficulties in Maintaining Social Functioning	None	Mild	Moderate	Marked*	Extreme*	Insufficient Evidence
3. Difficulties in Maintaining Concentration, Persistence or Pace	None	Mild	Moderate	Marked*	Extreme*	Insufficient Evidence
4. Repeated Episodes of Decompensation, Each of Extended Duration	None	One or Two	Three*	Four** or More		Insufficient

* Episodes of decompensation are exacerbations or temporary increases in symptoms or signs accompanied by a loss of adaptive functioning, as manifested by difficulties in performing activities of daily living, maintaining social relationships, or maintaining concentration, persistence or pace. Episodes of decompensation may be demonstrated by an exacerbation of symptoms or signs that would ordinarily require increased treatment or a less stressful situation (or combination of the two).

** If within one year your patent had more than three episodes of decompensation of shorter duration than two weeks or less frequent episodes of decompensation of longer duration than two weeks, please give the dates of each episode of decompensation.

B.   "C" Criteria of the Listings

1.   Complete this section if 12.02 (Organic Mental), 12.03 (Schizophrenic, etc.), or 12.04 (Affective) applies <u>and</u> the requirements in paragraph B of the appropriate listing are not satisfied.

NOTE: Item 1 below is more than a measure of frequency and duration. See 12.00C4 and also read carefully the instructions for this section.

☐   Medically documented history of a chronic organic mental (12.02), schizophrenic, etc. (12.03), or affective (12.04) disorder of at least 2 years' duration that has caused more than a minimal limitation of ability to do any basic work activity, with symptoms or signs currently attenuated by medication or psychological support, and one of the following:

☐   Repeated episodes of decompensation, each of extended duration

☐   A residual disease process that has resulted in such marginal adjustment that even a minimal increase in mental demands or change in the environment would be predicted to cause the individual to decompensate.

☐   Current history of 1 or more years' inability to function outside a highly supportive living arrangement with an indication of continued need for such an arrangement

☐   Evidence does not establish the presence of the "C" criteria

☐   Insufficient evidence to establish the presence of the "C" criteria (explain in Part IV, Consultant's Notes).

2.   Complete this section is 12.06 (Anxiety-Related) applies <u>and</u> the requirements in paragraphy B of listing 12.06 are not satisfied.

☐   **Complete** inability to function independently outside the area of one's home

☐   Evidence does not establish the presence of the "C" criteria

☐   Insufficient evidence to establish the presence of the "C" criterion (explain in Part IV, Consultant's Notes).

Summary of Step 5

Step 5 is the most complicated and difficult to understand of all the steps of the sequential evaluation. Most claimants are denied at Step 5, because the SSA concludes that a claimant is capable of performing some work in the national economy with his or her limitations.

Step 5 is designed to determine what work, if any, a claimant is capable of performing with the limitations that are the result of his or her disability.

A claimant's limitations will first be classified as to what weight he or she can lift and carry. This forms the claimant's exertional limitations, which are categorized as being able to perform sedentary, light, medium, or heavy work.

Thereafter, the claimant's age, education, and skills learned at his or her previous place of work will be factored into determining whether the claimant is or is not disabled. These are known as the grids.

If a claimant squarely fits within the grids, a determination is made as to whether the claimant is disabled.

If, because of physical or mental nonexertional limitations, the grids do not apply, the SSA will further modify the claimant's RFC to then determine if there is other work the claimant can do with his or her nonexertional limitations.

FILING THE INITIAL CLAIM   9

Part I of this book discusses the SSA's evaluation of a claim for Social Security Disability benefits. It explains how its very strict definition of disability differs from what a workers' compensation court or a long-term disability insurance carrier would consider to decide if someone was disabled. In addition, it explains the five-step sequential evaluation.

Accordingly, if you believe your physical or mental condition is severe, your disability causes you to be limited in your daily life, your condition has lasted or will last twelve months or longer, and you have doctors who support your position, you should file for benefits. To begin the process, there are three ways of making the initial application:

1. apply in person at a Social Security office;

2. contact the SSA by phone; or,

3. apply online at the SSA website at **www.socialsecurity.gov**.

> ### Practical Point
>
> Do not allow the SSA's definition of disability to be the determining factor as to whether or not you file for benefits. If you sincerely cannot work, you should apply. By doing so, the burden initially will shift to the SSA to decide if you are disabled. If you are turned down, the SSA must provide a written explanation of its reasons. Upon receiving a denial, you can then decide whether or not to appeal the decision.

Applying for Benefits by Phone

The SSA's toll-free phone number is 800–772–1213. This is the phone number for all Social Security inquiries, which may include questions regarding applying for Social Security numbers and death benefits, as well as disability. As a result, often you will be placed on hold, so please be patient. Note that the best time to call is midweek, as the SSA receives its greatest number of calls earlier in the week.

When you contact the SSA, your call will be answered by any one of many call centers managed by the SSA. Therefore, the person you are speaking to may be in your hometown or thousands of miles away. When the call is answered, be prepared to provide the following:

- your Social Security number;

- your date of birth;

- a telephone contact number; and,

- your mailing address.

The SSA representative will also ask you some very basic information about your disability so that a claim can be opened. You will then be told that an application package will be sent to you with instructions for completion. A complete discussion of the application information requirements is found in the following section.

Applying for Benefits in Person

Most people apply for benefits in person at the Social Security office located closest to where they reside. However, any Social Security office can take an initial application. If you do not know the location of the Social Security office nearest to you, you can call the SSA at 800–772–1213 and provide your zip code. The SSA will then provide a list of offices where you can file your application.

Upon arrival, inform the information clerk that you wish to apply for Social Security Disability benefits. You will then be asked if you would like to apply for benefits now or prefer to make an appointment for a later time. It is recommended that you make an appointment so that you can avoid what is usually a very long wait. If you wish to wait, you should go to the local office in the afternoon, as the morning tends to be the busiest time. Furthermore, the wait time is generally shorter toward the end of the week. Note that if you need an interpreter, the local office will provide one to you.

For all initial applications, you must produce the original or certified copy of your birth certificate and your Social Security number. If you do not have your birth certificate, the following are acceptable:

> **Practical Point**
>
> If you are having difficulty speaking or communicating, you can authorize someone, such as a family member, to initiate the phone call. That person will be asked to identify him- or herself and his or her relationship to you. Though someone will be acting on your behalf, a power of attorney is not necessary to simply obtain an application to file for benefits.

- school records;

- insurance policies;

- marriage certificate;

- passport;

- immigration or naturalization documentation;

- original family bible; or,

- a statement that is signed by the physician who witnessed your birth.

If you do not have a birth certificate or one of these acceptable documents, you will need to first obtain your birth certificate before the SSA can accept your application.

In addition to your birth certificate and Social Security number, the following is a list of the other information the SSA will need to begin processing your claim:

- medical information including:

- names, addresses, and phone numbers of all doctors, hospitals, and clinics;

  - patient ID numbers;

  - dates of medical care;

- names of medicines you are taking; and,

- any medical records in your possession;

- if you served in the military service, the original or certified copy of your military discharge papers for all periods of active duty;

- if you worked, your W-2 forms for the last year of work, or if you were self-employed, your federal income tax returns for the prior year (IRS Form 1040 and Schedules C and SE);

- if your disability is a result of an injury on the job, the date of your injury, any claim number, the name of your attorney if you are represented, and proof of any payments you are receiving;

- if married, the Social Security number and date of birth of your spouse and any minor children;

- name, address, and phone number of at least one person, not related to you, whom the SSA can use to get in touch with you;

Practical Point

Birth records can be obtained by writing to the county office of the state where you were born that maintains such records. All counties maintain websites that provide contact information. In addition, there are several online sites that can obtain birth records. Their fees average under $100. To find a site online, enter the search phrase "obtain birth certificates" in any search engine.

- a list of the kind of jobs that you did in the last fifteen years before you became disabled, including the occupation, name of employer, and a brief description of how you performed your job.

In addition to providing this information, be prepared to answer the following questions:

- your name at birth (if different from your current name);

- your place of birth (state or foreign country);

- if a public or religious record was made of your birth before age 5;

- whether you have ever filed for Social Security benefits, Medicare, or Supplemental Security Income, or whether anyone else has filed on your behalf;

- whether you were ever in the active military service before 1968, and if so, the dates of service and whether you have ever been eligible to receive a monthly benefit from a military or federal civilian agency;

- whether you or your spouse has ever worked for the railroad industry;

- whether you have earned Social Security credits under another country's Social Security system;

- whether you qualified for or expect to receive a pension or annuity based on your own employment with the federal government of the United States or one of its states or local subdivisions;

- whether you have filed or intend to file for workers' compensation or any public disability benefits;

- the names, dates of birth (or age), and Social Security numbers (if known) of any former spouses;

- the dates and places of each of your marriages, and for marriages that have ended, how and when they ended; and,

- the names of any unmarried children disabled before age 22.

LEGALLY SPEAKING

If you were born in another country, you will also need to provide proof of U.S. citizenship or legal residency in the United States.

Applying for Benefits Online

If you have access to a computer, you can apply online at the SSA's website, **www.socialsecurity.gov**. There are many links on the home page for beginning the application process. In addition, you will find a comprehensive checklist of all the items you will need to complete the initial application process.

Instructions for Filing Online

Before starting the application, make sure that you have read the online checklist and have the information ready. The checklist is found at **www.socialsecurity.gov/ disability/Adult_StarterKit_Checklist.pdf**.

To begin the application go to the website **www.socialsecurity.gov/applyfor disability/adult.htm**. Click on the "online application for Social Security Benifits," link, which will take you to a message page that reads:

Apply for Retirement/Disablity Spouse's Benefits

Restart Your Incomplete Application

Check Your Claim Status

Click on "Apply for Retirement/Disability/Spouse's Benifits" to begin the application.

After you enter your name, address, and Social Security number, a confirmation message will appear on the screen as follows:

Confirmation Number   Page 1 of 1

Social Security   # Social Security Benefit Application
Online
www.socialsecurity.gov

Confirmation Number for JOHN ████████

Your Confirmation Number Is ████████

In the event that you are unable to complete your online application for any reason, we will save your information for you. After waiting at least five minutes, you will be able to start this application again by selecting "Restart Your Incomplete Application" from the Social Security Claims page. You will need to enter your Social Security number and Confirmation Number to finish your application. If you lose your Confirmation Number and have not completed your application, you can start a new application and we will give you a new Confirmation Number. Your previous Confirmation Number will be deleted.

Please print this page (with your browser's printer) or write down your Confirmation Number. You may need it to complete your online application or to check the status of your claim.

Remember to guard your Confirmation Number carefully. Your Confirmation Number is the key to your application information!

- Don't put it where others can see it.
- Don't store it with other personal information, like your Social Security number.
- Don't give it to anyone else.
- Social Security employees will **never** ask for your Confirmation Number.

NOTE: If you are acting as an authorized representative for a client, you must complete and submit Form SSA-1696-U4 before using any information on this page.

If we do not receive your electronic application by 09/05/2007, you may lose benefits.

If you choose not to finish your Social Security application on the Internet, you should call 1-800-772-1213 toll-free to avoid any loss of benefits. If you are deaf or hard of hearing, call our toll-free "TTY" number, 1-800-325-0778.

Feedback

Print out this page. If you cannot complete the application in one sitting, you will need this confirmation number to return to the application. As the message warns you, protect this number and do not share it with anyone.

Click on the "continue" button to complete the application. Note that you cannot move to the next page if any information is missing. If information is not entered properly, that section will be highlighted in red.

After the last section of the application is completed, you will have an opportunity to edit each section. You should do so to ensure the accuracy of the information provided.

The last page is the submission page. Prior to clicking "submit," print the application, as you will not be able to do so once the application is submitted.

Prior to submitting, read the disclaimer. Note that only the person who is applying for benefits can click the "submit" button, as you are affirming that you personally provided the information, and the SSA is accepting your electronic signature verifying that you alone provided the information.

Immediately following your submission, an acknowledgment message will appear titled, "What you need to do now." It is five pages long and reproduced as follows. Print these pages, as they contain additional information that the SSA requires. Also, on page two is the address of the local Social Security office that has been assigned your file.

Social Security Benefit Application

Social Security
Online
www.socialsecurity.gov

What You Need to Do Now!

Thank You! Your electronic application has been received. Please print this screen now or write down the information that applies to you.

It will list the address where you sent your completed application, tell you how to provide more detailed medical information about your disability, advise you where to submit your documents, give you information about changes you must report and repeat the Confirmation Number you need to check the status of your claim on the Internet. You will not be able to return here if you go to another screen.

We cannot complete processing your claim until we have received and verified all of your required documents.

If you discover that something is incorrect on the electronic application you sent, please submit the corrections to the office displayed below under the heading "Where Do I Submit My Documents?", along with any documents.

If you indicated that you intend to file a Supplemental Security Income (SSI) application and we do not hear from you within 60 days, you may lose SSI benefits. Call our toll-free number at 1-800-772-1213 to arrange an appointment to file for SSI. If you are deaf or hard of hearing, call our toll-free TTY number, 1-800-325-0778. These claims cannot be applied for over the Internet.

Documents You Need to Submit to Social Security

You must submit your Original Birth Certificate or a Certified Copy of your birth certificate or other proof of birth to the office displayed below under the heading "Where Do I Submit My Documents?". AND, if applicable, you must also submit proof of your:

- Citizenship/Naturalization (if other than your U.S. birth certificate);
- U.S. Military Service (e.g., DD214 - Certificate of Release or Discharge from Active Duty);
- Wages from your employer for last year (e.g., copy of your W-2 form);
- Self-employment income for last year (e.g., IRS Schedules C and SE); and
- If we determine that you qualify for benefits as a spouse, we may also need proof of your marriage. We will contact you if necessary after we receive your application.

Note: If you have already proven your date of birth and citizenship status while filing a claim for another benefit administered by Social Security (e.g. Medicare, Supplemental Security Income, prior Social Security disability, etc.), you do not have to submit these proofs again.

Since you are applying for disability benefits, we will need the **Disability Report - Adult (SSA-3368)** and **Authorization To Disclose Information To The Social Security Administration (SSA-827)**, if you have not already submitted them to us.

Note: We will need one signed and dated SSA-827 for each of the medical sources that you list as soon as possible so we can begin evaluating your disability claim. We will also need two additional signed and dated SSA-827s in case we need to contact other sources at a later date.
We will also need, and can accept uncertified photocopies of, the following:

- Any <u>medical evidence</u> already in your possession regarding your disability.

- Award letters, pay stubs, settlement agreements or other proof of temporary or permanent <u>workers' compensation</u>-type benefits you received. The documents should show:
    - the date of your injury or illness;

    - the amount and effective date of your current payment and all increases or decreases within the last 17 months or, if later, since payments began;

    - if you receive workers' compensation, the type of payment (i.e., temporary partial, temporary total, permanent partial, permanent total, a lump sum or an annuity);

    - how often these payments are paid (e.g., weekly, bi-weekly, monthly, bi-monthly, etc.) or the period covered by a lump sum;

    - if benefits have already ended, the last day you were entitled to a payment and your last payment amount (if different than your regular payment amount);

    - your employer's name, address and phone number; and

    - if other than your employer, the name, address and phone number of the insurance carrier making the payments.

We must see your original birth certificate or other proof of age. We cannot accept photocopies unless they are certified by the office that issued the original. **If citizenship or naturalization is involved, we also must see your original documents.** For your convenience, we can accept uncertified copies of your military service papers, W-2 or IRS Schedule C or SE forms, medical information and documents related to your workers' compensation and/or similar benefits. **We will return all documents and photocopies to you unless you specifically tell us otherwise.**

Do not delay mailing or bringing in your documents, even if you do not have all the documents we need. We will help you get any other documents you need.

Where Do I Submit My Documents?

Please mail or take the documents we indicated we need to:

SOCIAL SECURITY
17075 NEWHOPE STREET
SUITE B
FOUNTAIN VALLEY, CA 92708

You can also mail or take your documents to a more convenient Social Security office.

If you want to submit your documents to a Social Security office other than the one you chose to process your claim, please select the <u>Office Locator</u> to identify the office of your choice. Mailing or taking your documents to a different Social Security office will not affect how your claim is processed.

Note: If you mail any documents to us, we must have your Social Security number so that we can match them with your claim. Please write your Social Security number on a separate sheet of paper and include it in the mailing envelope along with your documents. **Do not write anything on your original documents.** If you do not want to mail your documents or photocopies, you may bring them to the Social Security office where they will be examined and returned to you. Or, if a later office visit becomes necessary, you may bring them with you at that time.

Caution: Do not mail foreign birth records or any Department of Homeland Security (DHS) documents to us - especially those you are required to keep with you at all times. These documents are extremely difficult, time-consuming and expensive to replace if lost; and some cannot be replaced. Instead, bring them to your Social Security office where they will be examined and returned to you.

Note: DHS was formerly the Immigration & Naturalization Service (INS).

A Social Security Employee May Contact You For The Following Reason(s):

- We may need to verify the earnings history on your Social Security Statement.
- You indicated that you were not sure of the earnings history shown on your Social Security Statement or that you don't have one.
- You indicated that you have recent earnings you want included when we compute your benefits.
- We may need more medical information about your disabling condition.

Changes You Must Report and How to Report
If you are awarded benefits, you must tell us if:

- You change your address;
- You go outside the United States for 30 consecutive days or longer;
- Any beneficiary dies or becomes unable to handle benefits;
- The amount you expect to earn this or next year changes;
- You are confined to a jail, prison, penal institution, or correctional facility for conviction of a crime **or** you are confined to a public institution by court order in connection with a crime;
- You become entitled to a pension or annuity based on your employment that was not covered by Social Security **or** if such a pension or annuity stops;
- A stepchild becomes entitled to benefits on your record and you and the stepchild's parent divorce; or
- You change your marital status.

If you are less than full retirement age, and indicated that you have a disability, you must tell us if:

- Your medical condition improves so that you would be able to work, even though you have not yet returned to work;
- You go to work, whether as an employee or a self-employed person; or
- You apply for or receive a decision on benefits under any workers' compensation or similar type plan (including Black Lung benefits from the Department of Labor) or if the amount of such benefits changes.

How to Report

You can report by phone, mail or in person. Many changes can also be reported online at www.socialsecurity.gov. If you wish to report by phone, you may do so by calling **1-800-772-1213** toll-free. If you are deaf or hard of hearing, call our toll-free "TTY" number, **1-800-325-0778.**

If you do not report any of these changes and the change causes an overpayment, you may have to pay a penalty in addition to repaying the overpayment.

Since you applied for disability benefits...

you need to provide us with medical details related to your disability. This is in addition to any medical records you may have. If you have not already completed and submitted a **Disability Report - Adult (SSA-3368)** and the required number of **Authorization to Disclose Information to the Social Security Administration (SSA-827) forms**, you have the following choices to provide us with this information:

1. Use the 'Continue' button at the bottom of this page to proceed to another Social Security website where you will find the **Disability Report - Adult (SSA-3368)** and the **Authorization to Disclose Information to the Social Security Administration (SSA-827)**; or

2. Call **1-800-772-1213** (TTY **1-800-325-0778**) toll-free to arrange an appointment for us to help you complete the forms.

Note: If you choose option 1. and elect to go to the Disability Report - Adult (SSA-3368) Internet site, you must have a working printer connected to your computer.

Checking the Status of Your Claim

Information about the status of your claim will soon be available on the Internet. *Please wait at least 5 days before you check your claim status.* Just go to the Social Security Claims page at www.SocialSecurity.gov/applyforbenefits, select "Check Your Claim Status" and enter your Confirmation Number. Disability claims take longer to process than other types of Social Security claims because of the need to obtain sufficient medical evidence to show that you are disabled. It may take 90-120 days before "**Check Your Claim Status**" will reflect a final decision on your disability claim. The Confirmation Number for this claim is: 98423483

Remember to guard your Confirmation Number carefully. Your Confirmation Number is the key to your application information!

- Don't put it where others can see it.
- Don't store it with other personal information, like your Social Security number.
- Don't give it to anyone else.
- Social Security employees will **Never** ask for your Confirmation Number.

Voluntary Tax Withholding

If your claim is allowed and you would like to voluntarily have Federal Income Tax withheld from your Social Security benefits, please submit IRS Form W4-V to the office displayed above under the heading "Where Do I Submit My Documents?". You can obtain more information about tax withholding and obtain a copy of the form by entering this link to Voluntary Tax Withholding. The web address for Voluntary Tax Withholding is http://www.SocialSecurity.gov/taxwithhold.html.

How to Learn More About the Medicare Prescription Drug Program and/or File for

What You Need to Do Now!   Page 5 of 5

Extra Help With Medicare Prescription Drug Plan Costs

You can learn more about the Medicare Prescription Drug Program or apply for the extra help with costs related to this program on another Social Security website, **after you complete and submit your Disability Report - Adult (SSA-3368).** You will not be able to return to this page if you go to another website first. Therefore, you should copy or write down this web address, http://www.socialsecurity.gov/prescriptionhelp, so you can visit it later; or you may call our toll-free number at **1-800-772-1213** (TTY 1-800-325-0778) and ask about the Medicare Prescription Drug Program.

For a list of names of Medicare prescription drug providers in your area, contact the Centers for Medicare & Medicaid Services toll-free at **1-800-MEDICARE** (TTY 1-877-486-2048) or visit http://www.medicare.gov.

Frequently Asked Questions

If you have questions, please check our Frequently Asked Questions (FAQs) site. The web address for our FAQ site is **http://ssa-custhelp.ssa.gov.** Use the drop-down box titled **"Category"** to select **"Internet Benefit Claim."** Then select **"Search"** to see a list of questions that may provide the information you are seeking. Select any question to see the answer.

Feedback

Continue

The Inherent Problems of Applying Online

The major benefit of applying online is that it avoids the long *on hold* time that you may experience if applying by phone or the long wait that applicants often experience at the Social Security office. However, the online application process is still relatively new. Even though you can apply online, your application will ultimately be sent to the nearest Social Security office to where you reside, which may not be familiar with the online process. Accordingly, be prepared if some of the information that you provide does not find its way into the hands of the Social Security staff, causing you to duplicate your efforts.

> ### Practical Point
>
> As of the date of the writing of this book, online applications can only be taken for SSDI. SSI applications must be made by phone or in person.

Furthermore, prior to beginning the online application, there are very helpful links that explain what information you will need. The problem exists in the fact that if you do not have the necessary information, the program will not allow you to advance to the next page of the application. As a result, you will either have to abandon the online experience and apply in person or by phone, or enter information that is incorrect. You do not want to do the latter, as on the last page of the application you must sign a declaration that all the information contained in your application is true and correct.

To illustrate, if you have been married, divorced, and married again, one of the questions asked is, "Where were you divorced?" If your ex-spouse filed the papers and you did not contest the action, you may not be able to supply this information. Another question asks, "What is your former spouse's date of birth or age?" Sure, you could guess, but you might be wrong.

The site also limits how much information you may include for this entry. So if you abbreviate, do not use periods or dashes.

Note that even if you successfully filed your application online, the online experience does not remove the requirement of having direct, in-person contact with the SSA, as you will still have to appear in person to produce your birth certificate and Social Security number.

The biggest problem with online filings is that the word from the SSA that online applications have started has not filitered down to the local offices. As incredible as it may sound, I have received several calls from local offices advising me that they are not set up for an online application. As a result, my clients had to appear in person, and in a sense, start all over again. This causes even more confusion for both the applicant and SSA employees.

So, until all the bugs and quirks are worked out, no matter how computer savvy you may be, accept the fact that the technology is not there yet. Therefore, so as to not further delay the processing of your claim, I recommend that you apply by phone or in person.

Adult Disability Report

Whether you complete your application online, by phone, or in person, you will also need to complete the *Adult Disability Report* (Form SSA-3368-BK), which is reproduced as follows. The form is very straightforward and easy to complete. Note that it is to your advantage to provide all the information asked for in the report and not to leave any sections blank if they apply to your claim. Any information that you do not supply will delay the processing of your claim, as the SSA will request the information from you at a later time.

> ### Practical Point
>
> The site does not like keystrokes such as commas and slashes. Therefore, when imputing information, avoid using these keys. This is especially important for the section that asks you to list your disabilities. The following entry would not be accepted:
>
> **Diabetes/difficulty walking, high blood pressure**
>
> Instead, enter the information as follows:
>
> **Diabetes Difficulty Walking High Blood Pressure**

SOCIAL SECURITY ADMINISTRATION

Form Approved
OMB No. 0960-0579

DISABILITY REPORT
ADULT

For SSA Use Only
Do not write in this box.

Related SSN _____

Number Holder _____

SECTION 1- INFORMATION ABOUT THE DISABLED PERSON

A. **NAME** *(First, Middle Initial, Last)*

B. **SOCIAL SECURITY NUMBER**

C. **DAYTIME TELEPHONE NUMBER** *(If you have no number where you can be reached, give us a daytime number where we can leave a message for you.)*

_____   _____   ☐ Your Number   ☐ Message Number   ☐ None
Area Code   Number

D. Give the name of a **friend or relative** that we can contact (other than your doctors) **who knows about your illnesses, injuries or conditions** and can help you with your claim.

NAME _____   RELATIONSHIP _____

ADDRESS _____
(Number, Street, Apt. No.(If any), P.O. Box, or Rural Route)

_____ _____ _____   DAYTIME
City   State   ZIP   PHONE   _____ _____
                                               Area Code   Number

E. What is your **height** without shoes?   ___ ___   feet inches

F. What is your **weight** without shoes?   ___   pounds

G. Do you have a **medical assistance card**? (For Example, Medicaid or Medi-Cal) If "YES," show the **number** here: ☐ YES ☐ NO
_____

H. Can you **speak and understand English**? ☐ YES ☐ NO   If "**NO**," what is your preferred language? _____

NOTE: If you cannot speak and understand English, we will provide an interpreter, free of charge.

If you cannot **speak and understand English**, is there someone we may contact who speaks and understands English and will give you messages? ☐ YES ☐ NO   *(If "YES," and that person is the same as in "D" above show "SAME" here. If not, complete the following information.)*

NAME _____   RELATIONSHIP _____

ADDRESS _____
(Number, Street, Apt. No.(If any), P.O. Box, or Rural Route)

_____ _____ _____   DAYTIME
City   State   ZIP   PHONE   _____ _____
                                               Area Code   Number

I. Can you **read and understand English**?   ☐ YES ☐ NO

J. Can you **write more than your name in English**?   ☐ YES ☐ NO

FORM **SSA-3368-BK** (2-2004) EF (2-2004) Use 6-2003 edition Until Supply Exhausted   PAGE 1

Disability Report-Adult-Form SSA-3368-BK

SECTION 2
YOUR ILLNESSES, INJURIES OR CONDITIONS AND HOW THEY AFFECT YOU

A. What are the **illnesses, injuries or conditions** that limit your ability to work? _____

_____

_____

B. How do your illnesses, injuries or conditions limit your ability to work? _____

_____

_____

C. Do your illnesses, injuries or conditions cause you **pain**   ☐ YES   ☐ NO
   or **other symptoms**?

D. When did your illnesses, injuries or

Month	Day	Year

   conditions **first bother you**?

E. When did you become **unable to work** because

Month	Day	Year

   of your illnesses, injuries or conditions?

F. Have you **ever worked**?   ☐ YES   ☐ NO   *(If "NO," go to Section 4.)*

G. Did you **work at any time** after the date your
   illnesses, injuries or conditions first bothered you?   ☐ YES   ☐ NO

H. If "YES," did your illnesses, injuries or conditions cause you to: *(check all that apply)*

   ☐ **work fewer hours?** *(Explain below)*

   ☐ **change your job duties?** *(Explain below)*

   ☐ **make any job-related changes such as your attendance, help needed, or employers?**
      (Explain below)

_____

_____

_____

_____

I. Are you **working now**?   ☐ YES   ☐ NO

   If "NO," when did **you stop working**?

Month	Day	Year

J. Why did you **stop working**? _____

_____

_____

FORM **SSA-3368-BK** (2-2004) EF (2-2004) Use 6-2003 edition Until Supply Exhausted   PAGE 2

SECTION 3 - INFORMATION ABOUT YOUR WORK

A. List all the jobs that you had in the 15 years before you became unable to work because of your illnesses, injuries or conditions.

JOB TITLE (Example, Cook)	TYPE OF BUSINESS (Example, Restaurant)	DATES WORKED (month & year)		HOURS PER DAY	DAYS PER WEEK	RATE OF PAY (Per hour, day, week, month or year)	
		From	To				
						$	
						$	
						$	
						$	
						$	
						$	
						$	

B. Which job did you do the longest? _____

C. Describe this job. What did you do all day? (If you need more space, write in the "Remarks" section.)

_____

_____

D. In **this job**, did you:

Use machines, tools or equipment? ☐ YES ☐ NO

Use technical knowledge or skills? ☐ YES ☐ NO

Do any writing, complete reports, or perform duties like this? ☐ YES ☐ NO

E. In **this job**, how many total hours each day did you:

Walk? _____ Stoop? *(Bend down & forward at waist.)* _____ Handle, grab or grasp big objects? _____

Stand? _____ Kneel? *(Bend legs to rest on knees.)* _____ Reach? _____

Sit? _____ Crouch? *(Bend legs & back down & forward.)* _____ Write, type or handle small objects? _____

Climb? _____ Crawl? *(Move on hands & knees.)* _____

F. Lifting and Carrying *(Explain what you lifted, how far you carried it, and how often you did this.)*

_____

_____

G. Check **heaviest** weight lifted:

☐ Less than 10 lbs ☐ 10 lbs ☐ 20 lbs ☐ 50 lbs ☐ 100 lbs. or more ☐ Other _____

H. Check weight **frequently** lifted: *(By frequently, we mean from 1/3 to 2/3 of the workday.)*

☐ Less than 10 lbs ☐ 10 lbs ☐ 25 lbs ☐ 50 lbs. or more ☐ Other _____

I. Did you supervise other people in this job? ☐ YES (Complete items below.) ☐ NO (If NO, go to J.)

How many people did you supervise? _____

What part of your time was spent supervising people? _____

Did you hire and fire employees? ☐ YES ☐ NO

J. Were you a lead worker? ☐ YES ☐ NO

SECTION 4 - INFORMATION ABOUT YOUR MEDICAL RECORDS

A. Have you been seen by a **doctor/hospital/clinic** or anyone else for the illnesses, injuries or conditions that limit your ability to work?   ☐ YES   ☐ NO

B. Have you been seen by a **doctor/hospital/clinic** or anyone else for emotional or mental problems that limit your ability to work?   ☐ YES   ☐ NO

If you answered "NO" to both of these questions, go to Section 5.

C. List **other names** you have used on your medical records. _____

Tell us who may have medical records or other information about your illnesses, injuries or conditions.

D. List each **DOCTOR/HMO/THERAPIST/OTHER**. Include your **next appointment**.

1.
NAME	DATES	
STREET ADDRESS	FIRST VISIT	
CITY STATE ZIP	LAST SEEN	
PHONE _____ Area Code Phone Number	PATIENT ID # (If known)	NEXT APPOINTMENT
REASONS FOR VISITS _____		
WHAT TREATMENT WAS RECEIVED? _____		

2.
NAME	DATES	
STREET ADDRESS	FIRST VISIT	
CITY STATE ZIP	LAST SEEN	
PHONE _____ Area Code Phone Number	PATIENT ID # (If known)	NEXT APPOINTMENT
REASONS FOR VISITS _____		
WHAT TREATMENT WAS RECEIVED? _____		

SECTION 4 - INFORMATION ABOUT YOUR MEDICAL RECORDS

DOCTOR/HMO/THERAPIST/OTHER

3. NAME			DATES
STREET ADDRESS			FIRST VISIT
CITY	STATE	ZIP	LAST SEEN
PHONE *Area Code Phone Number*		PATIENT ID # (If known)	NEXT APPOINTMENT
REASONS FOR VISITS			
WHAT TREATMENT WAS RECEIVED?			

If you need more space, use Remarks, Section 9.

E. **List each HOSPITAL/CLINIC.** Include your **next appointment.**

1. HOSPITAL/CLINIC			TYPE OF VISIT	DATES	
NAME			☐ **INPATIENT STAYS** *(Stayed at least overnight)*	DATE IN	DATE OUT
STREET ADDRESS					
			☐ **OUTPATIENT VISITS** *(Sent home same day)*	DATE FIRST VISIT	DATE LAST VISIT
CITY	STATE	ZIP			
PHONE *Area Code Phone Number*			☐ **EMERGENCY ROOM VISITS**	DATE OF VISITS	

Next **appointment** _____ Your hospital/clinic **number** _____

Reasons for visits _____

_____

What **treatment** did you receive? _____

_____

What **doctors** do you see at this hospital/clinic on a regular basis? _____

_____

SECTION 4-INFORMATION ABOUT YOUR MEDICAL RECORDS

HOSPITAL/CLINIC

2. HOSPITAL/CLINIC			TYPE OF VISIT	DATES	
NAME			☐ **INPATIENT** STAYS *(Stayed at least overnight)*	DATE IN	DATE OUT
STREET ADDRESS					
CITY	STATE	ZIP	☐ **OUTPATIENT** VISITS *(Sent home same day)*	DATE FIRST VISIT	DATE LAST VISIT
PHONE			☐ **EMERGENCY ROOM** VISITS	DATE OF VISITS	
Area Code	Phone Number				

Next **appointment** _____ Your hospital/clinic **number** _____

Reasons for visits _____

_____

What **treatment** did you receive? _____

_____

What **doctors** do you see at this hospital/clinic on a regular basis? _____

_____

If you need more space, use Remarks, Section 9.

F. Does **anyone else have medical records or information** about your illnesses, injuries or conditions (Workers' Compensation, insurance companies, prisons, attorneys, welfare), or are you scheduled to see anyone else?

☐ YES *(If "YES," complete information below.)*   ☐ NO

NAME			DATES	
STREET ADDRESS			FIRST VISIT	
CITY	STATE	ZIP	LAST SEEN	
PHONE			NEXT APPOINTMENT	
Area Code	Phone Number			
CLAIM NUMBER (If any)				
REASONS FOR VISITS				

If you need more space, use Remarks, Section 9.

SECTION 5 - MEDICATIONS

Do you currently take any **medications** for your illnesses, injuries or conditions? ☐ YES

If "YES," please tell us the following: *(Look at your medicine bottles, if necessary.)* ☐ NO

NAME OF MEDICINE	IF PRESCRIBED, GIVE NAME OF DOCTOR	REASON FOR MEDICINE	SIDE EFFECTS YOU HAVE

If you need more space, use Remarks, Section 9.

SECTION 6 - TESTS

Have you had, or will you have, any **medical tests** for illnesses, injuries or conditions?

☐ YES ☐ NO   If "YES," please tell us the following: *(Give approximate dates, if necessary.)*

KIND OF TEST	WHEN DONE, OR WHEN WILL IT BE DONE? (Month, day, year)	WHERE DONE? (Name of Facility)	WHO SENT YOU FOR THIS TEST?
EKG (HEART TEST)			
TREADMILL (EXERCISE TEST)			
CARDIAC CATHETERIZATION			
BIOPSY--Name of body part			
HEARING TEST			
SPEECH/LANGUAGE TEST			
VISION TEST			
IQ TESTING			
EEG (BRAIN WAVE TEST)			
HIV TEST			
BLOOD TEST (NOT HIV)			
BREATHING TEST			
X-RAY--Name of body part _____			
MRI/CT SCAN Name of body part _____			

If you have had other tests, list them in Remarks, Section 9.

SECTION 7-EDUCATION/TRAINING INFORMATION

A. Check the highest grade of **school** completed.

Grade school: College:

0	1	2	3	4	5	6	7	8	9	10	11	12	GED	1	2	3	4 or more
☐	☐	☐	☐	☐	☐	☐	☐	☐	☐	☐	☐	☐	☐	☐	☐	☐	☐

Approximate **date** completed: _____

B. Did you attend **special education** classes? ☐ YES ☐ NO *(If "NO," go to part C)*

NAME OF SCHOOL _____

ADDRESS _____

(Number, Street, Apt. No.(if any), P.O. Box or Rural Route)

_____
               City   *State*   *Zip*

DATES ATTENDED _____ TO _____

TYPE OF PROGRAM _____

C. Have you completed any type of **special job training, trade or vocational school?**

☐ YES ☐ NO If "YES," what type?_____

Approximate date completed: _____

SECTION 8 - VOCATIONAL REHABILITATION, EMPLOYMENT, or OTHER SUPPORT SERVICES INFORMATION

Are you participating in the Ticket Program or another program of vocational rehabilitation services, employment services or other support services to help you go to work?

☐ YES (Complete the information below)   ☐ NO

NAME OF ORGANIZATION _____

NAME OF COUNSELOR _____

ADDRESS _____

(Number, Street, Apt. No.(if any), P.O. Box or Rural Route)

_____
           City   *State*   *Zip*

DAYTIME PHONE NUMBER _____ _____
                 Area Code   *Number*

DATES SEEN _____ TO _____

TYPE OF SERVICES OR
TESTS PERFORMED _____
        (IQ, vision, physicals, hearing, workshops, etc.)

SECTION 9 - REMARKS

Use this section for any added information you did not show in earlier parts of the form. When you are done with this section (or if you don't have anything to add), be sure to go to the next page and complete the blocks there.

SECTION 9 - REMARKS

_____

_____

_____

_____

_____

_____

_____

_____

_____

_____

_____

_____

_____

_____

_____

_____

_____

_____

_____

_____

_____

_____

_____

_____

_____

_____

_____

_____

_____

Name of person completing this form *(Please Print)*	**Date Form Completed** *(Month, day, year)*
Address *(Number and street)*	**e-mail address** *(optional)*
City **State**	**Zip Code**

When reviewing the form, pay particular attention to section 9. In completing this section, I advise my clients to "spill their guts." That is, explain in detail to the SSA why you are disabled. This is not the time to be modest. Even if something is embarrassing to you, write it down. The SSA needs to have a complete picture of why you cannot work so that it can fully evaluate your claim.

Along with the initial application and the Adult Disability Report, at some time during the application process you may need to complete a daily activities report known as *Activities of Daily Living*. This report details how you spend your day.

LEGALLY SPEAKING

Remember, it is very important that you do not make any false statements, as the SSA may prosecute any person who obtains benefits fraudulently.

In addition, the SSA may send to you to complete one or more of the following:

- if you are employed, a work activity report; or,

- if you are self-employed, an employment record and work activity report.

These reports allow you to explain how you performed your job. When completing the forms, provide as much information as possible and do not leave any section that is relevant blank, as that will only delay the processing of your claim.

In addition, someone acquainted with you may be asked to complete a third-party activities questionnaire. Similar to the daily activity report, this report is designed to elicit information about you from another person's point of view. The third-party questionnaire is helpful, as there may be certain details that you do not wish to reveal out of embarrassment but that the third party will mention.

Providing Medical Records

Regardless of the manner in which you choose to apply for benefits, your claim needs to be supported by medical records, which may include:

- records from doctors, hospitals, clinics, and therapists;

- reports from doctors from whom you are presently receiving treatment;

- lab tests, x-rays, and other records of diagnostic testing; and,

- lists of all medications you are taking.

Accordingly, you should provide copies of all medical documents to the SSA office that is assigned to your case as soon as possible, along with the names and addresses of all medical providers that you do not have records from. In addition, the SSA will require you to sign Form SSA-827, reproduced on page 92, which allows the SSA to contact your medical providers directly so that it can obtain any additional information that may be missing from your file. Note that medical records are confidential between you and your doctor, but with your written permission, your doctor can release those records.

WHOSE *Records to be Disclosed*	Form Approved OMB No 0960-0623
NAME *(First, Middle, Last)*	

SSN -- --	Birthday *(mm/dd/yy)*

SSA USE ONLY NUMBER HOLDER (If other than above)
NAME
SSN   --   --

AUTHORIZATION TO DISCLOSE INFORMATION TO
THE SOCIAL SECURITY ADMINISTRATION (SSA)

** PLEASE READ THE ENTIRE FORM, BOTH PAGES, BEFORE SIGNING BELOW **

I voluntarily authorize and request disclosure (including paper, oral, and electronic interchange):

OF WHAT   *All my medical records; also education records and other information related to my ability to perform tasks. This includes specific permission to release:*

1. All records and other information regarding my treatment, hospitalization, and outpatient care for my impairment(s) *including*, and **not limited to:**
   - Psychological, psychiatric or other mental impairment(s) (excludes "psychotherapy notes" as defined in 45 CFR 164.501)
   - Drug abuse, alcoholism, or other substance abuse
   - Sickle cell anemia
   - Records which may indicate the presence of a communicable or venereal disease which may include, but are not limited to, diseases such as hepatitis, syphilis, gonorrhea and the human immunodeficiency virus, also known as Acquired Immune Deficiency Syndrome (AIDS); and tests for HIV.
   - Gene-related impairments (including genetic test results)
2. Information about how my impairment(s) affects my ability to complete tasks and activities of daily living, and affects my ability to work.
3. Copies of educational tests or evaluations, including Individualized Educational Programs, triennial assessments, psychological and speech evaluations, and any other records that can help evaluate function; also teachers' observations and evaluations.
4. Information created within 12 months after the date this authorization is signed, as well as past information.

FROM WHOM

- All medical sources (hospitals, clinics, labs, physicians, psychologists, etc.) including mental health, correctional, addiction treatment, and VA health care facilities
- All educational sources (schools, teachers, records administrators, counselors, etc.)
- Social workers/rehabilitation counselors
- Consulting examiners used by SSA
- Employers
- Others who may know about my condition (family, neighbors, friends, public officials)

THIS BOX TO BE COMPLETED BY SSA/DDS (as needed) Additional information to identify the subject (e.g., other names used), the specific source, or the material to be disclosed:

TO WHOM   The Social Security Administration and to the State agency authorized to process my case (usually called "disability determination services"), including contract copy services, and doctors or other professionals consulted during the process. [Also, for international claims, to the U.S. Department of State Foreign Service Post.]

PURPOSE   Determining my eligibility for benefits, including looking at the combined effect of any impairments that by themselves would not meet SSA's definition of disability; and whether I can manage such benefits.
☐ Determining whether I am **capable of managing benefits** ONLY (check only if this applies)

EXPIRES WHEN   This authorization is good for 12 months from the date signed (below my signature).

- I authorize the use of a copy (including electronic copy) of this form for the disclosure of the information described above
- I understand that there are some circumstances in which this information may be redisclosed to other parties (see page 2 for details).
- I may write to SSA and my sources to revoke this authorization at any time (see page 2 for details).
- SSA will give me a copy of this form if I ask; I may ask the source to allow me to inspect or get a copy of material to be disclosed.
- I have read both pages of this form and agree to the disclosures above from the types of sources listed.

PLEASE SIGN USING BLUE OR BLACK INK ONLY | IF not signed by subject of disclosure, specify basis for authority to sign
INDIVIDUAL authorizing disclosure | ☐ Parent of minor   ☐ Guardian   ☐ Other personal representative (explain)

SIGN   Una
   t. . | (Parent/guardian/personal representative sign here if two signatures required by State law)   U.

Date Signed	Street Address		
Phone Number (with area code)	City	State	ZIP

WITNESS   *I know the person signing this form or am satisfied of this person's identity:*

SIGN Una
   t. | IF needed, second witness sign here (e.g., if signed with "X" above)
SIGN U.
Phone Number (or Address) | Phone Number (or Address)

This general and special authorization to disclose was developed to comply with the provisions regarding disclosure of medical, educational, and other information under P.L. 104-191 ("HIPAA"); 45 CFR parts 160 and 164; 42 U.S. Code section 290dd-2; 42 CFR part 2; 38 U.S. Code section 7332; 38 CFR 1.475, 20 U.S. Code section 1232g ("FERPA"); 34 CFR parts 99 and 300; and State law.

Form SSA-827 (6-2006) ef (06-2006) Use 2-2003 and Later Editions Until Supply is Exhausted   Page 1 of 2

Tips for Applying for Benefits

Regardless of the manner in which you choose to apply for benefits, the following are helpful suggestions for completing your application.

- Make sure to list all of your medical conditions, not just the one that is the worst. Social Security will look at all of your conditions together and how they affect you. A medical condition you leave out might limit you from work in a manner that you did not think of.

- You are not a doctor. Therefore, describe your medical conditions in nonmedical terms. For example, if you have difficulty walking, state that. You do not have to say that your diabetes has caused neuropathy in your feet.

- Submit as much medical evidence as you can. That includes medical reports and records. This will ensure that you give yourself the best chance of winning at this level. Note that if your claim is denied at the initial application stage, it may take months before another decision is made.

- Fill out the Social Security Disability or Supplemental Security Income application and all other forms completely. If you do not, Social Security will keep trying to get the information anyway and this will delay your claim.

Practical Point

Doctors are very busy treating patients and often have little time for filling out forms. To assist your case, you should call your doctor or the doctor's office manager to make them aware that you are filing for benefits, and to request that they cooperate when they are contacted by the SSA. In addition, request that your doctor provide you with a copy of any report that he or she prepares on your behalf. This is essential, as your doctor may be asked what your capabilities related to work are. If the information provided is inconsistent with what you have provided to the SSA, you will need to have the record corrected. Please refer to Chapter 11 for a complete discussion of developing your medical evidence.

- Have a family member or friend review your application before you submit it. There might be something important that you left out.

- Be truthful about your work history. Do not exaggerate a job title or description, as it could come back to haunt you. Remember, you are not applying for a job but applying for disability because you cannot work.

- Respond to questions from the SSA promptly, as any delay on your part will prolong the evaluation process. Even worse, if you do not cooperate, the SSA can deny your claim based on your lack of cooperation.

CONSULTATIVE EXAMINATIONS | **10**

For most claimants, it is a very long road they must travel to obtain benefits. Like any journey where you are not sure where you are going, you may encounter a bump in the road that could send you in the wrong direction. The problem, of course, is getting back in the direction that will lead to the SSA awarding you benefits.

In the world of the SSA, the bump in the road is often the *consultative examination*. It is here where many claims are decided against the claimant, resulting in the need to appeal the claim. As stated in earlier chapters, the appeal process is an even longer road to navigate.

Why Consultative Examinations May Be Required

The local Social Security office that has been assigned to your claim requires you to provide information to it that supports your claim for disability. This includes the names and addresses of your medical providers. This information is then sent to your state's office of Disability Determination Service (DDS) for the medical development of your claim. The DDS will then contact your treating doctors as well as all medical facilities where you have been seen in regard to your impairment. The DDS will request copies of medical records and will ask your doctors to complete questionnaires that will hopefully support your claim for disability.

Practical Point

Unlike many of the local Social Security office personnel who are often reluctant to provide you with their names, the DDS will be your link to your Social Security claim and you will be provided with the name of the person assigned to your claim, as well as his or her direct contact phone number.

Often, however, the DDS will schedule you to be seen by a doctor whom the DDS has contracted with for performing these examinations. The examination will be at no expense to you.

There are many reasons why a consultative examination may be necessary, including the following.

- Your medical records are not conclusive and therefore the DDS cannot fully evaluate the impairment that you allege to have.

- Your doctor or other treating facilities have not furnished the requested records.

- The records are not legible or are incomplete.

- Your doctor did not complete the requested questionnaire.

- Your doctor has made a diagnosis but is not a specialist in that field of medicine and therefore may not be qualified to render a medical opinion as to your diagnosis.

- You are claiming that you are disabled but the medical impairments that you are claiming are not ones for which you are under medical care.

Your Doctor May Also Perform the Consultative Examination

If the DDS contacts you to schedule a consultative examination, first inquire whether it will permit your doctor to serve as the *consultative examiner* (CE). Often, if your doctor's specialty includes the type of impairment you are claiming, the SSA may agree to allow your doctor to examine you. For example, if you have Hepatitis A, and are being treated by a gastroenterologist, the DDS will most likely allow him or her to examine you, as his or her medical specialty is in digestive disorders.

However, even if the DDS agrees, treating doctors are usually reluctant to perform the examination. The most often cited reason doctors give for declining to perform the exam is that the DDS pays very little and it is not worth the doctor's time. However, in most cases, your doctor will decline because he or she is your treating doctor, which does not include providing medical services for the purpose of rendering an opinion as to your disability. If you were denied benefits, however, you would point fingers at your doctor for not being more supportive. This would result in a breakdown of the doctor/patient relationship, which your doctor would prefer to avoid.

If your doctor does decline to be the CE, the DDS will arrange an appointment with another doctor with similar credentials.

The Inherent Problems Associated with Consultative Examinations

When a client is awarded benefits after a hearing before an administrative law judge, it is because the judge did not agree with the evaluation of the DDS. Since 75% of cases are granted at the hearing stage, this means the DDS is wrong 75% of the time. So why do they get it wrong 75% of the time?

To illustrate, you do not need to have a medical license to conclude that a person who is on a waiting list for a heart transplant is disabled, or that a claimant who has been taking medication but has still had more than a dozen seizures in the past twelve months resulting in six hospitalizations is unable to work. Still, these are two actual cases in which the DDS said that my clients were not disabled.

Although it would never be admitted, the DDS contracts with independent doctors to perform consultative examinations. These contracts are renewable. Even though the DDS does not pay a lot for the exam, a doctor still looks at his or her relationship with the DDS as a source of income. Arguably, if every claimant who was examined by the DDS doctor was found to be disabled, how long do you think his or her contract would continue? This is an unfortunate example where the power of money may interfere with a doctor's medical judgment.

> **Practical Point**
>
> The information gained from a physical consultative exam is essential to the DDS in determining whether you can perform any work that you have done in the last fifteen years. If you cannot, the evaluation will decide what your exertional limitations are and whether, with these limitations, you can perform any other type of work. This is Step 5 of the sequential evaluation as discussed in Chapter 7.

Types of Consultative Examinations

There are two types of consultative examinations. Depending on your claim, the DDS may schedule you for both. Note that regardless of whether one or multiple examinations are scheduled, the fee for the exam is paid by the SSA. You should never be asked to pay for any cost of the exam.

Physical Consultative Examinations

If your claim is for a physical impairment, your examination will include the doctor taking a history of your disability—that is, how long you have been ill and what treatment you are receiving. You will also be asked to provide the names of any medications you are taking and will be questioned if the medications are helping or causing any side effects.

The doctor should also conduct a physical examination. To illustrate, if you are claiming a back disorder, the doctor may ask you to bend and walk. He or she will also test your gripping strength so that he or she can determine how much you can lift.

Mental Consultative Examinations

If your claim is for a mental impairment, the DDS may schedule you to see its psychologist or psychiatrist. At the examination, the doctor will inquire about your ability to concentrate, follow instructions, and work in a group. If you are taking any medications, the doctor will ask if they are helping and if you are having any side effects.

Client Complaints about Consultative Examinations

People applying for Social Security Disability benefits are frustrated—and they should be. They are disabled, yet the government believes that they can work. With all the pressure that the clients must encounter in applying, the biggest complaints I hear from clients about the Social Security Disability process concern the consultative examinations. Aside from hearing that the medical offices are often shabby and that the staff is unprofessional, clients seem amazed that the examination is so brief. The following are actual comments as repeated by my clients.

"I complained about the difficulty I have walking but the doctor never examined the swelling in my legs."

"I told the doctor that I have chest pains but he never listened to my heart."

"The doctor started to ask me about my depression but then left the room and never came back. Fifteen minutes later his nurse said that the examination was completed."

What Does the DDS Do with the Consultative Doctor's Report?

After the doctor completes the examination, he or she sends his or her records and opinion as to whether you are disabled to the DDS, where a medical consultant reviews the information provided. Note that the CE's opinion is just that—an opinion only.

If the consultative doctor's opinion is that the claimant meets or equals the listings as discussed in Chapter 5, the DDS then considers his or her opinion. If it agrees, it will notify the local Social Security office that is handling the claim and shortly thereafter a benefit awards letter will be issued, provided the claimant also meets the nonmedical requirements for benefits as discussed in Chapter 3.

If the consultative doctor concludes that the claimant does not meet or equal the listings, he or she will then offer his or her opinion as to the claimant's exertional abilities (that is, how much the claimant can lift and carry). In addition, the doctor will note if the claimant has any other nonexertional limitations, such as whether the claimant should avoid exposure to noise or has difficulty sitting.

> ### Practical Point
>
> Remember that it is not the end of the road for you if your claim is denied. On the contrary, we were successful in obtaining benefits for both claimants previously mentioned by demonstrating that at Step 5 of the evaluation process, there were no jobs available that the claimants could perform. Please see Chapter 7 for a complete discussion of the evaluation process at Step 5.

With this information, the DDS will develop the claimant's residual functional capacity (RFC), which is discussed in Chapter 7. However, unless a claimant's RFC is very limiting, the claim will be denied.

The following are excerpts from denial letters of clients where a consultative doctor concluded that the claimants were not disabled.

"Though you have a back disorder, you can still lift and carry twenty pounds occasionally and ten pounds frequently and can stand or walk six to eight hours per day. As a result, you can do your previous job as a salesman and are therefore not disabled."

"Though you have aspergillosis, a severe pulmonary disease, and you should avoid all exposures to odors, you can still perform sedentary work."

In both examples, the consultative doctor first concluded that the claimant did not meet or equal the listings. Thereafter, based on the doctor's examination, the DDS evaluated the claimant's RFC for past and other work and determined that he or she was not disabled.

Dos And Don'ts for Consultative Examinations

Do:

- Show up on time. Although you may have to wait to be seen, it is best to arrive early.

- Stay focused on the questions that you are asked. It is okay to volunteer information so long as it relates to your disability.

- Take a family member or friend with you to the appointment and have him or her come into the examination room with you. Have your witness record what time the exam began and ended. Having a witness attend the examination may prove beneficial at a hearing if you need to contradict evidence in your file.

> ## LEGALLY SPEAKING
>
> If, after the examination, it is your opinion that the doctor did not fully inquire into the nature of your disability, or that the examination was too brief, you should contact the disability examiner assigned to your claim to file a complaint. In addition, you should send a letter expressing your concerns and dissatisfaction to the Social Security office where your initial claim was filed. This letter will become part of the record of your file and will be reviewed by the judge if your case goes to the hearing stage.

Don't:

- Ask the doctor if he or she believes that you are disabled.

- Be argumentative. Answer all the questions, even if you think they are ridiculous.

- Get upset with the doctor, especially if you think the examination was too brief.

- Ask the doctor for a copy of his or her report.

Developing Your Medical Evidence: Your Doctor's Role in Obtaining Benefits

11

Your treating doctor plays a key role in helping you obtain Social Security Disability benefits. This is because the Social Security regulations state that a treating doctor's opinion will be given greater weight than the SSA's consultative examiner in deciding a claim. Therefore, at your very first opportunity, you should inform your treating physician that you have applied for Social Security Disability benefits. He or she will then enter this information on your chart. Likewise, if you decide to retain an attorney, you should provide your doctor with your attorney's business card so that it can be attached to your file.

Getting the attention of your doctor can sometimes be frustrating. Therefore, it is important that you establish a contact with someone on your doctor's staff who is more reachable, especially if something urgent arises in your file that requires immediate attention. On occasion, we have sent a basket of muffins to a doctor's office to show our appreciation and to encourage the staff to respond to our future requests in a speedy manner.

Your Doctor Is Very Busy

Part of winning your case includes doctor cooperation, but your doctor receives requests for

---

Practical Point

Do not be surprised if your doctor is not familiar with the evaluation process (or, as I like to say, all the hurdles and hoops you have to jump through to prove that you are disabled). Doctors are not necessarily knowledgeable about how Social Security works, and often make the same assumption you made before you began reading this book: if a person cannot work, he or she must be disabled.

information on many of his or her patients. The problem for your doctor is that he or she is often trying to juggle treating patients and answering mail. However, if your doctor is already aware that you are applying, and you educate him or her about how long it takes for a case to be decided, he or she will hopefully respond to any requests from the SSA in a faster manner.

If You Have an Attorney

Although I have many friends who are physicians, in the world of doctors and lawyers it is like cats and dogs—the doctor senses something is bad when he or she is contacted by an attorney. Just the sight of an envelope from an attorney's office often raises concerns in the doctor's office that he or she may have done something wrong. In order to alleviate any initial concerns, tell your doctor that you have an attorney and that he or she will be contacting the office.

Ensure that Your Doctor Cooperates With the SSA and You

As previously mentioned, doctors spend their days treating patients and have very little time to answer correspondence. I have seen many claims that have been denied because a decision was made by the DDS without any medical documentation having been received from the claimant's medical providers.

Therefore, it is very important that you inform your doctor that his or her cooperation is greatly needed, and that he or she will be asked to provide copies of your records and may also have to complete a questionnaire that will ask what your limitations to do work are. You should also stress that the faster that the DDS receives the records, the sooner it will be able to evaluate your claim.

If Your Doctor Does Not Support You

I have had many cases in which a doctor takes the position that almost everyone can work. Sometimes this is because the doctor has his or her own philosophical agenda concerning persons who obtain governmental benefits that he or she believes they are not entitled to. It is the old story that "everyone should work and no one deserves a handout." As a result, the doctor may be reluctant to place his or her signature on any form that states you cannot be gainfully employed.

This is unfortunate because most people who apply for benefits are legitimately disabled and deserve to receive benefits.

You need to have a discussion with your doctor to determine whether he or she has any bias against a person applying for disability benefits. If he or she does, you should change doctors. If you discover any bias after he or she has provided an opinion to the DDS, it will make challenging any denial of benefits more difficult.

Who Are Acceptable Medical Providers?

You may have a great relationship with your doctor and believe that he or she is helping you. However, unless he or she is a recognized medical provider, the SSA will lend no merit to his or her records in support of your claim. Recognized medical providers include:

- licensed physicians;

- licensed osteopaths;

- licensed podiatrists;

- licensed optometrists;

- physical therapists;

- licensed or certified psychologists;

- licensed or certified social workers; and,

- licensed or certified mental health workers.

> ### Practical Point
>
> The recommendation to switch your medical provider is not made to encourage doctor shopping, which is frowned upon by both the legal and medical community. Instead, if you are disabled and your doctor does not believe you, regardless of whether you are applying for Social Security Disability benefits, you are with the wrong doctor.

Not on this list are doctors who provide medical services for acupuncture, homeopathic, or other alternative medicines.

Getting the Right Report from a Credible Source

Even if your doctor is licensed, if he or she is offering an opinion that is outside his or her scope of expertise, his or her opinion may not be valued. For example, if you are seeing a cardiologist for a heart problem and your claim for disability also results from a bulging disk in your lower back, your heart doctor's opinion that you require back surgery will probably not be considered by the DDS in evaluating your claim. Such an opinion would more properly be made by an orthopedist.

Obtaining Timely Reports

Just as it is important that the report is from your treating doctor, it is equally important that the records be timely. That is, you should have seen the doctor that you are stating is treating you recently. What qualifies as *recent* is debatable, but logic would hold that records within six months of filing your claim are timely. For example, if your disability is based on a back impairment that prevents you from sitting more than fifteen minutes, and you do not take pain medication, records from a doctor visit over two years ago will not be given the same weight as if you had just seen your physician.

Obtaining Accurate Records

A doctor's notations of your office visit are made for your doctor. He or she uses those notations to refer to when he or she sees you in a follow-up visit. Your doctor is not anticipating anyone else reading these notes and therefore they may not be completely accurate as they pertain to your claim for disability. For example, to obtain benefits based on diabetes, you must show that your blood sugar levels are not controlled despite compliance with taking prescribed medication; furthermore, you must show that the disease has progressed and is causing you to have problems with walking or vision. If your doctor has not documented your disease, his or her records will not be viewed as accurate.

Obtaining Sufficient Records

To be reliable, your doctor's opinion must be substantiated by medical findings. For example, if your doctor states that you have congestive heart failure, your record must include testing that was conducted to confirm this diagnosis. Without it, the record cannot be evaluated and the DDS will most likely order a consultative examination as discussed in Chapter 10.

Obtaining Legible Records

How many times have you heard the phrase "Doctors have the worst handwriting?" Well, more often than not it is true. Although many doctor offices now have chart notes transcribed, if the record is not legible, the SSA will not be able to evaluate it. Accordingly, you should inquire with the office staff if they have any problems with reading the doctor's notes. If they answer yes, kindly ask if someone in the office would review the file before it is sent to the DDS.

Compensating Your Doctor for His or Her Time

Doctors bill insurance plans for medical services that they perform. They cannot, however, submit a bill for the time it takes them to complete forms. For the doctor who seeks compensation for his or her time, this sometimes raises a problem for the claimant who is seeking the doctor's cooperation.

When the SSA requests records, it will compensate the doctor for copying charges and sometimes for completing a questionnaire. However, the doctor must first provide the information and then has to submit a bill for his or her time. This additional paperwork is often frowned upon by a busy doctor's staff. Fortunately, as a means of reducing time, most DDS offices allow records to be transmitted by fax, thereby avoiding the time it would take to copy records. The DDS will supply a cover sheet that is already preprinted with both the doctor's and your name on it for the doctor to send with the records.

Part of winning your case includes developing your medical evidence. As discussed later in this chapter, I use questionnaires for my client's doctor to complete. However, most doctors will charge you a report fee for completing the questionnaire. This may cause an unfortunate dilemma when your funds are extremely limited and the outcome of your case is being held up because your doctor has not been paid. In such situations, you should attempt to at least obtain your records directly. A patient is entitled to a copy of his or her file, and a doctor cannot withhold it from the patient.

Completion of questionnaires is often essential to proving your disability. Therefore, if you find yourself in a situation where your doctor is holding the questionnaire hostage until he or she receives payment, you should plead for his or her mercy in helping you. The following story may seem extreme, but when you have so much at stake, what my client did is surely understandable.

DAVE'S STORY

Dave retained our office after he received notice of his hearing. He was living in his car and surviving on food stamps. He was severely diabetic and the diabetes was causing him to have great difficulty walking. He was also losing sight in his right eye. His doctor, well aware of his situation, still demanded $100 to complete a questionnaire. Having exhausted all possibilities for borrowing the money, Dave showed up at his doctor's office and "camped out" in the waiting room. After several hours, the nurse gave him the completed form.

Developing the Medical Proof that You Meet or Equal the Listings

As has been discussed, the SSA evaluates your disability using a five-step sequential question process. To be awarded benefits at Step 3 of the sequential evaluation, your disability must *meet or equal* the medical listings as discussed in Chapter 5.

When the initial application was filed, you also completed a medical authorization, SSA 827, which allows the SSA to contact your medical providers to obtain records. Sometimes, the records may contain narrative reports, especially where you have had surgery, have had laboratory testing, or have completed other forms of diagnostic testing such as x-rays and MRI examinations.

More often, medical records are chart notes that are sometimes not legible or consist of only brief comments. As a result, the DDS must piece together all of this information and compare it to the medical listings to determine whether or not you meet or equal the listings. Because there are too many pieces of the puzzle, and the pieces are not neatly fitting together, the DDS in most cases

> **Practical Point**
>
> As the SSA moves into the electronic world for transmitting documents, some offices of the DDS are allowing medical records to be sent online, further reducing the time it takes for a doctor's office to comply.

has to order a consultative examination conducted by an SSA doctor to confirm your alleged reason for being unable to work. Aside from the many inherent problems associated with consultative examinations as detailed in Chapter 10, the consultative doctor also is at the disadvantage of working from chart notes that have been supplied to him or her that may not be in the best order or, even worse, are not readable.

As a result, claims are many times denied because your medical evidence does not support what you are claiming. To rectify this problem, Social Security Disability appeals attorneys have developed *medical questionnaires* (sometimes referred to as *medical interrogatories*) that are sent to the treating doctors to complete. Regardless of the disability, the interrogatories answer the following questions.

- What is the diagnosis?

- What is the prognosis?

- What are the symptoms?

- Are the symptoms severe enough that they would interfere with concentration?

- What are the clinical findings that support the diagnosis?

- What is the treatment?

- How long has this condition lasted?

- As a result of this condition, how are the patient's daily activities affected?

- As a result of this condition, would the patient have any work restrictions?

- As a result of this condition, how likely is it the patient would be absent from work?

The interrogatories ask the doctor to identify the elements of this list that you exhibit or your doctor finds as a result of testing he or she has conducted. Furthermore, it allows your doctor to explain why your impairment restricts you from doing daily activities. Remember, if you cannot perform daily activities in your home, you cannot be expected to be productive on the job.

The previous questions are reproduced in the Physical Residual Functional Capacities Questionnaire and can be found in Appendix A.

In the alternative, if the consultative examination concludes otherwise, the SSA may still deny the claims, basing its decision on the fact that you can still perform other work.

Strategy for Winning

In addition to asking the treating doctor questions that will assist the DDS in determining whether or not you meet or equal a listing, the questionnaires will also ask your doctor to render an opinion as to your ability to sit, stand, walk, lift, and bend. In addition, the doctor will be asked whether, with your disability, you would be likely to be absent from work. The answers to these questions are designed to demonstrate that with your limitations, at Step 5 of the sequential evaluation, you cannot be gainfully employed.

Please refer to Chapter 16, which discusses the hearing process and how to use the medical questionnaires to your advantage.

When to Obtain Medical Questionnaires

In terms of when to obtain medical questionnaires, it is the practice at my office to wait until at least the first denial before we ask the treating doctor to complete a questionnaire. We have adopted this policy not because we do not want to see that our clients get benefits sooner, but because at the initial application stage, there are several agencies involved in the claim. Specifically, the local Social Security district office acts as the fact gatherer collecting the information and the DDS is the evaluator of the information. Often there are time delays as information is being transferred back and forth. As a result, we sometimes do not know where to send the information.

Practical Point

You should never assume that simply because your doctor completes a questionnaire you will be awarded benefits. Provided the SSA has medical records that support the treating doctor's findings, the SSA may conclude that the claimant meets the listings.

LEGALLY SPEAKING

If you have the support of your doctor, and the SSA denies your claim, at the hearing stage you can argue before the judge that the SSA regulations state that the weight of a treating doctor should be considered over the finding of the consultative examination.

Submitting Questionnaires to Your Doctor

Assuming you have been denied benefits and have now filed for the first appeal, take the appropriate questionnaire to your treating doctor at your next appointment. During the visit, ask that he or she complete the form while you wait. Note that the form can be filled out by pen and the majority of the questions can be answered by checking boxes.

Once the report is completed, submit it to the SSA. However, where your claim is in the appeal process will determine where to submit your report. That is, if your claim is still being processed by the local Social Security office, send it there. However, if you have requested a hearing and have received an acknowledgment that your claim has been received by the Office of Disability, Adjudication, and Review (ODAR), you should send the report to that office.

- If you are at the Request for Reconsideration level, send the report directly to the DDS office that is evaluating the claim. You should also have a name of the person assigned to the claim. If the DDS is not handling the claim, send the report to the local Social Security office assigned to your claim.

- If you are at the Request for Hearing level, send the report directly to the ODAR once you have received an acknowledgment letter from the hearing office that your case has been received. *Do not* send the questionnaire to the local Social Security office, as that office has most likely packed up your file and shipped it to the ODAR. Sending any documents at this point to the local office will most likely mean those documents never reach your file.

For submitting questionnaires as well as any records, I have developed a simple transmittal form, produced as follows. Make sure that you include your name and Social Security number and specifically reference the questionnaire or any additional records you are submitting. In addition, include the date that the document was signed and the number of pages in the document. This way, if SSA discovers that a page was missing, you will be contacted. Of course, keep copies of everything that you submit.

Practical Point

Until the first denial, my office usually does not communicate with specific persons in the system to whom we can direct information. Therefore, to reduce the chances of our documents being lost or misdirected, we usually wait until the claim has been denied to submit interrogatories.

Practical Point

Doctors often have little time to complete reports. However, questionnaires are simple by design and take only minutes to complete. Impress this fact upon your doctor if he or she says that he or she will finish the report at a later time. It is very important that you leave your doctor's office with the report in hand.

Law Offices of

BENJAMIN H. BERKLEY
A PROFESSIONAL LAW CORPORATION
1440 North Harbor Boulevard, Suite 250, Fullerton, California 92835
Telephone (714) 871-6440 Facsimile (714) 871-9714
www.berkleylaw.net

March 22, 2007

Office of Disability Adjudication and Review
Social Security Administration
1120 W. La Veta., Ste 600
Orange, CA 928686

RE: CLAIMANT
      SOCIAL SECURITY NO.   :

To Whom It May Concern:

( )   Enclosed please find the following medical records to be added to the Claimant's exhibit List.

( )   Enclosed please find the following Medical Reports

( )   Enclosed please find brief for an OTR

(X) Other: APPOINTMENT OF REPRESENTATION
                   FEE AGREEMENT
                   SSA FORM 1695

Very truly yours,

BENJAMIN H. BERKLEY
BHB: cb
Enclosures

IF YOU ARE DENIED: THE FIRST APPEAL

12

If you are approved for benefits after filing your initial application, you will receive a letter from the local Social Security office that has been assigned to the processing of your claim. Thereafter, you will receive an *award letter*, which explains your monthly and retroactive benefits (if any). This information is discussed in detail in Chapter 18.

However, as previously stated, over 75% of all initial claims are denied benefits. Although some people file who would never qualify, the vast majority are legitimate claims that are denied for many reasons, including:

- the claimant's medical providers never sent all the records requested or what was received was not legible;

- the medical records were not properly evaluated;

- there are no current medical records; and,

- the claimant did not provide all the requested information required by the SSA to evaluate the claim.

Unfortunately, the SSA does not give you many chances to correct any defects in the initial paperwork that you submitted. It may ask for additional information, such as the name of your treating doctor. However, sometimes denials are made

Practical Point

To expedite the appeal process, the SSA is experimenting with certain areas of the country and eliminating the request for reconsideration stage. Instead, if your claim is denied, you must go to the next stage, which is the request for hearing. Ten states do not allow a reconsideration appeal stage. Social Security has eliminated the reconsideration appeal stage in: Alabama, Alaska, California (Los Angeles North and West areas), Colorado, Louisiana, Michigan, Missouri, New Hampshire, New York (Brooklyn and Albany areas), and Pennsylvania. In these states and areas, applicants whose claims are denied at the initial decision can appeal to an administrative law judge within sixty days of the decision notice. Again, it is very important that you read the denial letter, as it will state which appeal process must be filed.

without any medical information obtained. To illustrate, on the following page is an example of a typical denial letter.

In my client's case, even though medical records were submitted, the SSA took it upon itself to deny the case without properly developing the medical record. What is worse is that although the SSA is empowered to schedule a consultative examination for the purpose of developing the claim if there is insufficient evidence to render a decision, in this case no consultative examination was ever scheduled. Regardless, this claim was denied without being properly evaluated. See the discussion of consultative examinations in Chapter 10.

The First Appeal: The Request for Reconsideration

If your claim is denied—and most are—you will receive a letter from the SSA. Reprinted on page 117 is a typical denial letter. It is important that you read it carefully. Most importantly, do not become discouraged. Statistically, the odds are in your favor that your case will be approved at a later date. However, you must adhere to the very strict guidelines required to file your appeal.

SOCIAL SECURITY ADMINISTRATION
RETIREMENT, SURVIVORS, AND DISABILITY INSURANCE
Notice of Disapproved Claims

Telephone:
Date: September 27, 2006
Claim Number:

We are writing about your claim for Social Security disability benefits. Based on a review of your health problems you do not qualify for benefits on this claim. This is because you are not disabled under our rules.

The Decision on Your Case

The following report(s) were used to decide your claim:

GATEWAY INTERNAL MEDICINE report received 08/31/06
S & L MEDICAL GROUP/ANAHEIM report received 07/18/06

We have determined that your condition is not severe enough to keep you from working. We considered the medical and other information, your age, education, training, and work experience in determining how your condition affects your ability to work.

You said you were unable to work because of:

Rheumatoid arthritis, immobile shoulder, depression

The medical evidence shows that although you rheumatoid arthritis causes some problems for you, you are still able to get about in a sufficient manner. The records show that you are able to move your upper extremities in a satisfactory manner and your lower extremities have normal movement and good range of motion.

Although you may be depressed at times, you are able to think, act, and communicate in your own interest. You are able to adjust to ordinary emotional stresses and to get along with others as well as to do your usual activities and follow basic instructions.

All of the evidence in your file was considered in making our determination. We find this information sufficient. Your statements about how your condition prevents you from

(SSA-L443)

Page 2

working are not fully supported by the evidence in file.

We realize that your condition prevents you from doing your past job. However, it does not preclude all work activity. We considered your age, education and past work experience and concluded that you can do other work which requires less physical effort. Therefore, disability has not been established within the meaning of the law.

If your condition gets worse and keeps you from working write, call or visit any Social Security office about filing another application.

About the Decision

Doctors and other trained staff looked at this case and made these decisions. They work for the state but used our rules.

Please remember that there are many types of disability programs, both government and private, which use different rules. A person may be receiving benefits under another program and still not be entitled under our rules. This may be true in this case.

The Disability Rules

You must meet certain rules to qualify for disabled worker's Social Security benefits. You must have the required work credits and your health problems must:

o   keep you from doing any kind of substantial work (described below), and

o   last, or be expected to last, for at least 12 months in a row, or result in death.

Information About Substantial Work

Generally, substantial work is physical or mental work a person is paid to do. Work can be substantial even if it is part-time. To decide if a person's work is substantial, we consider the nature of the job duties, the skills and experience needed to do the job, and how much the person actually earns.

Usually, we find that work is substantial if gross earnings average over $860 per month after we deduct allowable amounts. This monthly amount is higher for Social Security disability benefits due to blindness.

A person's work may be different than before his/her health problems began. It may not be as hard to do and the pay may be less. However, we may still find that the work is substantial under our rules.

If a person is self-employed, we consider the kind and value of his/her work, including his/her part in the management of the business, as well as income, to decide if the work is substantial.

(SSA-L443)

Page 3

Other Benefits

Based on the application you filed you are not entitled to any other benefits besides those you may already be getting. In the future, if you may be entitled to benefits, you will need to file again.

If You Disagree With The Decision

If you disagree with this decision, you have the right to appeal. We will review your case and consider any new facts you have. A person who did not make the first decisions will decide your case.

o   You have 60 days to ask for an appeal.

o   The 60 days start the day after you get this letter. We assume you got this letter 5 days after the date on it unless you show us that you did not get it within the 5-day period.

o   You must have a good reason for waiting more than 60 days to ask for an appeal.

o   You have to ask for an appeal in writing. We will ask you to sign a form SSA-561-U2, called "Request for Reconsideration." You may request this form online at http://www.socialsecurity.gov/online/ssa-561.pdf.Contact one of our offices if you want help.

o   In addition, you have to complete a "Disability Report - Appeal" to tell us about your medical condition since you filed your claim. You may contact one of our offices or call 1-800-772-1213 to request this form. Or, you may complete this report online at http://www.socialsecurity.gov/disability/recon.

Please read the enclosed pamphlet, "Your Right to Question The Decision Made on Your Social Security Claim". It contains more information about the appeal.

New Application

You have the right to file a new application at any time, but filing a new application is not the same as appealing this decision. If you disagree with this decision and you file a new application instead of appealing:

o   you might lose some benefits, or not qualify for any benefits, and

o   we could deny the new application using this decision, if the facts and issues are the same.

(SSA-L443)

⌣   Page 4   ⌣

So, if you disagree with this decision, you should ask for an appeal within 60 days.

If You Want Help With Your Appeal

You can have a friend, lawyer, or someone else help you. There are groups that can help you find a lawyer or give you free legal services if you qualify. There are also lawyers who do not charge unless you win your appeal. Your local Social Security office has a list of groups that can help you with your appeal.

If you get someone to help you, you should let us know. If you hire someone, we must approve the fee before he or she can collect it. And if you hire a lawyer, we will withhold up to 25 percent of any past due Social Security benefits to pay toward the fee.

If You Have Any Questions

If you have any questions, you may call us toll-free at 1-800-772-1213, or call your local Social Security office at (714) 993-0276. We can answer most questions over the phone. You can also write or visit any Social Security office. The office that serves your area is located at:

> SSA DISTRICT OFFICE
> 3230 E IMPERIAL HIGHWAY
> STE 150
> BREA, CA 92821

If you do call or visit an office, please have this letter with you. It will help us answer your questions. Also, if you plan to visit an office, you may call ahead to make an appointment. This will help us serve you more quickly.

> Peter Spencer
> Regional Commissioner

Enclosures:
SSA Pub. No. 05-10058

KMJONE

(SSA-L443)

Completing the Request for Reconsideration

To file the Request for Reconsideration, you must use Form SSA-561-U2. This form, as well as all Social Security Disability forms, is available by contacting the SSA at 800–772–1213 or by visiting its website at **www.socialsecuirty.gov**. You can also pick up the forms at the local Social Security office where you initially filed your claim.

The Request for Reconsideration is reproduced on page 122 with some of the fields of the form filled in. Further, I have labeled the fields using letters of the alphabet, although please note that the fields are not labeled on the actual form. The form is quite simple to complete; generally, it asks for your name, Social Security number, address, and phone number. However, there are two sections that you must pay close attention to.

In completing field H, I do *not* recommend that you elaborate your reasons as to why you are appealing. Simply stating, "I am still disabled" is sufficient.

Furthermore, field I must be completed *only* if you are applying for SSI. In this box, always check "case review," as this will require the entire claim to be reviewed by the DDS. The other two choices are "informal" or "formal" conference. However, because the conference is not conducted by a judge, there is no benefit to you to choose either of these options.

Note that this form must be completed and sent to the SSA no later than sixty days from the date placed on the denial letter plus five days. The five days is to allow for mailing. If you fail to comply with the *sixty plus five day* requirement, you will need to begin the entire claim process again by making an initial application. The address of the office where you are to send the request will be found on the last page of the denial letter. In almost all cases, the address will be that of the office that processed your initial claim.

SOCIAL SECURITY ADMINISTRATION	TOE 710	Form Approved OMB No. 0960-0622

REQUEST FOR RECONSIDERATION

(Do not write in this space)

NAME OF CLAIMANT

(A) John Jones

NAME OF WAGE EARNER OR SELF-EMPLOYED PERSON *(If different from claimant.)*

(B)

CLAIMANT SSN	CLAIMANT CLAIM NUMBER (if different from SSN)
(C) 000 – 00 – 0000	– –

SUPPLEMENTAL SECURITY INCOME (SSI) OR SPECIAL VETERANS BENEFITS (SVB) CLAIM NUMBER

(D) – –

SPOUSE'S NAME *(Complete ONLY in SSI cases)*

(E)

SPOUSE'S SOCIAL SECURITY NUMBER *(Complete ONLY in SSI cases)*

(F) – –

CLAIM FOR *(Specify type, e.g., retirement, (disability) hospital /medical, SSI, SVB, etc.)*

(G)

(H) I do not agree with the determination made on the above claim and request reconsideration. My reasons are:

I am still disabled.

SUPPLEMENTAL SECURITY INCOME OR SPECIAL VETERANS BENEFITS RECONSIDERATION ONLY
(See the three ways to appeal in the How To Appeal Your Supplemental Security Income (SSI) Or Special Veterans Benefit (SVB) Decision instructions.)
"I want to appeal your decision about my claim for Supplemental Security Income (SSI) or Special Veterans Benefits (SVB). I've read about the three ways to appeal. I've checked the box below."

(I) ☑ Case Review   ☐ Informal Conference   ☐ Formal Conference

EITHER THE CLAIMANT OR REPRESENTATIVE SHOULD SIGN - ENTER ADDRESSES FOR BOTH

I declare under penalty of perjury that I have examined all the information on this form, and on any accompanying statements or forms, and it is true and correct to the best of my knowledge.

CLAIMANT SIGNATURE	SIGNATURE OR NAME OF CLAIMANT'S REPRESENTATIVE
(J) John Jones	☐ NON-ATTORNEY ☐ ATTORNEY

MAILING ADDRESS	MAILING ADDRESS
(K) 124 Main Street	

CITY	STATE	ZIP CODE	CITY	STATE	ZIP CODE
(L) Long Beach	(M) NY	(N) 11561			–

TELEPHONE NUMBER *(Include area code)*	DATE	TELEPHONE NUMBER *(Include area code)*	DATE
(O) (516) 432 - 0000	(P) 6/15/07	( ) –	

TO BE COMPLETED BY SOCIAL SECURITY ADMINISTRATION

See list of initial determinations

1. HAS INITIAL DETERMINATION BEEN MADE?	☐ YES ☐ NO	2. CLAIMANT INSISTS ON FILING	☐ YES ☐ NO

3. IS THIS REQUEST FILED TIMELY? (If "NO", attach claimant's explanation for delay and attach any pertinent letter, material, or information in Social Security office.)	☐ YES ☐ NO

RETIREMENT AND SURVIVORS RECONSIDERATIONS ONLY (CHECK ONE) REFER TO (GN 03102.125)

SOCIAL SECURITY OFFICE ADDRESS

☐ NO FURTHER DEVELOPMENT REQUIRED   (GN 03102.300)

☐ REQUIRED DEVELOPMENT ATTACHED

☐ REQUIRED DEVELOPMENT PENDING, WILL FORWARD OR ADVISE STATUS WITHIN 30 DAYS

ROUTING INSTRUCTIONS (CHECK ONE)	☐ DISABILITY DETERMINATION SERVICES *(ROUTE WITH DISABILITY FOLDER)*	☐ PROGRAM SERVICE CENTER	☐ DISTRICT OFFICE RECONSIDERATION
		☐ OIO, BALTIMORE	☐ CENTRAL PROCESSING SITE (SVB)
	☐ ODO, BALTIMORE	☐ OEO, BALTIMORE	

NOTE: Take or mail the **signed original** to your local Social Security office, the Veterans Affairs Regional Office in Manila or any U.S. Foreign Service post and keep a copy for your records.

Form SSA-561-U2 (9-2007) ef (9-2007)   Prior Edition May Be Used Until Exhausted

Claims Folder

Exceptions to the Sixty Plus Five Day Rule

You must have a very good reason as to why you were unable to file the Request for Reconsideration within the required time. Acceptable reasons include:

- you were in the hospital and can provide documentation;

- you moved and your mail was not forwarded; or,

- you were out of the country.

Late Filing

It is not a valid excuse if someone other than you was in the hospital. Furthermore, if the sixty plus five days have passed, you should immediately file the Request for Reconsideration and attach with it a letter explaining the reason for the late filing. Include with the letter any supporting documentation. It is also recommended that you file the request in person at the local Social Security office that has been assigned your claim.

SSA-3441-BK (Disability Report—Appeal)

In addition to Form 561-U2, you must file SSA-3441-BK (Disability Report—Appeal). If this form looks familiar, it is because you completed a similar form when you first made your initial application. However, because you are asking that the SSA take another look at your case, it requires that you update your information.

A new adult disability report is required to provide you with an opportunity to advise the SSA as to whether anything has changed in your medical condition, such as a new diagnosis, or whether the disability is causing further interference with your ability to perform your daily activities.

The form is reproduced on page 125. Unlike the Request for Reconsideration, in which you stated that your reason for filing the request is because you are still disabled, in completing this form you should provide as much information as available.

In addition, pay special attention to sections 7 and 10. In these sections, you should provide as much detail as possible to show how your daily activities have been impaired as a result of your disability. This is because if your daily life at home is affected by your medical condition, it is logical that you will not be able to perform your job.

SOCIAL SECURITY ADMINISTRATION

Form Approved
OMB No. 0960-0144

DISABILITY REPORT - APPEAL

For SSA Use Only -
Do not write in this box.

Related SSN _____ — ___ — ___

Number Holder _____

Date of Last
Disability Report _____

Individual
is filing: ☐ Reconsideration   ☐ Reconsideration for Disability Cessation   ☐ Request for ALJ Hearing

SECTION 1 - INFORMATION ABOUT THE DISABLED PERSON

A. NAME *(First, Middle Initial, Last)*

B. SOCIAL SECURITY NUMBER
___ — ___ — ___

C. DAYTIME TELEPHONE NUMBER *(If you do not have a number where we can reach you, give us a daytime number where we can leave a message.)*

(_____) _____ — _____   ☐ Your Number   ☐ Message Number   ☐ None
Area Code   Number

D. Give the name of a friend or relative that we can contact (other than your doctors) who knows about your illnesses, injuries, or conditions and can help you with your claim or case.

NAME _____   RELATIONSHIP _____

ADDRESS _____
(Number, Street, Apt. No.(If any), P.O. Box, or Rural Route)

_____ — _____   DAYTIME (_____) _____ — _____
City   State   ZIP   PHONE   Area Code   Number

SECTION 2 - INFORMATION ABOUT YOUR ILLNESSES, INJURIES, OR CONDITIONS

A. Has there been any change (for better or worse) in your illnesses, injuries, or conditions **since you last completed a disability report?**   ☐ Yes   ☐ No
If "Yes," please describe in detail:

_____
_____
_____

Approximate date the changes occurred:

Month	Day	Year

B. Do you have any new physical or mental limitations as a result of your illnesses, injuries, or conditions **since you last completed a disability report?**   ☐ Yes   ☐ No
If "Yes," please describe in detail:

_____
_____
_____

Approximate date the changes occurred:

Month	Day	Year

FORM SSA-3441-BK (1-2005) ef (12-2005) Use 2-2004 Edition Until Supply Is Exhausted

PAGE 1

C. Do you have any new illnesses, injuries or conditions since you last completed a disability report? ☐ Yes   ☐ No

If "Yes," please describe in detail.

_____

_____

_____

Approximate date the changes occurred:

Month	Day	Year

If you need more space, use Section 10 - REMARKS.

SECTION 3 - INFORMATION ABOUT YOUR MEDICAL RECORDS

A. Since you last completed a disability report, have you seen or will you see a doctor/hospital/clinic or anyone else for the illnesses, injuries, or conditions that limit your ability to work?   ☐ YES   ☐ NO

B. Since you last completed a disability report, have you seen or will you see a doctor/hospital/clinic or anyone else for emotional or mental problems that limit your ability to work?   ☐ YES   ☐ NO

C. List other names you have used on your medical records.

_____

_____

_____

If you answered "NO" to both A and B, go to Section 4 - MEDICATIONS.

Tell us who may have medical records or other information about your illnesses, injuries, or conditions since you last completed a disability report.

D. List each DOCTOR/HMO/THERAPIST/OTHER. Include your next appointment.

1. NAME			DATES
STREET ADDRESS			FIRST VISIT
CITY	STATE	ZIP	LAST VISIT
PHONE ( ) -- Area Code Phone Number	PATIENT ID # (If known)		NEXT APPOINTMENT
REASONS FOR VISITS			
WHAT TREATMENT DID YOU RECEIVE?			

2. NAME				DATES	
STREET ADDRESS				FIRST VISIT	
CITY		STATE	ZIP	LAST VISIT	
PHONE ( ) — Area Code Phone Number		PATIENT ID # (if known)		NEXT APPOINTMENT	
REASONS FOR VISITS					
WHAT TREATMENT DID YOU RECEIVE?					

If you need more space, use Section 10 - REMARKS.

E. List each HOSPITAL/CLINIC. Include your next appointment.

HOSPITAL/CLINIC	TYPE OF VISIT	DATES	
NAME	☐ INPATIENT STAYS (Stayed at least overnight)	DATE IN	DATE OUT
STREET ADDRESS	☐ OUTPATIENT VISITS (Sent home same day)	DATE FIRST VISIT	DATE LAST VISIT
CITY	STATE	ZIP	☐ EMERGENCY ROOM VISITS	DATES OF VISITS	
PHONE ( ) — Area Code Phone Number			

Next appointment _____   Your hospital/clinic number _____

Reasons for visits _____

What treatment did you receive? _____

What doctors do you see at this hospital/clinic on a regular basis? _____

If you need more space, use Section 10 - REMARKS.

PAGE 3

FORM SSA-3441-BK (1-2005) ef (12-2005)

F. Since you last completed a disability report, does anyone else have **medical records or information** about your illnesses, injuries, or conditions (for example, Workers' Compensation, insurance companies, prisons, attorneys, or welfare agency), or are you scheduled to see anyone else?   ☐ YES   ☐ NO

If "YES," complete information below:

NAME			DATES
STREET ADDRESS			FIRST VISIT
CITY	STATE	ZIP	LAST VISIT
PHONE ( ) – Area Code Phone Number			NEXT APPOINTMENT
CLAIM NUMBER (if any)			
REASONS FOR VISITS			

If you need more space, use Section 10 - REMARKS.

SECTION 4 - MEDICATIONS

Are you currently taking any **medications** for your illnesses, injuries or conditions?

☐ YES   ☐ NO

If "YES," please tell us the following: (*Look at your medicine containers, if necessary.*)

NAME OF MEDICINE	IF PRESCRIBED, GIVE NAME OF DOCTOR	REASON FOR MEDICINE	SIDE EFFECTS YOU HAVE

If you need more space, use Section 10 - REMARKS.

FORM SSA-3441-BK (1-2005) ef (12-2005)

SECTION 5 - TESTS

Since you last completed a disability report, have you had any medical tests for illnesses, injuries, or conditions or do you have any such tests scheduled?   ☐ YES   ☐ NO

If "YES," please tell us the following: *(Give approximate dates, if necessary.)*

KIND OF TEST	WHEN WAS/WILL TEST BE DONE? (Month, day, year)	WHERE DONE? (Name of Facility)	WHO SENT YOU FOR THIS TEST?
EKG (HEART TEST)			
TREADMILL (EXERCISE TEST)			
CARDIAC CATHETERIZATION			
BIOPSY -- Name of body part			
HEARING TEST			
SPEECH/LANGUAGE TEST			
VISION TEST			
IQ TESTING			
EEG (BRAIN WAVE TEST)			
HIV TEST			
BLOOD TEST (NOT HIV)			
BREATHING TEST			
X-RAY – Name of body part			
MRI/CT SCAN – Name of body part			

If you need more space, use Section 10 - REMARKS.

SECTION 6 - UPDATED WORK INFORMATION

Have you worked since you last completed a disability report?   ☐ YES   ☐ NO

If "YES," you will be asked to give details on a separate form.

SECTION 7 - INFORMATION ABOUT YOUR ACTIVITIES

A. How do your illnesses, injuries, or conditions affect your ability to care for your personal needs?

_____

_____

B. What changes have occurred in your daily activities since you last completed a disability report?

If none, show "NONE." _____

_____

_____

If you need more space, use Section 10 - REMARKS.

SECTION 8 - EDUCATION/TRAINING INFORMATION

Have you completed any type of **special job training, trade or vocational school since you last completed a disability report?**   ☐ YES   ☐ NO

If "YES," describe what type: _____

_____

_____

Approximate date completed: _____

SECTION 9 - VOCATIONAL REHABILITATION, EMPLOYMENT, or OTHER SUPPORT SERVICES INFORMATION

Since you last completed a disability report, have you participated in the Ticket Program or another program of vocational rehabilitation services, employment services or other support services, to help you go to work?   ☐ YES ☐ NO

If "YES," complete the following information:

NAME OF ORGANIZATION   _____

NAME OF COUNSELOR   _____

ADDRESS   _____
                        (Number, Street, Apt. No.(if any), P.O. Box, or Rural Route)

_____
                        City   *State*   *ZIP*

DAYTIME PHONE NUMBER   ( ) ___ _____
                        Area Code   *Number*

DATES SEEN   _____   TO   _____

TYPE OF SERVICES OR
TESTS PERFORMED   _____
                        (IQ, vision, physicals, hearing, workshops, etc.)

SECTION 10 - REMARKS

Use this section for any additional information you did not show in earlier parts of this form. When you are finished with this section (or if you don't have anything to add), be sure to go to the next page and complete the blocks there.

_____

_____

_____

_____

_____

_____

_____

_____

_____

_____

_____

_____

_____

_____

_____

_____

_____

_____

_____

_____

_____

_____

_____

SECTION 10 - REMARKS

_____
_____
_____
_____
_____
_____
_____
_____
_____
_____
_____
_____
_____
_____
_____
_____
_____
_____
_____
_____
_____
_____
_____
_____
_____

Name of person completing this form (Please print)	Date Form Completed (Month, day, year)
Address (Number and street)	e-mail address (optional)

City	State	ZIP

To demonstrate the importance of providing as much information in the Disability Report as possible, the following are two cases for your evaluation. Based on the information provided in the disability report, which one would make you more inclined to conclude that the claimant is disabled?

Example 1:

A 45-year-old female worked in a nail salon for the last fifteen years. She stopped working because her asthma condition has worsened over the years. The smell from the products used in the salon made her ill. Her doctor told her to stop working and that she must carry an inhaler and use it when she has a breathing attack.

In section 7 she states she is having shortness of breath and tires easily when she puts on her clothes and washes her hair. In section 10 she states that her use of the inhaler has increased since she originally filed.

Example 2:

The facts are the same as in the previous example, but in section 7 she adds that the fragrance from any shampoo causes her to have an asthma attack. She also says that she cannot do her laundry because the smell from the laundry detergent makes her gasp. In section 10 she states that her daughter cannot wear any perfume in the house, as it affects her breathing.

Analysis:

Although the claimant in the first example may eventually be found to be disabled, she will probably have to file a second appeal and appear before a judge, since her claim is not as strong as that in the second example. In the first example, she can probably work in an office setting. However, in the second example, with the added facts that she reacts to all smells and fragrances, there is probably no work available, as it is commonplace for both women and men to wear fragrances and therefore no work environment is immune from fumes and odors. When the DDS reviews the disability report in Example 2, it will provide more insight into the claim.

SSA-827 (Authorization to Disclose Information to the Social Security Administration)

In addition to Form 561-U2 and SSA-3441-BK, you must file SSA-827 (Authorization to Disclose Information to the Social Security Administration). When you made the initial application for benefits, you completed this same form, which allows your doctors to release information about you.

However, you may have changed doctors, had testing, or been a patient in a hospital that the SSA was not aware of. As a result, the SSA requires that you provide a current authorization. The form is reproduced on page 92. Note that the form must be witnessed but the witness can be anyone who is over the age of 18. Make sure that you include the address of the witness.

In addition to the previously listed forms, you may also be required to complete the following:

- a daily activities questionnaire, and

- a pain questionnaire if you have pain.

These forms are discussed in Chapter 9.

> **Practical Point**
>
> Do not withhold any details that may help your case. Even if revealing something about your condition may be embarrassing, get over it! It is your claim and your financial future is at stake.

Supplementing the Request for Reconsideration

Along with the required forms, you should also send to the SSA any additional medical information that was previously not provided. This may include medical records, tests, and lab results from medical providers that the SSA did not previously receive information from.

In addition, you should include information from other entities that support your claim for disability. Examples include:

Practical Point

If you decide to mail the forms, mail them by certified mail, return receipt requested, so that you have proof that they were received on time.

- a finding of disability from a workers' compensation court;

- a finding of disability from a disability insurance carrier;

- a finding of disability from a state or other federal disability office;

- letters or records from a school you were attending that show excessive absences or that show you withdrew from the program;

- employment attendance records from your last employer that show excessive absences from work prior to becoming disabled; or,

- school records of performance.

JOHN'S STORY

John was in a very serious car accident that resulted in brain damage. After months of therapy, John had difficulty with his memory as well as problems following simple instructions. Prior to applying for benefits, he enrolled in a school for brain-injured adults so that he could hopefully improve his skills. However, each time he enrolled, he had to withdraw, as he could not keep up with the work load. When John applied for Social Security Disability benefits, he was denied, but when he appealed, he included the attendance records that showed his inability to remain in school. On reconsideration, his claim was approved.

Once all the forms are completed, bring or mail them to the Social Security branch office that sent you the denial letter. The address of the branch office can be found on page four or five of the denial letter. If you cannot find the address of the office that is handling your claim, you can contact the SSA at 800–772–1213, and it will provide the address to you. If you bring the papers in person, make sure that you keep a copy and have the clerk stamp the Request for Reconsideration showing that you filed within the sixty-day time limit.

What Happens Next

Practical Point

Only 5% of cases that are reviewed at the request for reconsideration stage are approved for benefits. Again, you cannot get frustrated and give up. Your option is to go to the next appeal stage and file a request for a hearing.

Once all the forms are received by the local office, any new medical records not previously provided, along with any additional information, will be sent by the local SSA office to the DDS for a second evaluation. The DDS may then contact you if it requires additional information about how your medical condition affects your ability to work. It may also have you complete additional forms that ask about your daily activities.

As discussed in Chapter 10, the DDS may also decide to schedule you for a consultative examination if you were previously not examined by an SSA doctor, or it may schedule another examination if the information in your claim is not sufficient for the DDS to make a complete evaluation. In addition, if you are claiming a disability that was not evaluated before, it may be necessary to schedule a subsequent consultative exam. To illustrate, if you initially claimed that you had a physical impairment but you are now claiming that you are depressed, the DDS will want you to have a psychiatric review by an SSA doctor.

The request for reconsideration appeal process generally takes four to six months. Unless a claimant has been diagnosed with a terminal illness, there is no practical way of speeding up the process. I also do not recommend that you contact the local office of the SSA to check the status of your claim unless more than six months have passed. This is because, sometimes when a file is pulled, it is not always put back in the same place and instead is placed at the bottom of the pile. It sounds incredible but it is too often true!

What to Do While You are Waiting

For too many claimants, waiting for a decision causes financial havoc. Bills have to be paid and creditors are not often sympathetic to your situation. Chapter 17 provides information for what to do while you are waiting.

Filing a New Application While the Request for Reconsideration Is Being Decided

In addition to appealing a denied claim, a claimant has the option of filing a new initial application. To do so, you may make a new application by phone, in person at a local Social Security branch office, or online at **www.socialsecurity.gov**. Follow the procedures as discussed in Chapter 9.

Filing a new application is recommended if your condition has *seriously* worsened or you have a new impairment that was not evaluated in your prior application. For example, if you previously filed claiming a disability for diabetes that has now resulted in an amputation of a lower limb, your condition has *seriously* worsened.

However, if you are simply asking the SSA to take another look at your case, your new application will most likely be denied under the principal of *res judicata*. This is a Latin phrase that means an issue has already been evaluated and decided.

Therefore, a claim can be denied simply because there is nothing new or there is no material that would change the previous decision. Using the previous example, if the claimant with diabetes had not had a lower limb amputated, his or her new claim would be denied because there were no material changes to the condition, which had already been evaluated.

If You Never Hear on Your Initial Claim

It takes approximately four to six months for the SSA to process an initial application. This includes the gathering of all your supporting documentation and having the DDS evaluate your claim. Part of the delay is due in part to the time it takes to contact your doctors and have them respond.

You should receive a written response within this time period. If you do not, you should call the local SSA office assigned to your claim to learn your case status. If you are informed that you have been denied and that a letter was sent out, immediately inquire as to the address where the letter was mailed.

- If the address that the SSA sent the letter to was incorrect, notify the SSA so that it can send the letter to the correct address. Thereafter, upon receipt, file the Request for Reconsideration, along with a letter explaining why the request is being filed late.

- If the address provided by the SSA was correct, and you did not receive the letter, you should still file the Request for Reconsideration and follow the information previously provided for a late filing. However, in most cases, your request will be denied, as you are well outside the sixty-day rule. In such matters, I recommend that you also file a new application for benefits so that you do not lose any additional time.

If You Are Denied Again: The Second Appeal

13

As stated in Chapter 12, only 5% of decisions are reversed at the request for reconsideration stage. Those cases typically involve claimants who have been diagnosed with a terminal condition that will probably result in death. Therefore, you should not be surprised if you receive a second denial letter of your claim.

A typical second denial letter is found on page 140.

If you are denied a second time, read the letter very carefully.

In the letter, the section titled "The Decision on Your Case" explains the SSA's reasons why your claim was denied a second time. As stated previously, you should not become upset or angry at the decision. You know you are disabled, and now you will have an opportunity to speak directly to a judge to explain your disability.

Request for Hearing Before an Administrative Law Judge

The procedure for filing the second appeal is very similar to the process of filing the Request for Reconsideration. However, unlike the Request for Reconsideration, when appealing your denial a second time, you are requesting a hearing wherein an administrative judge will decide your case. At this hearing, you will be able to offer testimony as well as have witnesses testify on your behalf.

Please refer to Chapters 14 and 16, which discuss preparing for the hearing and the hearing process.

SOCIAL SECURITY ADMINISTRATION
RETIREMENT, SURVIVORS, AND DISABILITY INSURANCE
Notice of Reconsideration

Telephone: ▮▮▮▮▮
Date: JAN 10, 2002
Claim Number: ▮▮▮▮▮

You asked us to take another look at your claim for Social Security disability benefits. Someone who did not make the first decision reviewed your case, including any new facts we received, and found that our first decision was correct.

The Decision on Your Case

The following report(s) were used to decide your claim in addition to those listed on our previous notice
S & L MEDICAL GROUP/ANAHEIM report received 12/28/2006
S & L MEDICAL GROUP/ANAHEIM report received 01/04/07

We have determined that your condition is not severe enough to keep you from working. We considered the medical and other information, your age, education, training, and work experience in determining how your condition affects your ability to work.

You said you are unable to work because of: knee replacement surgery, arthritis, stomach problems and depression.

Though you do have discomfort in your knee and arthritis, the evidence shows you are still able to move about and to use your arms, hands and legs in a satisfactory manner. The evidence shows that although you have stomach problems your condition can be controlled. Therefore it does not prevent you from working. Though you may be at times, your records show that you are able to think, communicate and act in your own interest. The evidence shows you are able to adjust to ordinary emotional stresses, and to get along with others, as well as to do your usual activities and to remember and follow basic instructions. The evidence does not show any other impairment which would significantly restrict you from

(SSA-L928)

Page 2

performing work related functions. Based on your description of the job you performed as an Inventory Supervisor, we have concluded that you have the ability to perform this same type of work as it is usually performed in the national economy.

If your condition gets worse and keeps you from working write, call or visit any Social Security office about filing another application.

About the Decision

Please remember that there are many types of disability programs, both government and private, which use different rules. A person may be receiving benefits under another program and still not be entitled under our rules. This may be true in this case.

The Disability Rules

You must meet certain rules to qualify for disabled worker's Social Security benefits. You must have the required work credits and your health problems must:

o   keep you from doing any kind of substantial work (described below), and

o   last, or be expected to last, for at least 12 months in a row, or result in death.

Information About Substantial Work

Generally, substantial work is physical or mental work a person is paid to do. Work can be substantial even if it is part-time. To decide if a person's work is substantial, we consider the nature of the job duties, the skills and experience needed to do the job, and how much the person actually earns.

Usually, we find that work is substantial if gross earnings average over $860 per month after we deduct allowable amounts. This monthly amount is higher for Social Security disability benefits due to blindness.

A person's work may be different than before his/her health problems began. It may not be as hard to do and the pay may be less. However, we may still find that the work is substantial under our rules.

(SSA-L928)

Page 3

If a person is self-employed, we consider the kind and value of his/her work, including his/her part in the management of the business, as well as income, to decide if the work is substantial.

Other Benefits

Based on the applications you filed you are not entitled to any other benefits besides those you may already be getting. In the future, if you think you may be entitled to benefits, you will need to file again.

If You Disagree With The Decision

If you disagree with this decision, you have the right to request a hearing. A person who has not seen your case before will look at it. That person is an Administrative Law Judge (ALJ). The ALJ will review your case again and consider any new facts you have before deciding your case.

o   You have 60 days to ask for a hearing.

o   The 60 days start the day after you get this letter. We assume you got this letter 5 days after the date on it unless you show us that you did not get it within the 5-day period.

o   You must have a good reason for waiting more than 60 days to ask for a hearing.

o   You have to ask for an appeal in writing. We will ask you to sign a form HA-501-U2, called "Request for Hearing." You may complete this form online at http://www.socialsecurity.gov/ha-501.pdf. Contact one of our offices if you want help.

o   As part of the appeal process, you also need to tell us about your current medical condition. We provide a form for doing that, the "Disability Report - Appeal". You may contact one of our offices or call 1-800-772-1213 to request this form. Or, you may complete this report online at http://www.socialsecurity.gov/disability/hearing.

How the Hearing Process Works

(SSA-L928)

Page 4

The ALJ will mail you a letter at least 20 days before your hearing to tell you its date, time and place. The letter will explain the law in your case and tell you what has to be decided. Since the ALJ will review all the facts in your case, it is important that you give us any new facts as soon as you can.

The hearing is your chance to tell the ALJ why you disagree with the decision in your case. You can give the ALJ new evidence and bring people to testify for you. The ALJ also can require people to bring important papers to your hearing and give facts about your case. You can question these people at your hearing.

Please read the enclosed pamphlet "Your Right To An Administrative Law Judge Hearing and Appeals Council Review Of Your Social Security Case." It has more information about the hearing.

It Is Important To Go To The Hearing

It is very important that you go to the hearing. If for any reason you can't go, contact the ALJ as soon as possible before the hearing and explain why. The ALJ will reschedule the hearing if you have a good reason.

If you don't go to the hearing and don't have a good reason for not going, the ALJ may dismiss your request for a hearing.

New Application

You have the right to file a new application at any time, but filing a new application is not the same as appealing this decision. If you disagree with this decision and you file a new application instead of appealing:

o   you might lose some benefits, or not qualify for any benefits, and

o   we could deny the new application using this decision, if the facts and issues are the same.

So, if you disagree with this decision, you should ask for an appeal within 60 days.

If You Want Help With Your Hearing

You can have a friend, lawyer, or someone else help you. There are groups that can help you find a lawyer or give you free legal services if you qualify. There are

(SSA-L928)

Page 5

also lawyers who do not charge unless you win your appeal. Your local Social Security office has a list of groups that can help you with your appeal.

If you get someone to help you, you should let us know. If you hire someone, we must approve the fee before he or she can collect it. And if you hire a lawyer, we will withhold up to 25 percent of any past due Social Security benefits to pay toward the fee.

If You Have Any Questions

If you have any questions, you may call us toll-free at 1-800-772-1213, or call your local Social Security office at (714) 502-9249. We can answer most questions over the phone. You can also write or visit any Social Security office. The office that serves your area is located at:

> SSA DISTRICT OFFICE
> 300 S HARBOR BLVD
> STE 310
> ANAHEIM CA 92805

If you do call or visit an office, please have this letter with you. It will help us answer your questions. Also, if you plan to visit an office, you may call ahead to make an appointment. This will help us serve you more quickly.

> Peter Spencer
> Regional Commissioner

Enclosures:
SSA Pub. No. 70-10281

VLDAVI

(SSA-L928)

Completing the Required Forms

On page three or four of the denial letter, you will find a section titled "If You Disagree with the Decision." This section explains how to appeal the decision. You must file the Request for Hearing no later than sixty days from the date of the notice that your claim was denied a second time. In addition, you are granted five extra days for mailing. To appeal the second denial, you must use the SSA forms, which are:

- HA-501-U5 (Request for Hearing by Administrative Law Judge);

- SSA-3441-BK (Disability Report— Appeal); and,

- SSA-827 (Authorization to Disclose Information to the Social Security Administration).

> ### Legally Speaking
>
> Please see the discussion on "Late Filing" on page 123 in Chapter 12, as this also applies to filing a Request for Hearing.

These forms are available by contacting the SSA at 800–772–1213 or visiting its website at **www.socialsecurity.gov**. You can also pick up the forms at the local office where you initially filed your claim.

Form HA-501-U5
(Request for Hearing by Administrative Law Judge)

Form HA-501-U5 is reproduced on page 147 with sample information provided in the various fields of the form. Note that in completing field E, do not elaborate your reasons as to why you are requesting a hearing. Simply stating, "I am still disabled" is sufficient.

In field F, always state that you have additional evidence to submit, even if you do not have the evidence available at the time you are filing for the Request for Hearing. Additional evidence can always be submitted at a later time and many judges will even allow you to bring evidence to court on the day of the hearing.

Practical Point

Until 2006, the ODAR was known as the Office of Hearings and Appeals (OHA). I mention this only because many offices have not changed their letterhead to reflect the new name. So if you receive a letter from either the OHA or ODAR, it is the same office.

In field G, always check that you want to appear at the hearing. The benefit of appearing is to allow the judge to see with his or her own eyes and hear with his or her ears why you are claiming that you are disabled. To simply submit evidence without the opportunity to appear would seem self-defeating.

Form SSA-3441-BK (Disability Report—Appeal)

A new adult disability report is required to provide you with an opportunity to advise the SSA as to whether anything has changed in your medical condition, such as a new diagnosis, or whether the disability is causing a further interference with your ability to perform your daily activities.

This form is found on page 125. You have already completed this form twice but now have to do it again, as the SSA requires that you provide any updated information. Please see the discussion of this form in Chapter 12, as well as the two examples of how important providing detailed information is on page 133.

SOCIAL SECURITY ADMINISTRATION
OFFICE OF DISABILITY ADJUDICATION AND REVIEW

Form Approved
OMB No. 0960-0269

REQUEST FOR HEARING BY ADMINISTRATIVE LAW JUDGE
*(Take or mail the **signed original** to your local Social Security office, the Veterans Affairs Regional Office in Manila or any U.S. Foreign Service post and keep a copy for your records)*

See
Privacy Act Notice

1. CLAIMANT NAME	CLAIMANT SSN	2. WAGE EARNER NAME, IF DIFFERENT
John Jones	000-00-0000	
3. CLAIMANT CLAIM NUMBER, IF DIFFERENT	4. SPOUSE'S NAME, IF NOT WAGE EARNER	SPOUSE'S CLAIM NUMBER OR SSN
- -		- -

5. I REQUEST A HEARING BEFORE AN ADMINISTRATIVE LAW JUDGE.   I disagree with the determination made on my claim because:

I am still disabled.

An Administrative Law Judge of the Social Security Administration's Office of Disability Adjudication and Review or the Health and Human Services will be appointed to conduct the hearing or other proceedings in your case. You will receive notice of the time and place of a hearing at least 20 days before the date set for a hearing.

6. I have additional evidence to submit.   ☒ Yes   ☐ No

Name and address of source of additional evidence:

Martin Klein, MD
202 S. Broadway, Ryan, NJ

(Please submit it to the hearing office within 10 days. Your servicing Social Security Office will provide the address. Attach an additional sheet if you need more space.)

7. Do not complete if the appeal is a Medicare issue.

Check one of the blocks:

☒ I wish to appear at a hearing.

☐ I do not wish to appear at a hearing and I request that a decision be made based on the evidence in my case. (Complete Waiver Form HA-4608)

You have a right to be represented at the hearing. If you are not represented but would like to be, your Social Security office will give you a list of legal referral and service organizations. If you are represented and have not done so previously, complete and submit form SSA-1696 (Appointment of Representative) unless you are appealing a Medicare issue.

Regardless of the issue you are appealing, you should complete No. 8 and your representative (if any) should complete No. 9. If you are represented and your representative is not available to complete this form, you should also print his or her name, address, etc., in No. 9.

I declare under penalty of perjury that I have examined all the information on this form, and on any accompanying statements or forms, and it is true and correct to the best of my knowledge.

8. (CLAIMANT'S SIGNATURE)	(DATE)	9. (REPRESENTATIVE'S SIGNATURE/NAME)	(DATE)
John Jones			

ADDRESS
124 Main Street

(ADDRESS) ☐ ATTORNEY;   ☐ NON ATTORNEY;

CITY	STATE	ZIP CODE	CITY	STATE	ZIP CODE
Long Beach	NY	11564-			-

TELEPHONE NUMBER	FAX NUMBER	TELEPHONE NUMBER	FAX NUMBER
(516) 432-0000	( ) -	( ) -	( ) -

TO BE COMPLETED BY SOCIAL SECURITY ADMINISTRATION-ACKNOWLEDGMENT OF REQUEST FOR HEARING

10. Request received for the Social Security Administration on _____ by: _____

(Date)   (Print Name)

(Title)   (Address)   (Servicing PO Code)   (PC Code)

11. Was the request for hearing received within 65 days of the reconsidered determination?   ☐ YES   ☐ NO
If no is checked, attach claimant's explanation for delay; and attach copy of appointment notice, letter, or other pertinent material or information in the Social Security office.

12. Claimant is represented   ☐ Yes   ☐ No
☐ List of legal referral and service organizations provided

13. Interpreter needed   ☐ Yes   ☐ No
Language (including sign language): _____

14. Check one: ☐ Initial Entitlement Case
☐ Disability Cessation Case
☐ Other Postentitlement Case

16. HO COPY SENT TO: _____   HO on _____

☐ CF Attached: ☐ Title II;   ☐ Title XVI;   ☐ Title VIII;   ☐ T XVIII;
☐ Title II CF held in FO   ☐ Electronic Folder
☐ CF requested   ☐ Title II;   ☐ Title XVI;   ☐ Title VIII;   ☐ T XVIII
(Copy of email or phone report attached)

17. CF COPY SENT TO: _____   HO on _____

☐ CF Attached: ☐ Title II;   ☐ Title XVI;   ☐ T XVIII
☐ Other Attached:

15. Check all claim types that apply:

☐ RSI only	(RSI)
☐ Title II Disability-worker or child only	(DIWC)
☐ Title II Disability-Widow(er) only	(DIWW)
☐ SSI Aged only	(SSIA)
☐ SSI Blind only	(SSIB)
☐ SSI Disability only	(SSID)
☐ SSI Aged/Title II	(SSAC)
☐ SSI Blind/Title II	(SSBC)
☐ SSI Disability/Title II	(SSDC)
☐ Title XVIII	(HI/SMI)
☐ Title VIII Only	(SVB)
☐ Title VIII/Title XVI	(SVB/SSI)
☐ Other - Specify:	

Form HA-501-US (5-2007) ef (5-2007)
Destroy Prior Editions

TAKE OR SEND ORIGINAL TO SSA AND RETAIN A COPY FOR YOUR RECORDS

Form SSA-827 (Authorization to Disclose Information to the Social Security Administration)

You have previously seen this form, but a new authorization is required so that your doctors can release information about you. Furthermore, as many months have passed since your initial claim was filed, it is very possible that you are seeing a different doctor. Without this authorization, the SSA would not be able to obtain your new information.

The form is reproduced on page 92. The form must be witnessed. Witnesses can be anyone over the age of 18. Make sure that you include the address of the witness.

Once all the forms are completed, bring or mail them to the Social Security branch office that sent you the denial letter. The address of the branch office can be found on page four or five of the denial letter. If you cannot find the address of the office that is handling your claim, you can contact the SSA at 800–772–1213, and someone will provide the address to you. If you bring the papers in person, make sure that you keep a copy and have the clerk stamp the Request for Hearing showing that you filed within the sixty-day time limit.

What Happens Next

Once the forms are filed, the local branch office of the SSA that sent you the denial letters will forward the file to the Office of Disability, Adjudication, and Review (ODAR), which will schedule your case for a hearing.

Once your file is received, the ODAR will send you written acknowledgment that your file has been received. A typical acknowledgment letter is shown on the following page.

At this time, if you have additional medical evidence to submit, you should send it to the ODAR. However, to ensure that your records are received and placed in your file, it is advisable to attach a cover letter as follows on page 150.

SOCIAL SECURITY AD[   ]NISTRATION

Office of Disability Adjudication and Review
1120 W La Veta Ave
Suite 600
Orange, CA 92868
Tel: (714)246-8275 / Fax: (714)246-8271

February 7, 2007

Benjamin H. Berkley
1440 N. Harbor Blvd.
Ste. 250
Fullerton, CA 92835

Dear Benjamin H. Berkley:

We have received your client's request for a hearing before an Administrative Law Judge (ALJ). This letter tells you about the hearing process and things that you should do now to prepare for the hearing. We will mail a Notice of Hearing to you and your client at least 20 days before the date of the hearing to tell you its time and place.

The Hearing

At the hearing, you and your client may present her case to the ALJ who will hear and decide it. The ALJ will consider the issue(s) you or your client has raised and the evidence now in her file and any additional evidence you provide. The ALJ may consider other issues as well and, if necessary, change parts of the previous decision that were favorable to your client. The Notice of Hearing will state the issues the ALJ plans to consider at the hearing.

Because the hearing is the time to show the ALJ that the issues should be decided in your client's favor, we need to make sure that her file has everything you want the ALJ to consider. You and your client are responsible for submitting needed evidence. After the ALJ reviews the evidence in the file, he or she may request more evidence to consider at the hearing.

Providing Additional Evidence

If there is more evidence you want the ALJ to see, get it to us as soon as possible. If you need help, you should contact us immediately. You may ask the ALJ to issue a subpoena that requires a person to submit documents or testify at your hearing.

You May See The Evidence In Your File

If you wish to see the evidence in your client's file, you may do so on the date of the hearing or before that date. If you wish to review the file before the date of the hearing, please call us.

ODAR
800 East Colorado Blvd.
Pasadena, California 91101

Re: James Jeter
SSN: 000–00–0000

To Whom It May Concern:

I am in receipt of your acknowledgment that my case has been received by your office and will soon be scheduled for a hearing.

Enclosed please find the following:

1. Medical report from Neal Dorf, M.D., dated December 23, 2007
2. MRI report from Newport Open MRI, dated November 11, 2007

I wish that these records be added to my file and be made part of the record.

Respectfully yours,

Receiving the acknowledgment letter is not an indication that a hearing will soon be scheduled. In fact, from the time that you receive the acknowledgment that your file has been received by the ODAR, it typically takes anywhere from six to eighteen months for a hearing to be scheduled. The time does vary greatly among different parts of the country, as some states have fewer judges available and the SSA has not expanded the court system.

On-the-Record Decisions

Shortly after the case is received by the ODAR, it will be assigned to a *senior case technician*. The senior case technician's responsibility is to review the case and make a determination about whether benefits should be granted without the need for a hearing. This is known as an *on-the-record decision* and is more fully discussed in Chapter 15.

Understanding the Hearing Letter and Preparing for the Hearing

14

Depending upon where in the United States you reside, sometime within nine months to as long as two years after you have filed your request for a hearing, you will receive a hearing package from the Office of Disability, Adjudication, and Review (ODAR). Included in this package will be the following:

- a notice that your hearing has been scheduled;

- additional forms for you to complete and bring to the hearing;

- an acknowledgment card of the hearing; and,

- a list of the medical records (list of exhibits) contained in your file.

> **Practical Point**
>
> If you are represented, the court will contact your attorney directly before the hearing is scheduled. This is done as a courtesy to attorneys, as they may have another matter already scheduled on the same day.

A copy of a typical hearing notice is reproduced on page 152.

The Hearing Letter

The hearing letter will advise you of the date and time of the hearing. It will also list the name of the judge who will hear your case. It is most important that you read this letter very carefully, as it outlines the issues that will be discussed at the hearing. In addition, it will list whether the court has scheduled any experts to offer testimony regarding your claim. Please see the discussion on page 161 about medical and vocational experts.

 **SOCIAL SECURITY ADMINISTRATION**

Refer To:

Office of Disability Adjudication and Review
3116 W. March Lane
Suite 100
Stockton, CA 95219
Tel: (209)477-3103 / Fax: (209)477-3394

February 15, 2007

NOTICE OF HEARING

I have scheduled your hearing for:

Day: Tuesday   **Date:** March 20, 2007   **Time:** 11:00 AM
    Pacific (PST)

Room: **Address:** Downey ODAR
    8345 Firestone Blvd.
    Suite 210
    Downey, CA 90241

It Is Important That You Come To Your Hearing

I have set aside this time to hear your case. If you do not appear at the hearing and I do not find that you have good cause for failing to appear, I may **dismiss** your request for hearing. I may do so without giving you further notice.

Complete The Enclosed Form

Please complete and return the enclosed acknowledgment form to let me know you received this notice. Use the enclosed envelope to return the form to me within 5 days of the date you receive this notice. We assume you got this notice 5 days after the date on it unless you show us that you did not get it within the 5-day period.

If You Cannot Come to Your Scheduled Hearing

If you cannot come to your hearing at the time and place I have set, call this office immediately. Also mail in the form right away.

See Next Page

If you object to the set time and place, but do not request a change at the earliest possible opportunity at which you could do so before the time set for the hearing, I will rule on your request based on our standards for deciding if there is a good reason for not timely filing a request and our standards for deciding if there is a good reason for changing the time and place of a scheduled hearing. I will apply these standards in considering any objection to the set time and place that is not timely submitted.

To request a change, you must state why you object to the time or place set. You also must state the time and place you want the hearing held. You should do this in writing if at all possible.

If I find you have a good reason, I will reschedule the hearing for a time and place I set. I will also mail you another notice at least 20 days before the date of the hearing.

Travel Costs

When you, a representative, or needed witnesses will travel more than 75 miles one way to the hearing, we can pay certain travel costs. I am enclosing a sheet telling about our rules for doing that. Please call me if you want more information.

Issues I Will Consider In Your Case

The hearing concerns your application of September 28, 2005, for a period of disability and Disability Insurance Benefits under sections 216(i) and 223(a) of the Social Security Act.

I will decide if you have enough earnings under Social Security to be insured for Disability Insurance Benefits. If you do, I must decide if you became disabled while insured.

Under the Act, I may find you disabled for those benefits only if you have a physical or mental impairment that:

- has prevented you from doing any substantial gainful work; and

- has lasted 12 straight months or can be expected to last for that time or result in death

To decide if you are disabled, I will follow a step-by-step process until I can make a decision. The issues in this process concern:

- any work you have done since you got sick;

- the severity of your impairment(s); and

- your ability to do the kind of work you did in the past and, considering your age, education and work experience , any other work that exists in the national economy.

Our regulations explain the rules for deciding if you are disabled and, if so, when you came disabled. These rules appear in the Code of Federal Regulations, Title 20, Chapter III, Part 404, Subpart P.

See Next Page

More About The Issues

If I find that drug addiction and/or alcoholism is an issue, I also will decide whether it is a contributing factor material to the determination of your disability. Further, if drug addiction or alcoholism is a contributing factor material to the determination of your disability, I will find you not disabled pursuant to Sections 223(d)(2) and 1614(a)(3) of the Social Security Act as amended by Public Law 104-121.

If you qualify for benefits based on disability, I will also decide if your disability continues. I will consider whether there has been any medical improvement in your impairment(s) or whether one of the exceptions to medical improvement stated in the regulations applies. Unless certain exceptions apply, I will find you still disabled if you have not become able to work.

If You Have Objections

If you object to the issues I have stated, or to any other aspect of the scheduled hearing, you must tell me in writing why you object. You must do this at the earliest possible opportunity before the hearing.

You May Submit Additional Evidence And Review Your File

If there is more evidence you want to submit, get it to me right away. If you cannot get the evidence to me before the hearing, bring it to the hearing. If you want to see your file before the date of the hearing, call this office.

Your Right To Request a Subpoena

I may issue a subpoena that requires a person to submit documents or testify at your hearing. I will issue a subpoena if it is reasonably necessary for the full presentation of your case.

If you want me to issue a subpoena, you must submit a written request. You should submit the request as soon as possible before the hearing. The request must identify the needed documents or witnesses and their location, state the important facts the document or witness is expected to prove, and indicate why you cannot prove these facts without a subpoena.

What Happens At The Hearing

- You may review your file. If you wish to do so, please arrive 30 minutes before the time set for the hearing. Call us if you want more time.

- You will have a chance to testify and tell me about your case.

- You (and your representative) may submit documents, present and question witnesses, state your case, and present written statements about the facts and law.

See Next Page

 Page 4 of 4

- I will question you and any other witnesses about the issues. You and any other witnesses must normally testify under oath or affirmation.

- We will make an audio recording of the hearing.

My Decision

After the hearing, I will issue a written decision explaining my findings of fact and conclusions of law. I will base my decision on all the evidence of record, including the testimony at the hearing. I will mail a copy of the decision to you.

If You Have Any Questions

If you have any questions, please call or write this office. Our telephone number and address are shown on the first page of this notice.

Howard K. Treblin
Administrative Law Judge

Enclosures

cc: Benjamin H. Berkley
1440 N. Harbor Blvd.
Ste. 250
Fullerton, CA 92835

Practical Point

Upon receiving the letter, calendar the date immediately. In addition, share the information with a family member or friend so that he or she can remind you of the date. This advice especially applies to people who are having issues with memory.

Practical Point

In some parts of the country, the list of exhibits is sent to the claimant prior to the date of the hearing. Regardless of when it is received, it is important that you review your file at the earliest opportunity.

The Acknowledgment Card

Accompanying the letter will be an acknowledgment card that you must complete and return to the court. As the court has set aside a specific time to hear your claim, it wants to make sure that you will be there. Accordingly, upon receipt, complete the card and return it to the court immediately.

List of Exhibits

Also included in the hearing package will be a document titled "List of Exhibits." This is a list of all the medical evidence that has been created by the SSA, as well as the evidence submitted by you. Often, there may be a medical report or other record that you submitted that is missing from this list. Therefore, you should review this list carefully. In addition, you should call the ODAR to make an appointment to review the documents listed on the exhibit list.

Additional Forms

In addition to the letter, the court may include forms that concern the following topics, which should be completed and brought with you on the day of the hearing:

- current medications that you are taking;

- any recent medical treatment; and,

- your work background.

The forms addressing these topics are reproduced on page 158. The purpose of these forms is to allow the court to update any information on your claim so as to be assured that the administrative law judge (ALJ) has the most current information available when deciding your claim.

Reviewing the File and Its Exhibits

Upon receipt of the hearing package, you should call the court and arrange a time to review your file. This is very important, as there may be records that you have submitted that are missing from the list of exhibits. In addition, taking a look at your file will give you an opportunity to review the reports by any consultative examining doctors. This is critical, because it will provide an insight as to why your claim has been denied and what you will need to prove so the judge can approve your claim.

Because courts are so backlogged, the courts require that you arrange a specific time to review your file. As you review the file, pay special attention to the consultative reports that are numbered by the list of exhibits. To find the physical consultative report, first look at the list of exhibits. The list might read as follows:

Exhibit 4F: Physical report by James Jones, State Doctor, dated March 31, 2007.

By turning to the section of your file that contains the medical records, you can flip through that section until you find Exhibit 4F.

Social Security Administration
Office of Disability Adjudication and Review

Form Approved
OMB No.0960-0292

CLAIMANT'S RECENT MEDICAL TREATMENT

A. To be completed by Hearing Office staff

Claimant's Name: Mary C. Mitten	SSN: 546-04-1989	The last time your case was brought up-to-date:

B. To be completed by claimant

Please Answer the Following Questions:

1) Have you been treated or examined by a doctor (other than a doctor at a hospital) since the above date? ☐ Yes ☐ No

(List the names and addresses of doctors who have treated or examined you since the above date and the dates of treatment or examination. If possible, you should submit an updated report from these doctors to the Administrative Law Judge prior to the date of your hearing.)

DOCTORS' NAME(S)	ADDRESS(ES)	DATE(S)

2) What have these doctors told you about your condition?

3) Have you been hospitalized since the above date? ☐ Yes ☐ No
(If so, please state the name and address of the hospital, the reasons why you were hospitalized and the nature of the treatment you received.)

Name of Hospital	Address of Hospital (include ZIP code)

If more space is needed use the back of the form

**PLEASE READ THE PRIVACY ACT
STATEMENT ON THE NEXT PAGE**

Form HA-4631 (8-1996) ef (10-2004)
Issue Old Stock

Social Security Administration
Office of Headings and Appeals

Form Approved
OMB No. 0960-0292

CLAIMANT'S RECENT MEDICAL TREATMENT

A. To be completed by hearing office

(Claimant and Social Security Number)	(Wage Earner and Social Security Number) (Leave blank if same as claimant)	The last time we brought your case up-to-date was:

B. To be completed by the claimant

PLEASE PRINT

Please Answer the Following Quetions:

(1) Have you been treated or examined by a doctor (other than a doctor at a hospital) since the above date? ⟶ ☐ Yes ☐ No

(If yes, please list the names,addresses and telephone numbers of doctors who have treated or examined you since the above date. Also list the dates of treatment or examination. If possible, send updated reports from the doctor to the Administrative Law Judge before the date of your hearing.)

DOCTORS NAME(S)	ADDRESS(ES) &TELEPHONE NO.(S)	DATE(S)

(2) What have these doctors told you about your condition?

(3) Have you been hopitalized since the above date? ⟶ ☐ Yes ☐ No

(If yes, please list the name and address of the hospital. Also, explain why you were hospitalized and what treatment you received.)

Name of Hospital	Address of Hospital (Include ZIP Code)

Reason for hospitalization:

Treatment received:

Form HA-4631(8-96) Issue Old Stock	**PLEASE READ PRIVACY ACT STATEMENT ON REVERSE**	If more space is needed, use additional sheet.

Social Security Administration
Office of Disability Adjudication and Review

Form Approved
OMB No.0960-0300

CLAIMANT'S WORK BACKGROUND

A. To be completed by Hearing Office

Claimant and Social Security Number:	Wage Earner and Social Security Number (Leave blank if same as claimant):	The last time we brought your case up-to-date was:
Mary C. Mitten 546-04-1989		

B. To be completed by the claimant

PLEASE PRINT

Start with your most recent job, and list that and any work performed within the past 15 years.

DATE OF EMPLOYMENT (APPROXIMATELY)	NAME OF EMPLOYER AND LOCATION OF EMPLOYMENT	DUTIES PERFORMED
FROM		
TO		
FROM		
TO		
FROM		
TO		
FROM		
TO		

PLEASE READ THE PRIVACY ACT STATEMENT ON THE NEXT PAGE   If more space is needed use additional sheets

Form **HA-4633** (3-1994) ef (10-2004)
Issue Old Stock

After you review the list of exhibits, make sure that every report you filed did in fact make it into the court's file. If it did not, immediately send another copy of the report to the ODAR. Also, if you are still waiting for records or a completed questionnaire from your doctor, call the doctor to explain that a hearing has been scheduled and it is essential that you obtain the records.

After reviewing the file, it is a good idea to make copies of those sections of the file that you may want to refer to during the hearing. You may make photocopies of all or any portion of your file at no charge by using the photocopier that the SSA provides at every ODAR. Be prepared, however, to wait your turn in line, as there is usually only one copier available.

Medical and Vocational Experts

Somewhere in the body of the letter, it may state that the court has scheduled a medical or vocational expert to appear with you at the hearing. An expert's testimony may be required because the judge, based on the evidence that you have submitted, will have questions that he or she needs answered and it is felt that your testimony alone will not be sufficient to provide the answers needed.

The fact that experts are scheduled should not be viewed positively or negatively. Often, the scheduling of experts is a personal preference of the judge. Some judges are confident that they can make the correct decision based on your testimony as well as what has been provided in the file and will rarely require expert testimony. Other judges, no matter how obvious the case may appear, always schedule experts. Therefore, regardless of whether an expert will appear or not, if you have the medical evidence that will support your testimony, your chances of receiving benefits are in your favor.

Vocational Experts

A vocational expert will explain to the judge what type of work you performed in the last fifteen years. This is not as simple as it sounds, as not all work is performed the same way. To illustrate, assume that you took phone orders sitting at a desk, but at times, you went into the warehouse and pulled parts from boxes that were placed on shelves. Your past work may be rated "light," as you were sitting as well as standing and pulling. The vocational expert would then testify whether you can still perform "light" work. If the expert testifies that you can, you may not be found disabled. However, see the discussion of the grids found in Chapter 7 for more information.

Medical Experts

A medical expert is necessary when there is a question as to whether your impairment meets or equals the medical listings as discussed in Chapter 5. As previously stated, if you are found to meet or equal the listings, you are disabled. However, if your medical record has not been developed fully and the court cannot with certainty conclude whether you meet or equal a listing, the expert will help explain the medical records. In doing so, the medical expert may ask you some questions about your symptoms and limitations. Based on your answers, he or she will be able to offer an opinion to the judge.

You may have already been examined by a doctor that the SSA sent you to for evaluation. That experience was possibly upsetting because the doctor may have spent very little time understanding your problem. You should not, however, draw the conclusion that the expert for the judge will be biased against you. From experience, I have always felt that the court-appointed medical experts are very fair in assisting the judge.

Preparing for the Hearing

Waiting for the hearing date to arrive has been frustrating, and now that the date itself is looming, you probably feel anxious. To alleviate any additional stress associated with getting to the court, it is my recommendation that you drive to the court a day or more before the hearing. This will familiarize you with where the court is located. In addition, if the court is in an area that you are not familiar with, you will want to know how long it will take to get to the hearing so that you can allow the proper amount of time for travel and parking.

REQUESTING AN ON-THE-RECORD DECISION

As previously discussed, the time from making the initial application to having a hearing scheduled can take two years or more. Also, even though the SSA has annually requested that more staff as well as judges be hired, Congress routinely has cut the budget for hiring. As a result, there are inherent case delays in the processing of claims because the hearing offices are greatly understaffed.

In addition, though a case has been transferred to a hearing office, until it reaches the point where it is ready to be scheduled, little if any new work has been done on the file. Therefore, even though you have filed your Request for Hearing within the sixty days as you are required to do, your file has literally sat in some office collecting dust.

However, there is a way of speeding up the process—requesting an *on-the-record decision* (OTR).

On-the-Record Decisions

An on-the-record decision occurs when the evidence already submitted is sufficient to render a favorable decision without the need for a hearing. That is, nothing more will be gained by the judge meeting with you in person as the medical evidence meets or equals the medical listings of disability, or for vocational reasons, you are disabled according to the grids. (For a further discussion of the medical listings, see Chapter 4. For a further discussion of the grids, please see Chapter 7.)

A request for an OTR requires getting the attention of the hearing office so that your file can be moved from storage and brought to the attention of a Social Security attorney who works in the hearing office. To do so, you must make your request in writing. However, it is advisable that you delay making your request until your file has been received, as discussed in Chapter 14.

After you have reviewed the medical listings and the grids, and are of the belief that your case either meets or equals the listings or meets the five-step sequential evaluation, call the office and ask if the case has been assigned to a judge. In most cases, that probably has not yet occurred. Regardless, ask the clerk for the name of the staff attorney to whom you can address your request for an OTR. If the ODAR has no staff attorney (and many now do not, due to budget cuts), request the name of a senior staff member, senior case technician, or hearing case manager to address your request.

When making your written request for an OTR, remember that you are asking the court to grant you benefits because it is your position that the evidence meets or equals the medical listings or vocationally you cannot work. Therefore, your request must do more than simply state that you are disabled. Instead, you must identify the evidence in your file that satisfies your claim for disability. You are presenting a legal brief that weaves the facts with the law and reaches the conclusion that you are disabled.

In preparing to submit your request for an on-the-record decision, you will want to state your case with as much understanding of your disability as possible. In reviewing your records and medical questionnaires, you may find yourself at a loss trying to explain what your doctor has said about you. Furthermore, the medical listings are highly technical, using language that is more commonly understood by members of the medical community. The following resource materials are available at your public library to assist you in drafting your brief:

- *The Merck Manual of Diagnosis and Therapy of Diseases*, which is an encyclopedia of diseases, including symptoms and treatments;

- *The Professional Guide to Diseases* (published by Springhouse Corporations), which is written for health care providers such as those in the nursing field, explaining diseases and their treatments, and includes listings of very rare diseases;

- *Merriam-Webster Medical Dictionary*, which provides comprehensive coverage of medical terminology (buy the paperback edition);

- *Dictionary of Medical Acronyms and Abbreviations*, which is a very useful guide since doctors love to abbreviate;

- *Dorland's Illustrated Medical Dictionary, 30th Edition*;

- *Physician's Desk Reference, 61st Edition*; and,

- *Harrison's Principles of Internal Medicine, 16th Edition*.

In addition to these sources, there are many paperback encyclopedias of medications that provide information on drugs by manufacturer, their generic brand name, and possible side effects.

Finally, I highly suggest reviewing Gray's *Anatomy*. The illustrations are extremely helpful in understanding spinal and musculoskeletal impairments as well as all systems of the body.

Drafting an OTR Brief

To illustrate a claim where an OTR decision may be warranted, suppose the following. You are 49 years old and have worked for the last fifteen years in an office doing phone sales and most recently as a security guard. You are having trouble walking and writing. You have been diagnosed with diabetes. Your doctor has completed a medical questionnaire that has not been submitted.

In writing your brief, you should first review the medical listings. The following is a sample request for an OTR.

Stacy Klein, Senior Technician
Office of Disability, Adjudication, and Review
1120 West La Veta Avenue, Suite 600
Orange, California 92868

Re: Anna Belle Sitzer
SSN: 111–11–1112

Dear Ms. Klein,

Please consider my claim for a possible on-the-record decision. My request is based on the fact that it is my position that I meet listings 9.08.

Specifically, in 2005, I was complaining about loss of feeling when walking as well as pain and loss of feeling in my hands. It was becoming more and more difficult for me to do my job as a security guard since I could not stand on my feet. After having two episodes where I blacked out, I made an appointment with my doctor. He promptly ordered blood work and told me that my blood sugar was very high. He diagnosed me with diabetes and also told me that the disease had affected my ability to move. Although I am on insulin, my sugar levels are still high. Furthermore, I have not returned to work.

Listing 9.08 describes neuropathy as the "significant and persistent disorganization of motor function in two extremities resulting in sustained disturbance of gross and dexterous movements, or gait and station."

In the medical report prepared by Byron Meeker, M.D., who made my original diagnosis, he cites this listing and identifies his objective findings. (See his report attached, dated May 12, 2005.)

Previously, you have been provided with all of my laboratory results as well as my doctor's treating notes.

For the above reasons, I request a favorable decision.

Very truly yours,

As with all documents sent to Social Security, it is advisable that you send your OTR request by certified mail, return receipt requested. This way, you have written proof that the information was received. However, once you mail the documents, there is nothing further required on your part at this time.

Upon review, the court will do one of the following:

- grant your request for an OTR;

- request additional information from you in support of your request; or

- not respond. Instead, the case will be scheduled for a hearing.

If the request is granted, you will receive a Notice of Decision from the court. This will be followed by a letter from the SSA explaining your monthly benefits, as well as the amount of past due benefits. Please read this notice very carefully. Favorable decisions and award benefits are discussed in Chapter 18.

Alternatively, the court may require additional information before a decision can be rendered. If this occurs, take this as a positive sign, as the court is saying, "We want to grant you benefits but just need another piece of the puzzle."

The information may be something as simple as another copy of a record that was not legible, or the court may want a statement from your doctor that you are still under his or her care. Regardless of the request, provide the information as soon as possible.

> ## Practical Point
>
> Even if your request is denied, the paperwork that you submitted will remain as a permanent part of your file. Furthermore, when the judge prepares for the hearing, he or she will also review your request. This often works in your favor, as it provides a summary for the judge from the claimant's point of view in deciding what the central issue of your claim is. Therefore, although there may not have been sufficient enough information to grant your request on the record, the judge may be more focused on your limitations in deciding your claim.

LEGALLY SPEAKING

Even when the evidence is overwhelmingly in your favor, OTR decisions are not as common as one might believe. This is not because the court questions the evidence, but because the ALJ wants to have had the opportunity to meet with you so that he or she can, with assurance, make a favorable decision. Note that even the judge's decisions are reviewed by the Appeals Council as a means of quality assurance to make sure the judge is doing his or her job correctly. Therefore, if there is the slightest doubt of whether to award benefits, the judge will schedule a hearing.

As hearings may take as long as two years to schedule, it is difficult to place a timeline as to when you would hear on your request for an OTR. Therefore, do not be discouraged if you do not hear anything for several months. However, if the court eventually schedules a hearing, then you will know that your request for an OTR was denied.

THE HEARING

16

After months and perhaps years of waiting, the day has arrived for your hearing. The following discussion will explain how the hearing is conducted and what to expect. It will also dispel any preconceived presumptions you may have about the process.

Arriving for the Hearing

You should plan to arrive about thirty minutes before the hearing. As you enter the hearing office, you may have to go through a metal detector. Regardless, upon arrival, you will be asked to sign in by printing and signing your name and noting the time that you arrived. This way the clerk can alert the judge that you are present. Be prepared to also show proper photo identification

The Hearing Venue

When people think about going to court, they imagine walking up the white marble stairs of the U.S. Supreme Court and then entering a large room with wood-paneled walls as they stare at the judge's bench where the almighty presides.

In the world of SSA hearings, the venues are not quite that elaborate. Although the SSA does have some sites where a traditional type of hearing room exists, many sites are located in office buildings where the SSA rents space and has converted offices into hearing rooms.

Reviewing Your File

By arriving early, you will be given one last opportunity to examine your file. This is especially important if you have recently submitted new medical records, as you will want to make sure that they have been entered into the file.

Immediately Prior to the Hearing

A few minutes prior to the scheduled time for your hearing, the judge's clerk will introduce him- or herself to you and ask if you have any additional information. At this time you can provide the clerk with any new information. You will also hand the clerk the three completed forms that the court sent to you, along with the hearing letter. These forms are discussed in Chapter 14. If you are planning to have anyone else testify on your behalf, such as your spouse or friend, advise the clerk and he or she will make a note on the file for the judge.

The Hearing Room

When your case is called, you will be escorted by the judge's clerk to the hearing room. If experts are also scheduled, they are often already seated in the room when you enter.

Note that most hearing rooms are very small and consist of only a table and chairs where you and the witnesses sit. The seat on which the judge sits is called the bench and may be slightly elevated. Seated near the judge will be his or her hearing assistant, who will tape-record the proceedings.

Practical Point

If you have submitted evidence to the court within the last thirty days, you should take a copy of any records with you to the hearing. This way, if they are not in the file, the court can make a copy from what you supply.

When the judge enters the room, it is expected that you rise from your seat to show respect. Most judges will signal for you to immediately sit down. The judge, depending on his or her own personal style, may or may not be wearing a black robe.

Meet the Administrative Law Judge

An administrative law judge (ALJ) is appointed by the Social Security Administration. Prior to the judge's appointment, he or she may have had a varied background as an attorney. He or she may have been in private practice representing Social Security claimants or in some other area of the law. He or she may also have been an administrative judge for a different branch of the government, including handling military cases for the United States Army. Regardless, all judges are experienced in administrative law. Further, as part of their requirements to remain on the bench, they must attend continuing education classes so that they remain fully up to date with the ever-changing Social Security regulations.

How a Hearing is Conducted

Let me first dispel some myths. First, the hearing is an administrative hearing. This means that the rules that would normally apply to a courtroom do not apply here. There is no jury, there are no side bars, and this is not the O.J. Simpson trial. There is no opposing attorney. In fact, some judges do not even wear a black robe.

Upon taking the bench, the judge will ask if you have reviewed the file and are in agreement that the records contained in the file should be entered into evidence. There is no reason to object to the evidence in the file being admitted unless the file contains evidence from a different claimant. Otherwise you should answer that the file may be introduced into evidence. If you have any questions before the judge begins the hearing, you should ask them now. Note, at this point, your questions should be very general in nature. Do not ask anything specific about your claim, as the recorder has not yet been turned on.

The Order of the Hearing

At the start of the hearing, the judge will ask you and any witnesses to take an oath to tell the truth. This is not a religious oath that you are "swearing unto God," but instead an oath in which you are stating that your testimony will be truthful.

After taking the oath, the judge will ask that you say and spell your name and recite your Social Security number. In addition, the judge will ask that you verify your current mailing address. This is required so that the court has the correct address to which to mail the decision.

Practical Point

If you have witnesses who will be appearing on your behalf, the judge may ask that they remain outside the hearing room until he or she calls them in for questioning.

Since this is an administrative hearing, you can speak informally. There is no need for "I object" or "Let the record show." The judge, however, should be treated with respect and addressed as "Your Honor."

The hearing can be as short as five minutes, but generally takes twenty to thirty minutes. Prior to asking you about your disability, the judge will make an opening statement about the hearing that will include:

- that the judge is not part of the SSA office that previously denied the claim and therefore you should be assured that he or she is not biased by any previous decision;

- that the hearing is being tape-recorded and that the official record of the hearing will consist of both oral testimony and the records that have been submitted;

- that one person will speak at a time and that all witnesses will be placed under oath; and,

- that you will be given a reasonable time after the hearing to submit any additional information that would support your claim.

The judge will then either first question you or the experts. If the experts are examined first, this is because you have provided all the information necessary to support your position that you are disabled, and if you gave testimony, you would only be providing information that is already part of the record.

Your Testimony

If the ALJ begins with your testimony, he or she will ask you a series of questions that will cover the following areas:

- statistical information including your full name, Social Security number, date of birth, highest grade in school completed, higher education, vocational training, and any certificate or degrees achieved;

- work experience for the past fifteen years including names of employers, dates of employment, job descriptions, how the work was performed, and why you left the job;

- medical history including when an injury first occurred or when a diagnosis was made;

- current treatment including names of doctors, their specialties, length of treatment, type of treatment, and medications prescribed;

- physical complaints including questions about severity and location of pain and other physical impairments such as shortness of breath and fatigue;

- mental impairments including issues regarding concentration, following instructions, and stress;

- physical functioning restrictions including questions about the length of time you can sit, stand and walk, lift and carry, bend, twist, kneel, stoop, travel, and manipulate objects with your hands;

LEGALLY SPEAKING

When you represent yourself, the judge will conduct the questioning. It is not necessary to give an "opening statement," as the court is well aware of what you are seeking. Furthermore, you should stay focused on the question you are being asked and limit your responses to the question. Most importantly, you should not volunteer information. Before the judge concludes the hearing, however, you will be given an opportunity to explain to the court anything that you feel the judge needs to know that you were not asked. In addition, you will have an opportunity to summarize your case by making a closing statement, which is simply a summary of your case.

- questions about "good days and bad days" to elicit information about how you spend your day;

- questions about daily activities including driving, housework, and shopping;

- questions about personal care including dressing, bathing, and hygiene; and,

- questions about social functioning including whether you attend any activities on a regular basis, participate in sports, and have any hobbies.

How to Conduct Yourself During the Hearing

Because Social Security hearings are administrative, the hearing does not follow the formal requirements that would be found in other courts. To illustrate, unlike the many court television programs where attorneys are jumping up and down raising objections to testimony and evidence trying to be admitted, the judge typically asks the questions. In addition, it is not an adversary hearing, as the SSA is not represented by an attorney. Therefore, the judge will decide what is or is not relevant. However, despite the informal setting, you should still conduct yourself appropriately.

Addressing the Court

When talking to the judge, it is proper to address the judge as "Your Honor." This would apply both to answering his or her questions and providing information.

Submitting New Information

The hearing notice that you received specified that all new information should be submitted to the court no later than twenty days before the hearing. Some judges very strictly enforce this policy, although most will allow you to introduce evidence at the time of the hearing if you are not represented. If you have new information, provide it to the judge's hearing assistant *before* the case is called.

This way the assistant can show it to the judge before he or she takes the bench so that he or she is familiar with it, as it may alter the questions he or she will ask you. Do not hold on to the information and plan on dramatically announcing that you have it during the hearing. The hearing is not a time for courtroom dramatics and the judge will not appreciate your attempt at surprise.

Do Not be Argumentative

The judge's role is to independently decide your claim, and he or she will state at the beginning of the hearing that any prior decisions that have been made on your case will not influence his or her decision. You should sincerely believe this. From experience I can tell you that I have never found a judge who I believed was biased against my client before the hearing.

However, a judge's open-mindedness can be influenced by the attitude that you display in court. Accordingly, if you argue with the judge or any expert, or do not cooperate with the hearing process, the judge will admonish you. If your attitude does not change, it is almost certain to influence the outcome.

JOE'S STORY

Joe came to my office after attending the hearing on his own. The judge terminated the hearing, giving Joe two weeks to "get his act together" and strongly suggesting that he retain an attorney. Joe told me that he was annoyed by the judge's line of questioning, because he thought that the judge thought he was a liar. Before I took the case, I called the court and spoke with the hearing assistant, who confirmed that the claimant was rude and indignant. The judge, being a very fair person, gave the claimant a second chance, when he could have easily ended the hearing and delivered a denial decision. In preparing for the hearing, I instructed Joe on how he was to act. He complied and we won his case.

Answer the Questions with Details

You have waited so long to tell your story to the judge. Now that the moment has arrived, you must take full advantage of the time that you will be allotted. Note that most hearings last less than twenty to thirty minutes. It is in that time that you must convince the judge why the SSA was wrong in its prior decisions.

Note that by the time you walk into court, the written part of your claim has been documented. Now, you must explain to the court so that the judge can see with his or her eyes and hear with his or her ears how your disability affects your ability to be gainfully employed.

This is the time for you to express what is in the written record. To illustrate, if your doctor says that you have shortness of breath, tell the judge how, after taking a few steps, you must stop to catch your breath. Tell the judge how opening the door to the refrigerator to reach for a container of milk is difficult. Explain how you cannot hook your bra or reach over your head to shampoo your hair.

The following are two illustrations of how the same question can be answered. You be the judge. Which response better paints a picture of someone who is disabled?

ALJ: Where do you have pain?

Client: In my hands, back, and feet.

ALJ: Is the pain constant or sometimes?

Client: Sometimes.

Compare this example with a different response to the same question as follows.

ALJ: Where do you have pain?

Client: In my hands, back, and feet. I can't even hold a brush to brush my hair. My daughter has to help me. It is difficult to brush my teeth. I also have trouble dressing myself. I can't button my clothes because I have pain in the tips of my fingers. I wear slip-on shoes because I cannot bend down to tie my shoes. It seems there is nothing I can do to relieve the pain.

ALJ: Is the pain constant or sometimes?

Client: Only if I lie down is the pain slightly diminished. Otherwise, there is nothing I can do to relieve the pain.

You must take full advantage of the time you are allowed to answer the questions. Of course you have pain, and it is documented in all the previously submitted medical reports. However, you must convince the judge that performing simple, everyday tasks is very difficult if not impossible. Logically, if you cannot work in your home, then you cannot perform on the job.

Be an Actor

It is said that everyone has his or her fifteen minutes of fame. In fighting for your benefits, look at the time you have to impress the judge as your fifteen minutes.

When I prepare a client for testifying, I often ask if he or she ever performed in a school play or ever made a public speech. I like to make this reference, as testifying before a judge is your opportunity to shine. The spotlight is on you.

Remember that the Judge is Observing You

Although the hearing does not begin until the judge asks the hearing assistant to turn on the tape recorder, from the moment the judge enters the courtroom he or she is observing you. These observations will help him or her form an opinion about your case. Anything that he or she perceives negatively will make it that much more difficult for you to win your case.

To illustrate, say you have stated in the record that you are in constant pain and cannot sit for more than fifteen minutes without shifting your weight. However, the hearing has now lasted twenty minutes and you remain seated, appearing very comfortable. If you truly cannot sit, then stand up, or alternate between sitting and standing. It is that simple.

The court does not want your pain to be aggravated by the hearing, but it does have years of experience in spotting a claimant who is faking symptoms.

Your Body Language Can Tell More about Your Claim than Your Testimony

When I first meet a client, it is my policy to go out into the waiting room, announce my name, shake my client's hand, and follow him or her into my office. During this time, I am making some initial observations. Specifically, is he or she walking with assistance or limping? Is he or she walking slowly? Does he or she seem disoriented or confused? Is the person who accompanied the client doing all the talking?

I make these observations to compare with the information we gathered about the client when he or she first contacted our office. To illustrate, the client may have said on the phone that he or she has great difficulty walking as a result of a back injury and that he or she has difficulty getting up from a sitting position. If, when I first meet my client, he or she jumps out of the chair and then proceeds to walk into my office in a straight line, his or her body movements will raise questions in my mind as to his or her credibility and how he or she will be perceived by the judge.

RHONDA'S STORY

With twenty-nine years of experience, it is not often I can say I am not prepared for a hearing. Perhaps because I am of the male gender, I was caught off guard in this situation.

Rhonda was 48 and had worked as an administrative assistant for the past sixteen years. Her job included word processing and data entry. Due to a car accident, she injured her neck and upper back. Her main complaints were loss of feelings in her hands and fingers. She also said it was difficult to manipulate small objects. Her doctor reports supported her complaints.

When we entered the hearing room, the judge was already seated. Prior to starting the hearing, she made a few remarks to Rhonda that I thought were intended to put her at ease. The judge commented on Rhonda's hair style, as my client wore her hair in a tight curl. The judge further asked her where she went to have her hair done and Rhonda replied that she did her hair herself. All along, I thought that this was idle chitchat between two women, and so I paid no attention to the conversation.

However, once the hearing began and the questions turned to exertional impairments, the judge focused on hand manipulation and asked several questions about Rhonda's grooming, including styling her hair.

I left the hearing knowing I had lost and was not surprised when I received the judge's decision that concluded that despite the medical record, my client was not credible and therefore the judge was not convinced that she had hand problems. She concluded that my client could return to sedentary work.

In retrospect, it is not that I would want my client to deceive the court. However, your credibility is at stake. Your words as well as your actions will be judged.

American Idol and the Likeability Factor

Whether or not you are a fan of the popular show *American Idol,* you are probably aware that the first audition involves idol hopefuls facing three judges. Before the audition starts, they are asked, "Why are you here?" After the contestant sings (or attempts to sing), Randy, Paula, and Simon offer their critiques. Along with the evaluation of whether the contestant can carry a tune is a discussion of whether he or she is likeable. That is, will the viewing public buy the contestant's records not only because he or she can sing, but also because they like him or her?

At your hearing, the judge is also making an evaluation that extends beyond the documents that have been submitted and what you have said. The judge is deciding if he or she likes you and thus believes you. If there is any doubt as to whether or not you are disabled, if the judge likes you, he or she will decide in your favor.

Dos And Don'ts about Testifying

Do:

- Answer the question that is being asked. Make sure your answer is complete and answers the question to the best of your ability.

- Speak clearly and audibly. Be confident yet respectful.

- Practice prior to the hearing in describing how your disability prevents you from working and how your daily life is impaired. Tell your story. This is your most important opportunity to prove your case. Give specific examples, such as how it is difficult to bathe or dress yourself or how you cannot remember simple instructions.

- Be yourself.

- Talk to the judge. Do not look away. Direct your testimony into the judge's eyes.

- Organize your thoughts.

- Be sincere.

Don't:

- Make the judge go fishing for your answer. Be prepared.

- Volunteer information that is not asked. If there is something that you want to add, you will be given an opportunity to make a statement at the end of the hearing.

- Be shy, arrogant, or rude.

- Answer questions in a robotic manner.

- Ramble.

- Make a political statement about how you have been treated unfairly by the SSA.

Video Hearings

In certain parts of the country, the SSA is experimenting with conducting hearings by video conference. That is, the judge may be at one location while you are at another. This is being implemented for those situations in which the claimant may have to travel a great distance to the closest court and a video hearing may be more convenient. At this time, video conferences are not mandatory if you prefer to have your hearing in person.

If you are offered the option of appearing by video, it is my opinion that you should turn it down and appear in person. This allows the judge to meet you and observe you and hopefully feel your pain and discomfort in a way that would not be possible by video.

Expert Testimony

The majority of hearings are conducted without the need for experts, because the judge has a very good understanding of the medical reports and your limitations, and generally the judges are sympathetic and compassionate. They will decide in your favor if there is any doubt as to whether you are disabled. However, there are times when the medial reports are not conclusive or there is a question as to whether you are capable of doing some type of work even though it might not be the job you had before you became disabled.

Medical Experts

If the hearing will have a medical expert, do not assume the expert is biased against you. Even if the SSA had previously ordered a consultative examination, the medical expert is most likely not familiar with that doctor or associates with him or her.

The role of the medical expert is to assist the judge in explaining the reports and the alleged disability. The medical expert will also be asked to give an opinion as to whether or not you meet or equal the listings as discussed in Chapter 5. You will recall that if you meet the listings, the hearing does not need to go any further, as you will be awarded benefits. If the expert says that you do not meet or equal the listings, the judge will then ask the medical expert to give an opinion as to the severity of your impairments and to discuss your limitations. This will assist the judge in forming questions to ask the vocational expert as to your ability to perform your previous work and whether or not you can do any other type of work.

You will also be given an opportunity to ask the medical expert questions.

Practical Point

Be familiar with the listings so that your questions can cover the elements of the impairment. Also, be prepared to question the doctor as to long-term side effects of certain medications, and whether these side effects can affect your ability to work.

Specifically, you should question him or her to make sure that he or she reviewed your doctor's reports. You should also ask what is missing from the record that would allow him or her to change his or her opinion. If, from the expert's answer, you become aware of something that is missing from your file, such as a test report or lab work that satisfies the doctor's needs, you should inform the judge that the information is available but that you need to have the hearing rescheduled to give you sufficient time to obtain the records.

In preparing for the hearing, understand that the purpose of the medical expert is to assist the judge. Most claimants who have previously been seen by a Social Security doctor for a consultative examination have already had a bad experience because the doctor appeared unsympathetic or the examination was very brief. Be assured that the fact that there is a doctor at your hearing acting as a medical expert signals that the judge is making a very thorough analysis of your claim.

Vocational Experts

Steps 4 and 5 of the sequential evaluation address vocational factors. If the impairment does not meet or equal the medical listings, the question becomes whether the claimant can perform his or her previous work or any other work for which he or she is trained. The role of the *vocational expert* (VE) is to explain to the judge exactly what type of work the claimant did and whether he or she can return to that type of work. If he or she cannot, the question becomes whether he or she has learned any skills that would allow him or her to do other work.

Understanding your previous work is very important in developing your case. As an example, if you have had back surgery and you were a waitress for fifteen years, the VE may ask if you have ever worked as a cashier. This is very important because although you can no longer lift plates and trays, and therefore cannot be a waitress, you are able to be a cashier, which does not require lifting.

At the hearing, the judge will ask the VE hypothetical questions. Depending on the VE's responses, you may want to ask questions. The following is a typical hypothetical.

> **ALJ:** Mr. VE, assume a client who is 55 years old, had back surgery, and still has constant pain in his back that runs down his legs. He has constant numbness in his right leg. He cannot lift more than five pounds, but can sit more than thirty minutes and stand for ten minutes. He needs to take frequent breaks to rest. Can the claimant return to work as a truck driver?

> **VE:** No.

ALJ: Is there any other work he can do?

VE: Your Honor, the file shows that the claimant also worked as a salesman. Because he can sit for thirty minutes, and because sales do not involve lifting, I believe he can do this type of work.

Your examination of the VE would follow this question path:

Claimant: My past work was as a car salesman, and this is a job that requires sitting and standing. Is that correct?

VE: Yes.

Claimant: Would you agree that a car salesman spends the majority of his time on his feet?

VE: Yes.

Claimant: When showing a car, would you agree that the average customer will look at a car for more than ten minutes?

VE: Probably.

Claimant: If a car salesman had to take unscheduled breaks when he is showing a car, would he be productive on this job?

VE: Well, probably not as productive as his manager would like.

Claimant: Because my doctors say that I cannot stand for more than ten minutes and need to take breaks, would it be safe to assume that the number of available jobs as a car salesman would be seriously decreased if the job description would include allowing the employee to take unscheduled breaks?

VE: Probably yes.

From this example, you can see that your goal is to develop a hypothetical that forces the expert to conclude that you cannot work.

> ### Practical Point
>
> If the VE tells the judge that there is no work that you can perform, do not further question the VE. You won!

Listen carefully to the types of jobs that the VE says that you can do. Often, the VE forgets to consider medical restrictions when listing the types of jobs that you are capable of performing. For example, once I had a hearing where my client suffered from severe rheumatoid arthritis. His treating doctor said he must avoid all exposure to extreme heat and cold. The VE said, with confidence, that although my client could no longer work as a printer, he could be an inspector. He then said the client was qualified to be a sausage inspector. He was quite embarrassed when I asked him, "Isn't it true that sausage is kept in a cold environment to avoid spoilage?" We won the case.

Your Own Witnesses

As part of the administrative process, you are entitled to present your own witnesses if you feel that their testimony would add credence to your claim. Remember, however, that the court wants to hear testimony that is relevant—that is, it must have aid in supporting your claim. Likewise, if a person's testimony is simply a repeat of whatever you have already said, nothing new has been learned and the judge has the authority to limit or dismiss your client's testimony.

Having Your Doctor Testify

During my initial interview with a client, I ask if he or she is under medical care. Invariably, the answer is yes, but then the client continues by saying, "My doctor said that he would do whatever he can to help me get benefits and would be happy to testify in court if he needed to."

Although I appreciate hearing this, in the real world, doctors get paid for treating patients. No matter how benevolent they appear to be, when it comes to going to court, they want to be paid for their time. This is only logical, since the doctor is losing income during the time that he or she is away from the office. In my twenty-nine years of practicing Social Security law, I have never had a doctor offer to appear at a hearing without seeking a fee for services.

Therefore, in place of your doctor's testimony, it is important that you obtain the most up-to-date medical records that your doctor has of you in his or her file. In addition, if you are claiming that your disability affects your ability to sit, stand, or walk, or limits you from lifting, your doctor should complete the appropriate medical questionnaire as discussed in Chapter 11 and found in Appendix A.

LEGALLY SPEAKING

Unlike other court proceedings, where a witness's testimony is subject to cross-examination by the opposing party, the SSA does not have an attorney appearing on its behalf at the hearing. Therefore, you may submit letters, reports, and other records from your doctor, and these can be used as substitutes for your doctor's testimony.

Other Witnesses

When considering who should testify, think of calling someone who can articulate your disability perhaps even better than you can. For example, if your chief complaint is pain, call someone who sees how you live with your pain day after day. Find someone who can tell the judge the difficulty you have trying to dress yourself or get out of bed.

Also, your witnesses may be able to offer testimony about your condition that perhaps is embarrassing for you to talk about.

RISHA'S STORY

Risha had bowel cancer. As a result of her radiation, she often soiled herself, as her treatment burned the nerves that affect our ability to control bowel movements. This was extremely embarrassing for her to talk about, although such testimony is very important in proving that a person cannot work if he or she will have to take unscheduled bathroom breaks. After her initial testimony, she stepped out of the hearing room and her husband explained to the court how chronic the problem was.

The Waiting Game: How Do You Survive?

17

The most frustrating aspect of running a Social Security Disability law practice is trying to offer solutions to clients' financial problems while they wait for benefits. It is sad enough that you are disabled and cannot work. The added stress applied by bill collectors may only aggravate your medical condition.

Some people who have applied for benefits may be receiving compensation from a workers' compensation claim or a long-term disability insurance policy. For most, however, state disability benefits may have already run out or the claimant has been without any source of income for many months or years. Even when a claimant is married and the other spouse is working, the loss of one income due to a disability quickly turns into a financial nightmare. We have had clients who have lost their homes in foreclosure, had vehicles repossessed, and have been forced to move in with family members or even live on the streets.

The questions most often asked by our clients include:

"How do I pay my bills if I have no money coming in?"

"I am going to lose my house. Is there any way of stopping the foreclosure?"

"Does the SSA ever advance money while it is deciding a case?"

"What if I work part-time? Will that hurt my chances of getting benefits?"

What further adds to our frustration is that there is no accurate timetable that I can refer to in order to advise my clients when they can expect to receive benefits.

In some cases, I have obtained benefits for my client upon making the initial application even when I thought the claim would be denied. In other cases, where I believed the medical evidence was very supportive, the case took two years from the time the client filed the initial application before we had a hearing and the judge granted benefits.

Claimants are often at the mercy of the disability system, but that does not always mean that the rest of the world is sympathetic to their plight. Landlords want their rent, finance companies want the car payment made on time, and doctors want to be paid for their services.

There are no simple answers when you are battling a disability and trying to financially survive. However, there are some short-term solutions.

Consider Filing Bankruptcy

The bankruptcy laws were drastically changed in October 2005. Under the new law, the government has set limits as to how much you can earn annually to qualify to file, and the income limit varies from state to state as the cost of living differs. For example, in California, if you are single and earn less than $43,100, you would be eligible to file. If you were married and had two children, you could file if your income did not exceed $70,700.

By filing bankruptcy, you would no longer be responsible for payment on your unsecured debts, which include credit cards, medical bills, utilities, and back rent. However, if you are making a house or car payment, you would need to continue making these payments or the creditor may exercise its right to repossess or foreclose on the property.

Bankruptcy is an extreme option and you should consult with a bankruptcy attorney before making any decision to file.

Negotiate with Your Creditors

If you are saddled with credit card debt, it is best to recognize the problem rather than ignore it. If you do not make payments on your credit card debts, the company will turn the account over to a collection agency. Thereafter, you could be sued and have your assets attached. If you own a home, the creditor could put a lien on your home, which would prevent you from selling the house until the debt is paid.

Many large creditors like MBNA and Citibank offer forbearance programs. That is, if they are aware of some special circumstance such as an illness, they may agree to suspend or *forbear* payments for a set period of time. During this time, interest may or may not continue to accrue.

Likewise, if you are having difficulty making your vehicle or house payment, contact the lender before your loan becomes delinquent and ask if they offer a forbearance program. Such programs typically last three to six months to allow you time to make up the back payments.

Apply for General Relief

If you have no income, you may be eligible to receive general relief. Each state has its own welfare program that offers assistance to indigent persons. Benefits may include income for dependent children as well as food stamps. If you do receive Social Security benefits, you may have to reimburse the state agency for any money that you received. To apply, contact your local state office.

If You Are About to Become Homeless

If your living situation is such that you may become homeless, the county or city where you reside may provide information about shelters. Some shelters require that you are looking for work, which is contradictory to your position since you are filing for disability benefits. Check with the Department of Social Services in your state for more information. In addition, most local police departments offer vouchers to stay from one to four nights in a local motel at no expense to you.

Presumptive Disability

The general rule is that until you have been found to be disabled, Social Security Disability benefits do not begin. The one exception is if you qualify for what is known as *presumptive disability*. That is, in cases of extreme hardship, the SSA will make a one-time advance against your benefits if your disability is one that can be determined by observation. Such conditions include:

- total blindness in both eyes;

- total deafness;

- amputation of two limbs;

- amputation of a leg at the hip; and,

- total bed confinement.

The SSA may also find for presumptive disability if the disability can be confirmed by the local Social Security office without the need for developing the medical evidence. For example, if someone is under hospice care for a terminal illness, the SSA would be able to verify this information in a short period of time.

The emergency cash advance, however, does not exceed the federal benefit rate, which is presently set at about $600. An applicant for presumptive disability would apply for this emergency benefit when making an initial application for SSI at the local Social Security office.

> **Practical Point**
>
> All states offer an emergency cash benefit if you are homeless and without any financial assistance. In California, the cash benefit is $200. To verify your eligibility, contact your state's office of social services.

Contact Your Congressperson and Senator

Most of us have very little contact with our representatives in Congress, but come election time, our mailboxes are flooded with political flyers seeking our vote. As an agency of the federal government, the SSA must answer to the members of Congress, and our representatives want to know of any improprieties that may involve any agency of the federal government. Over the past twenty-nine years, I have had many clients who have asked their representatives to assist in the disability process. This has, on occasion, been a successful move—especially when the case had been dragging.

The Dangers of Working Part-Time

Chapter 2 discusses the definition of disability. It includes a finding that you cannot be gainfully employed. Under the SSA guidelines, gainful employment means that you do not have income from wages that exceeds what your state has established as the maximum allowed.

The dilemma occurs, however, when you must balance between putting food on the table for you and your family to survive and how the SSA will view the fact that you are working. Too often, I have seen judges conclude that any type of work raises a presumption that a disability does not result in *marked* limitations if the claimant is able to attend to some type of work on a regular basis. Recall that in Chapter 2 the definition of disability also includes the requirement that your impairment results in marked limitations. As a result, it is always my advice to clients to avoid any attempt to work, no matter how few the hours may be, so as to avoid the presumption.

ROY'S STORY

Roy was a real estate appraiser and had his real estate license. He filed for disability, alleging vertigo, which can be extremely disabling as you are constantly dizzy and have issues with maintaining your balance. He stopped working as an appraiser, but when the bills were piling up, his friend offered him a job on weekends at a new housing development. His job duties were limited to sitting in a show room trailer greeting prospective buyers who came to tour the models. He received a small salary for the two-days-a-week work. Roy appeared at the hearing without any attorney and the judge jumped all over Roy for his claim that he could not work at his former job but "somehow managed to show up every Saturday and Sunday." Roy's claim was denied.

The Dangers of Attending School

No one can put a price on education, and as the saying goes, "it is never too late to learn." Although I embrace this saying, the timing of getting an education could interfere with your chances of getting Social Security Disability benefits. The SSA can be easily confused about why you are in school while you are claiming that you are disabled. The presumption is that if you are able to attend classes, you would also be able to get to work every day on time and be productive on the job. Accordingly, so as to not distract from your claim, you are advised to put school on the back burner.

Favorable Decisions 18

The last comment that the ALJ will make before the hearing closes will be that he or she will put the decision in writing and that it will be mailed to you at the address that you have provided. At this point, there is nothing more that you can do to improve your case, as it is in the hands of the court. Of course, those parting words will continue to resonate in your brain as the days and weeks following the hearing tick by, but finally, a manila envelope will appear in your mail. Hopefully, about a third of the way down the first page will appear the words "Notice of Decision—Fully Favorable." If so, your struggle is finally over. The court has agreed with what you have known all along—that you are disabled.

The next part of the letter explains that you will receive a letter explaining your benefits from another office of the SSA. Typically, this follow-up letter will arrive within thirty to forty-five days. You should mark your calendar for the receipt of the next letter.

Do not, however, be overly concerned by the section of the favorable decision letter that begins with the heading "The Appeals Council May Review the Decision on Its Own."

Even though the judge who heard your case has granted you benefits, all cases are subject to being reviewed by the Appeals Council, which in favorable decisions serves as a means of providing quality control to the judicial system. That is, the Appeals Council needs to make sure that the ALJ followed the correct sequential evaluation method in making the decision. An extremely small percentage of favorable decisions are reviewed by the Appeals Council, since the majority of its work is taken up by reviewing unfavorable cases as discussed in Chapter 19.

Partially Favorable Decisions

It is not uncommon for an ALJ to decide that you are disabled but disagree with the date that you claim your disability began. If this is the case, he or she will issue what is known as a *partially favorable decision.*

VERN'S STORY

Vern is 54 years old. He stopped working on February 14, 2005, because of back pain. After receiving state disability for one year, he filed for SSDI and gave his onset date (the date that he claimed he was disabled) as the last date that he worked. After a series of tests and failed procedures, he had back surgery in November 2005. The surgery did not relieve the pain and a pain management doctor recommended a morphine pump to be inserted. This was done in March 2006. As a result of the morphine, Vern had difficulty with concentration and memory.

At the hearing, the ALJ considered Vern's testimony that he was having difficulty with sitting and walking when he stopped work. However, in evaluating Step 5 of the sequential evaluation, the court felt that Vern was able to perform sedentary work up until the time when he received the morphine pump. The judge concluded that the availability of jobs that Vern could perform was greatly diminished if he was taking a prescribed narcotic prescription. As a result, the ALJ issued a favorable decision but changed the onset date from February 14, 2005, to March 2006.

When a decision is partially favorable, you must decide whether to accept the judge's decision or appeal. If you agree to accept, there is nothing further that you will need to do, and you will receive your benefits letter, as discussed later. If you decide to appeal the decision, you must file an appeal as discussed in Chapter 12.

However, in making your decision about whether to accept the court's decision or appeal, you should weigh the length of time it has already taken you to get to this point and how much longer it will take for the Appeals Court to decide. Furthermore, if you decide to appeal, your monthly benefits will not commence until the appeal has been decided. Likewise, you will not receive any retroactive benefits until the court rules on your appeal.

The Award Letter

Whether your claim was approved at the initial application, Request for Reconsideration, Request for Hearing, or after a hearing, you will receive a letter from the SSA explaining your benefits. Most letters are generated from the SSA's processing center in Baltimore, Maryland. However, if you are closely approaching retirement age, you may instead receive a letter from a local processing office. Regardless, your letter will look something like the sample letter on page 196.

Notice that the letter contains the following information:

- the amount of the past-due benefits;

- the amount of the monthly benefits;

- the date that disability benefits begin;

- how the benefits were calculated; and,

- an explanation of any offsets.

LEGALLY SPEAKING

When the court decides on a different onset date than what you originally stated in the initial application, this change in date will affect the amount of any retroactive benefits. Depending upon the monthly benefit amount that you are entitled to, the difference could be very significant.

Social Security Administration
Retirement, Survivors and Disability Insurance
Notice of Award

Office of Central Operations
1500 Woodlawn Drive
Baltimore, Maryland 21241-1500
Date: May 5, 2007
Claim Number:

You are entitled to monthly disability benefits beginning February 2004.

The Date You Became Disabled

We found that you became disabled under our rules on November 15, 1999. This is different from the date given on the application.

Our records show that you became disabled on November 15, 1999. By law, we can pay benefits no earlier than 12 months before the month of filing. Since you filed for benefits on February 17, 2005, monthly payments will begin February 2004.

What We Will Pay And When

- You will receive $643.50 for May 2007 around June 13, 2007.

- After that you will receive $737.00 on or about the second Wednesday of each month.

- Later in this letter, we will show you how we figured these amounts.

The day we make payments on this record is based on your date of birth.

Your Benefits

The following chart shows your benefit amount(s) before any deductions or rounding. The amount you actually receive(s) may differ from your full benefit amount. When we figure how much to pay you, we must deduct certain amounts, such as Medicare premiums. We must also round down to the nearest dollar.

Beginning Date	Benefit Amount	Reason
February 2004	$752.70	Entitlement began
December 2004	$773.00	Cost-of-living adjustment

See Next Page

573-13-6759HA

December	2005	$804.60	Cost-of-living adjustment
December	2006	$831.10	Cost-of-living adjustment

Other Government Payments Affect Benefits

We are holding your Social Security benefits for February 2004 through April 2007. We may have to reduce these benefits if you received Supplemental Security Income (SSI) for this period. We will not reduce your past-due benefits if you did not get SSI benefits for those months.

However; we will withhold part of any past-due benefits to pay your representative. Later in this letter, we will tell you more about the money we are withholding to pay your representative. When we decide how much you are due for this period, we will send you another letter.

Information About Medicare

You are entitled to medicare hospital insurance beginning February 2006 and medical insurance beginning May 2007.

We did not give you medical insurance earlier because we did not process it timely. If you want these benefits earlier, you can choose medical insurance benefits beginning February 2006. To start benefits earlier, within 30 days after the date of this notice, you must tell us in writing that you want medical insurance benefits beginning February 2006. In addition, you must:

- pay us $1,347.50 (this covers premiums due from February 2006 through April 2007); or

- tell us we can withhold this amount from the check.

If you want benefits beginning February 2006 but find it hard to pay the premium amount in a lump sum, ask us about other ways to pay the money.

We will send you a Medicare card. You should take this card with you when you need medical care. If you need medical care before receiving the card and your coverage has already begun, use this letter as proof that you are covered by Medicare.

IMPORTANT: A new law changes how premiums for Medicare Part B are calculated for some higher income beneficiaries, generally individuals with incomes higher than $80,000 and couples with incomes higher than $160,000. Social Security will be contacting the Internal Revenue Service, and if we determine that you have to pay a higher premium, we will send you a notice explaining our decision, and the higher amount will be effective May 2007. For more information, visit www.socialsecurity.gov on the Internet or call us toll-free at 1-800-772-1213 (TTY 1-800-325-0778).

Information About Representative's Fees

We have approved the fee agreement between you and your representative.

Your past-due benefits are $29,768.00 for February 2004 through March 2007. Under the fee agreement, the representative cannot charge you more than $5,300.00 for his or her work. The amount of the fee does not include any out-of-pocket expenses (for example, costs to get copies of doctors' or hospitals' reports). This is a matter between you and the representative.

If we approve your claim for SSI, the representative may be able to charge an additional amount for his or her work. We will send you another letter about SSI telling you the additional amount of the fee, if any, he or she can charge.

How To Ask Us To Review The Determination On The Fee Amount

You, the representative or the person who decided your case can ask us to review the amount of the fee we say the representative can charge.

If you think the amount of the fee is too high, write us within 15 days from the day you get this letter. Tell us that you disagree with the amount of the fee and give your reasons. Send your request to this address:

Social Security Administration
Office of Disability Adjudication and Review
Attorney Fee Branch
5107 Leesburg Pike
Falls Church, Virginia 22041-3255

The representative also has 15 days to write us if he or she thinks the amount of the fee is too low.

If we do not hear from you or the representative, we will assume you both agree with the amount of the fee shown.

Information About Past-Due Benefits Withheld To Pay A Representative

Because of the law, we usually withhold 25 percent of the total past-due benefits to pay an approved representative's fee. We withheld $5,300.00 from your past-due benefits to pay the representative.

We are paying the representative from the benefits we withheld. Therefore, we must collect a service charge from him or her. The service charge is 6.3 percent of the fee amount we pay, but not more than $77, which is the most we can collect in each case under the law. We will subtract the service charge from the amount payable to the representative.

The representative cannot ask you to pay for the service charge. If the representative disagrees with the amount of the service charge, he or she must write to the address shown at the top of this letter. The representative must tell us why he or she disagrees within 15 days from the day he or she gets this letter.

Other Social Security Benefits

The benefit described in this letter is the only one you can receive from Social Security. If you think that you might qualify for another kind of Social Security benefit in the future, you will have to file another application.

573-13-6759HA   Page 4 of 7

Your Responsibilities

The decisions we made on your claim are based on information you gave us. If this information changes, it could affect your benefits. For this reason, it is important that you report changes to us right away.

We have enclosed a pamphlet, "What You Need To Know When You Get Disability Benefits". It will tell you what must be reported and how to report. Please be sure to read the parts of the pamphlet which explain what to do if you go to work or if your health improves.

A provider of employment or vocational rehabilitation services may contact you about getting help to go to work. The provider may be a State vocational rehabilitation agency or a provider under contract with the Social Security Administration.

If you go to work, special rules allow us to continue your cash payments and health care coverage. For more information about how work and earnings affect disability benefits, call or visit any Social Security office and ask for the following publications:

- Social Security - Working While Disabled...How We Can Help (SSA Publication No. 05-10095).

- Social Security - If You Are Blind--How We Can Help (SSA Publication No. 05-10052).

Other Information

We are sending a copy of this notice to BENJAMIN H BERKLEY.

Do You Disagree With The Decision?

You have already been notified of your appeal rights regarding the decision made by the Administrative Law Judge and what you must do to have that decision reexamined. If you believe that any other determination made by us in carrying out the Administrative Law Judge decision is incorrect, you may also request that part of your case be reexamined.

If you want this reconsideration, you may request it through any Social Security office. If additional evidence is available, you should submit it with your request. We will review your case and consider any new facts you have. A person who did not make the first decision will decide your case. We will correct any mistakes. We will review those parts of the decision which you believe are wrong and will look at any new facts you have. We may also review those parts which you believe are correct and may make them unfavorable or less favorable to you.

- You have 60 days to ask for an appeal.

- The 60 days start the day after you get this letter. We assume you got this letter 5 days after the date on it unless you show us that you did not get it within the 5-day period.

- You must have a good reason for waiting more than 60 days to ask for an appeal.

- You have to ask for an appeal in writing. We will ask you to sign a Form SSA-561-U2, called "Request for Reconsideration". Contact one of our offices if you want help.

Please read the enclosed pamphlet, "Your Right to Question the Decision Made on Your Social Security Claim". It contains more information about the appeal.

Things To Remember For The Future

Doctors and other trained staff decided that you are disabled under our rules. But, this decision must be reviewed at least once every 3 years. We will send you a letter before we start the review. Based on that review, your benefits will continue if you are still disabled, but will end if you are no longer disabled.

Please tell us if there is a change in the mailing address and/or direct deposit information. We need this information to make sure payments are deposited timely and important notices regarding your payments reach you.

If You Have Any Questions

We invite you to visit our website at www.socialsecurity.gov on the Internet to find general information about Social Security. If you have any specific questions, you may call us toll-free at 1-800-772-1213, or call your local Social Security office at 1-714-246-8158. We can answer most questions over the phone. If you are deaf or hard of hearing, you may call our TTY number, 1-800-325-0778. You can also write or visit any Social Security office. The office that serves your area is located at:

SOCIAL SECURITY
FIFTH FLOOR
1851 EAST FIRST STREET
SANTA ANA, CA 92705

573-13-6759HA

If you do call or visit an office, please have this letter with you. It will help us answer your questions. Also, if you plan to visit an office, you may call ahead to make an appointment. This will help us serve you more quickly when you arrive at the office.

Michael J. Astrue
Commissioner
of Social Security

Practical Point

When benefits are approved, the SSA sends the information to several different offices, including the office that actually issues the check. Sometimes, and probably because of automation, the first check is issued before the award notice is sent. As a result, if you have asked that your benefits check be automatically deposited into your checking or savings account, you may wake up to see a large balance in your account. Before you spend the money, it is strongly advised that you wait to receive your benefits letter so that you can verify the SSA's calculations.

LEGALLY SPEAKING

If you are applying for both SSDI and SSI, the onset date may differ and therefore the retroactive benefit period you may be entitled to may also differ.

For SSDI cases, you may also be entitled to retroactive benefits if it was decided that your disability began on a date prior to your application. This is known as the *onset date*. For example, if you applied for benefits in July 2006 and alleged that you were disabled as of July 2005, you would be entitled to retroactive benefits. However, by law the SSA will not pay retroactive benefits for more than twelve months. Furthermore, the first five months of disability do not count. To be even stingier, the SSA starts counting the five months beginning with the first day of the first month after you were found to be disabled. To illustrate, if you were disabled as of July 2005, your retroactive benefits would go back to January 2006 as the five-month elimination period begins with August, which is the first month after the month that you were found to be disabled.

For SSI cases, the onset date is determined by the date of your application. Therefore, even if you alleged that you were disabled two years prior to filing your initial application, the earliest you could receive benefits is the date that you made your application. In calculating retroactive benefits, benefits would begin on the first month following the date of the application.

JANE'S STORY

Jane applied for SSI on January 2, 2007. She had a stroke in February 2006. Although the DDS determined that she was disabled in February 2006, her benefits began in February 2007, as that was the first month following her application.

Medicare and Medicaid

In addition to receiving a monthly check from the SSA, you may be entitled to receive Medicare, Medicaid, or both.

Medicare

If you are awarded SSDI, you will also be entitled to receive *Medicare*, which will cover the costs associated with your future medical care. However, Medicare benefits do not commence until you have been receiving SSDI for twenty-four months. The one exception to this rule is if you have been diagnosed with ALS (also known as Lou Gehrig's disease). In such cases, Medicare benefits will commence with the date that you are entitled to receive your first benefits check.

Medicaid

Medicaid is a poverty program that provides for medical coverage for persons receiving SSI benefits. Unlike Medicare, which imposes a twenty-four-month waiting period, Medicaid eligibility begins the first month that you qualify for SSI. If you are approved for SSI, you will get Medicaid.

Benefit Offsets

One of the biggest misconceptions about Social Security Disability law involves how other benefits you are already receiving affect the amount you can receive from the SSA. Even though you may have paid into the Social Security system for

Practical Point

If you have applied for both SSDI and SSI, you may be entitled to receive both types of medical coverage.

many years, if you are receiving benefits from some other source, you may not be eligible for SSDI, or the amount that you will receive from SSDI may be reduced.

The SSA may offset the monthly amount that you are entitled to if you receive or have received any of the following:

- a settlement from a workers' compensation claim;

- workers' compensation advances against a future settlement;

- past and ongoing workers' compensation benefits;

- benefits received from state welfare programs such as General Relief and AFDC; or,

- advance payments from the SSA against your benefits.

Your monthly Social Security Disability benefits, including benefits payable to your family members, are added together with your workers' compensation or other public disability payment.

If the total amount of these benefits exceeds 80% of your average current earnings, the excess amount is deducted from your Social Security benefits.

TAMIKA'S STORY

Before Tamika became disabled, her average current earnings were $4,000 a month. Tamika, her spouse, and their two children would be eligible to receive a total of $2,200 a month in Social Security Disability benefits. However, Tamika also receives $2,000 a month from workers' compensation.

Because the total amount of benefits she would receive ($4,200) is more than $3,200 (80% of her average current earnings), Tamika's family's Social Security benefits will be reduced by $1,000.

Your Social Security benefit will be reduced until the month you reach age 65 or the month you stop receiving your other benefits stop, whichever comes first.

Overview of Workers' Compensation Offsets

If you were injured as a result of an on-the-job injury, it is quite common to file for both workers' compensation benefits and Social Security benefits. This is because your injury may prevent you from returning to your previous work, and because of your age or lack of training to perform other work, you may be disabled under the Social Security Disability regulations. Assuming you do qualify for SSDI, the monthly amount of benefits you are entitled to will be offset by the benefits you receive from workers' compensation.

To illustrate, let us presume the following facts:

- you are a construction worker who suffered a very serious injury that made your right arm useless;

- you also suffered a back injury that prevents you from lifting more than ten pounds;

- you are 58 and your employer has elected not to retrain you;

- you settled with your employer's workers' compensation insurance carrier for $90,000, which you received as a lump sum;

- when you applied for SSDI, you had not worked for over a year;

- at your SSDI interview, based on your earnings record, you are told that if you get benefits, you will receive $1,900 per month; and,

- your application is completed and your doctors support your claim that you are disabled.

All is going well until you receive a letter from the SSA. It begins with the comforting words, "Based on the information provided, you are qualified to receive benefits."

However, the letter goes on to say that because you are receiving benefits from a workers' compensation recovery, your monthly SSDI benefits have been reduced to "0." Zero! How can that be? In the world of SSA, your benefits can be reduced by other earnings that you are receiving. Since the $90,000 is classified as earnings, until the $90,000 is exhausted, your SSDI benefits will not begin.

Exhausting your SSDI benefits does not mean that you have to first spend the $90,000. Instead, the SSA will divide the $90,000 by $1,900, the amount you would receive but for the offset. Accordingly, your benefits will begin approximately forty-seven months after the date that the SSA determined you were disabled.

Getting Around a Workers' Compensation Offset

If your workers' compensation case has not settled yet, make sure your attorney is aware that you are filing for SSDI. Further, in negotiating your case, your attorney should seek a monthly award instead of a lump sum. Although there still will be an offset, you may be entitled to receive benefits earlier, but at a reduced amount.

Use the same example as above, but now assume that instead of taking your award from workers' compensation as a lump sum, you received $1,200 per month. Based on the $90,000 award, you would receive $1,200 per month for seventy-five months. Since you are entitled to $1,900 per month for SSDI, the SSA will reduce your monthly award by only $700. As a result, you do not have to wait seventy-five months before your benefits begin.

Public Welfare Programs

Claimants who receive public assistance from state welfare programs, such as Aid to Families with Dependent Children (AFDC) and General Relief, are required to reimburse those programs upon receipt of a past-due benefits award. Social Security will automatically do this by offsetting that amount. This is because the claimant provided Social Security with the information that he or she was receiving public assistance when he or she first applied for benefits.

Advance Payment Cases

In rare cases, Social Security may have paid a claimant a monthly benefit in advance of an award. Typically, this occurs only in those cases where death will result in twelve months. You may ask why the claimant is entitled to receive benefits when his or her case has not been approved. Once again, there is no logic. In any event, Social Security will offset all the advances that were made against the amount of the past-due benefits check the claimant receives.

> ### Practical Point
>
> To understand the reason for the offset, please note that Social Security Disability benefits are to provide financial assistance because you cannot work, but the workers' compensation settlement represents payment for the period you did not work. To collect from both sources would equate to having two jobs at the same time.

Long-Term Disability Benefits

Similar to workers' compensation, *long-term disability insurance* carriers impose a different definition of disability from the SSA. However, if you have a long-term disability policy that you have obtained or was offered by your employer, one of the conditions of applying and receiving benefits is that you must also file for SSDI. This is because long-term disability benefits are considered as a supplement to SSDI, and any money you receive from your long-term disability carrier will be reduced by your SSDI award.

Again, let us presume the following facts:

- You are 60 years old and have been diagnosed with systemic lupus, which is affecting your heart function.

- You have worked for an aerospace company in management. As part of your benefits, you have a long-term disability policy that pays $3,500 per month.

- Your application for long-term disability benefits is approved but one of the requirements for keeping the benefits is that you apply for SSDI.

- Your claim for SSDI benefits is approved and in the Notice of Award you are informed that you are entitled to receive $2,200 per month.

LEGALLY SPEAKING

Do not assume that your workers' compensation attorney is aware of the SSA's right to offset benefits. Discuss the issue of offsets with your attorney at the same time that settlement of your job injury case commences.

Because you are already receiving $3,500 per month from long-term disability, your insurance carrier will offset the amount you will receive from SSDI, and your new monthly amount from long-term disability will be $1,300.

If you receive Social Security Disability benefits and one of the following types of public benefits, your Social Security benefits will *not* be reduced:

- Veterans Administration benefits;

- State and local government benefits, if Social Security taxes were deducted from your earnings; or,

- Supplemental Security Income (SSI).

Unfavorable Decisions and Your Right to Appeal

19

The majority of claimants are awarded benefits at the Request for Hearing stage. That is because, for the first time in the application process, you are able to testify as to how your disability restricts your daily life and impairs your ability to work. More than 75% of cases decided by administrative law judges are approved.

If you receive an unfavorable decision from the administrative judge after a hearing, there are still options that remain available to you. They are:

- appealing your case to the Appeals Council;

- filing a new claim; or,

- appealing to the Appeals Council and concurrently filing a new claim.

Appeals Council Appeals

Upon receiving your unfavorable decision, read it carefully, as it will also provide very specific information for appealing your case to the Appeals Council. Its role is to review the judge's decision and consider your argument as to why the judge was wrong in reaching the decision that he or she did. The most common example of judicial error occurs if the judge did not review evidence that was submitted.

After reading the decision of the administrative law judge, you may ask the Appeals Council (AC) to review the decision. As such, you are saying that the

ALJ made a mistake. Upon receipt of your request, the AC will review the tape of the hearing and compare the contents of the tape with the judge's decision. In addition, the council will review the list of exhibits.

Following its review, the AC will take one of the following actions:

- grant the review;

- deny the review;

- dismiss the case; or,

- remand the case.

> **Practical Point**
>
> The AC will allow you to submit additional medical evidence when you file for the review. Evidence that is highly supportive of your disability that was not reviewed by the ALJ will strengthen your chances of the AC granting a review.

If the AC grants the review, it is because the AC believes that the judge's decision was erroneous as it was decided by improperly applying the law. For example, if you were claiming that you were disabled because you met the medical listing 12.06 as you suffer from panic attacks, but the ALJ denied the claim, applying the medical listing 12.09 because he or she felt your past alcohol abuse was the contributing factor causing your disability, it is likely the AC would review the case, provided you have supporting evidence that distinguishes your panic attacks from your prior history of drinking.

If the AC denies the review, this is because it has read the ALJ's decision and agrees with it. It is the opinion of the AC that the ALJ's decision was correct and there is no legal basis to change the decision.

If the AC dismisses the review, it means that the AC did not read the ALJ's decision. This result is the most common and most likely occurs because your request for review was not supported by any facts. Unlike when additional evidence is submitted along with your request, the AC in the majority of cases will "rubber stamp" the prior ALJ's decision where there is no apparent reason to consider reviewing it.

If the AC remands the case, the case will be sent back to the ALJ who first heard the case for a new hearing. By remanding the case, the AC is asking the ALJ to further develop the evidence so that the AC can make a decision on your claim. If this occurs, it gives the ALJ an opportunity to make a favorable decision.

An appeal to the Appeals Council must be made within sixty days of the date of the unfavorable decision. You should use SSA Form HA-520-U5, shown on page 212. This form is available online at the SSA's website, **www.socialsecurity.gov**. It is also available at all local Social Security offices. In addition to completing the form, if you have any additional evidence that further supports your claim, you may submit it with the form. Make sure to keep a copy of everything that you submit to the SSA.

Note, in lieu of the form, the Appeals Council will accept a letter from you stating that you wish to appeal the judge's decision. Your letter should contain the information in the sample letter found on page 213.

SOCIAL SECURITY ADMINISTRATION/OFFICE OF HEARINGS AND APPEALS

Form Approved
OMB No. 0960-0277

REQUEST FOR REVIEW OF HEARING DECISION/ORDER
(Do not use this form for objecting to a recommended ALJ decision.)
*(Take or mail the **signed original** to your local Social Security office, the Veterans Affairs Regional Office in Manila or any U.S. Foreign Service post and keep a copy for your records)*

See Privacy Act Notice

1. CLAIMANT	2. WAGE EARNER, IF DIFFERENT
3. SOCIAL SECURITY CLAIM NUMBER – –	4. SPOUSE'S NAME AND SOCIAL SECURITY NUMBER *(Complete ONLY in Supplemental Security Income Case)*

5. I request that the Appeals Council review the Administrative Law Judge's action on the above claim because:

ADDITIONAL EVIDENCE

If you have additional evidence submit it with this request for review. If you need additional time to submit evidence or legal argument, you must request an extension of time in writing now. If you request an extension of time, you should explain the reason(s) you are unable to submit the evidence or legal argument now. If you neither submit evidence or legal argument now nor within any extension of time the Appeals Council grants, the Appeals Council will take its action based on the evidence of record.

IMPORTANT: Write your Social Security Claim Number on any letter or material you send us.

SIGNATURE BLOCKS: You should complete No. 6 and your representative (if any) should complete No. 7. If you are represented and your representative is not available to complete this form, you should also print his or her name, address, etc. in No. 7.

I declare under penalty of perjury that I have examined all the information on this form, and on any accompanying statements or forms, and it is true and correct to the best of my knowledge.

6. CLAIMANT'S SIGNATURE DATE	7. REPRESENTATIVE'S SIGNATURE	☐ ATTORNEY ☐ NON-ATTORNEY
PRINT NAME	PRINT NAME	
ADDRESS	ADDRESS	
(CITY, STATE, ZIP CODE)	(CITY, STATE, ZIP CODE)	
TELEPHONE NUMBER FAX NUMBER ( ) – ( ) –	TELEPHONE NUMBER FAX NUMBER ( ) – ( ) –	

THE SOCIAL SECURITY ADMINISTRATION STAFF WILL COMPLETE THIS PART

8. Request received for the Social Security Administration on _____ by: _____
       (Date)   (Print Name)

_____ (Title)   _____ (Address)   _____ (Servicing FO Code)   _____ (PC Code)

9. Is the request for review received within 65 days of the ALJ's Decision/Dismissal?   ☐ Yes   ☐ No

10. If "No" checked: (1) attach claimant's explanation for delay; and
                      (2) attach copy of appointment notice, letter or other pertinent material or information in the Social Security Office.

11. Check one: ☐ Initial Entitlement ☐ Termination or other	12. Check all claim types that apply:
APPEALS COUNCIL OFFICE OF HEARINGS AND APPEALS, SSA 5107 Leesburg Pike FALLS CHURCH, VA 22041 - 3255	☐ Retirement or survivors (RSI) ☐ Disability-Worker (DIWE) ☐ Disability-Widow(er) (DIWW) ☐ Disability-Child (DIWC) ☐ SSI Aged (SSIA) ☐ SSI Blind (SSIB) ☐ SSI Disability (SSID) ☐ Health Insurance-Part A (HIA) ☐ Health Insurance-Part B (HIB) ☐ Title VIII Only (SVB) ☐ Title VIII/Title XVI (SVB/SSI) ☐ Other - Specify: _____

Form **HA-520-U5** (5-2003)   ef (05-2005)
Destroy Prior Editions

TAKE OR SEND ORIGINAL TO SSA AND RETAIN A COPY FOR YOUR RECORDS

Your name

Your address

Your Social Security Number

To: Appeals Council

To Whom It May Concern:

On July 31, 2007, I appeared before Judge Craig Lerner.

The records will show that I am claiming I am disabled because I suffer from grand mal seizures that are not controlled with medication.

At the hearing, I was unable to produce my medical records for the past year, which show that I have been seen in the emergency room six times complaining of seizures. Attached please find those records.

It is my opinion that had those records been available for review by the judge, his decision would have been favorable. I therefore ask that the Appeals Council remand my case to Judge Lerner for a subsequent hearing.

Respectfully yours,

Once the form or letter is completed, mail the request to the following address:

5107 Leesburg Pike
Falls Church, Virginia 22041

It is advised that you send the request by certified mail, return receipt requested.

In the alternative, you can deliver the form to the local Social Security office that was originally assigned your claim. This is also the office that was listed on the first and second denials that you received.

When completing the form, you must provide a reason why you are requesting a review, as the AC will not take it upon itself to try to figure it out. Possible reasons may include:

> **Practical Point**
>
> *Do not* send your request to the ODAR, as there is no guarantee that it will be forwarded to the correct office.

- you were not given an adequate opportunity to present your case;

- the ALJ failed to consider your treating doctor's reports;

- you have new evidence that was not reviewed by the ALJ and that further supports your claim; and,

- the ALJ did not take into consideration all of your reasons for claiming you were disabled.

If you are seeking a review based on the fact that you were not given sufficient time to testify, the taped recording will either support or dismiss your claim.

MURRAY'S STORY

Murray claimed he was disabled due to a car accident that left him little use of his left arm. In addition, he suffered a severe brain injury that caused him to have memory loss. The ALJ's decision to deny the claim made little reference to his mental problems. The AC remanded the case back to the ALJ for further development.

Federal Court Appeals

The AC is the last step in the appeals process. If you are unsuccessful at the AC level, and the AC dismisses your case, the only remaining option is to file a lawsuit in federal District Court. The lawsuit must be filed within sixty days of receiving notice of dismissal from the Appeals Council. However, unlike the appeals process, which is an administrative law process whereby the strict rules of evidence practiced in courtrooms are not applicable to a Social Security Disability hearing, there are very strict rules of court that must be followed in federal court. Furthermore, in federal court, the judges are looking for legal errors made by the SSA, including the ALJ.

The federal court process is beyond the scope of this book, and very few claimants represent themselves and instead seek attorney representation. For a discussion of how to find an attorney, please see Chapter 23.

Filing a New Claim

The SSA does not restrict whether or not you can file another claim if a present claim is at the Appeals Council for review. Because the Appeals Council review may take several months, and if your disability has worsened to the point where you believe you may get benefits at the initial application stage, you should file a new claim. If your AC claim is successful, you will still be entitled to receive retroactive benefits based on your earlier claim.

> ### Practical Point
>
> There is only one Appeals Council located in Falls Church, Virginia, and this court handles requests for reviews from all over the United States. This office is extremely overloaded and terribly understaffed. As a result, it is not uncommon for the AC to take up to one year to respond to a request. Therefore, I recommend that you file a new claim for disability. This way, while the second claim is working its way through the evaluation process, you are not losing any additional time in the event that the earlier AC review is denied.

ANATOMY OF A SOCIAL SECURITY DISABILITY CASE

20

The following time line is based on an actual case. The claimant contacted our office after her initial application for benefits was denied. It is presented to illustrate both the inherent time delays in the processing of a claim as well as what is required to successfully develop the claim. Note that although this case went all the way to a hearing before a judge, many claimants are awarded benefits earlier in the process.

Jackie is 47 years old and has worked over twenty years in banking. Most recently, she was a branch manager. Four years ago, she was diagnosed with rectal cancer. Fortunately, after surgery and several rounds of chemotherapy and radiation, she was pronounced cancer free. Except for the time when she had surgery, she was able to work and missed very few days. She was also fortunate that the chemotherapy did not cause any severe side effects. However, about a year after she completed treatment, she developed severe pain in her lower back and abdomen. Tests showed that the radiation had burned the surrounding nerves and caused a condition known as lipidemia, which can be very disabling. As a result, sitting became difficult and standing on her feet was worse. After frequent absences from work, she went on state disability. After collecting benefits for a year and not being able to return to work, she decided to file for SSDI.

Time Line

2/14/05

Jackie files her claim at her local Social Security office. She tells the Social Security clerk that she cannot work due to pain. Within a few days, she also supplies the names and addresses of all her doctors and signs an authorization allowing the SSA to obtain her records.

5/14/05

Jackie receives in the mail and promptly completes a daily activities questionnaire, which asks information about how her disability affects her daily life. She also completes a pain questionnaire.

7/09/05

Jackie is contacted by the Disability Determination Services, informing her that a physical and mental consultative examination has been scheduled.

7/30/05

Jackie attends the physical examination. The doctor asks her a few questions about her pain, how long she can sit and stand, and what medications she is taking. He does not examine her, and the whole examination lasts only fifteen minutes.

7/31/05

Jackie attends the mental examination where she is asked questions about her depression. She did say on her pain questionnaire that she was depressed and that she could not work, but she did not think that her inability to work was solely due to the depression. After twenty minutes, the examination is concluded.

8/05/05

Jackie receives a letter from the SSA, saying that her claim is denied. The letter states, "Although you have pain, you can still stand six out of eight hours per day. . . and are not disabled."

9/03/05

Jackie meets with our office and we agree to accept representation. In evaluating her case, we determine that though her cancer is in remission, the combined effects of the radiation and chemotherapy cause such pain that it prevents her from working. We file the first appeal (the Request for Reconsideration) but advise our client that she will most likely be denied a second time and that her best chance of success is at the hearing level. Over the next three months, we collect all Jackie's medical records and provide them to the SSA, as there were several medical providers that the SSA had not obtained records from.

12/28/05

Jackie is once again denied benefits. In her second denial letter, the SSA does not list the additional records that we provided. It does cite that, "upon taking a second look at your claim, nothing has changed." We immediately file for a Request for Hearing. In addition, we have her treating doctor complete both a pain questionnaire and a Residual Functional Capacity questionnaire, which address the issues as to how long Jackie can sit, stand, walk, lift, and pull. It also asks how often Jackie can be expected to be absent from work in a thirty-day period.

4/09/06

The ODAR assigned to Jackie's case sends an acknowledgment that the case has been received. We thereafter file with the court the questionnaires we have received from Jackie's treating doctors.

4/15/06

We file with the court a Request for an On-the-Record Decision, citing the questionnaires, applying specific references to Jackie's limitations, and asking the court to approve the claim. We do not hear anything on our request.

6/15/06

The court contacts our office to schedule a hearing for 8/14/06.

8/2/06

We meet with Jackie to prepare for the hearing. We review with Jackie the line of questioning she can anticipate and the areas that she needs to provide detailed information.

8/14/06

The hearing is conducted and Jackie provides information on how she is in constant pain even with the pain medication she takes daily. Furthermore, she cannot do housework, make her bed, or shop for food. She also cannot drive except to her doctor. Standing on her feet is the most painful, and even when sitting she needs to keep her feet elevated. A vocational expert tells the judge that he believes Jackie can no longer perform work as a bank manager, as that work requires standing, walking, and sitting. However, she could still do sedentary type work. When we question him about her doctor saying that Jackie would be expected to be absent from work at least four times per month, the expert testifies that there is no work available for her.

9/20/06

Jackie receives her favorable decision letter followed forty-five days later by her retroactive benefits check.

Commentary

From the time Jackie filed her initial claim to when she received her check, more than nineteen months had passed. Even though it was ultimately proven that she was disabled, there was no method available for speeding up the process. Instead, if you sincerely believe that you are disabled, you must work within the system—and never doubt that you will succeed.

TURNING A LOSING DECISION INTO A VICTORY

21

If your initial claim for benefits is denied, you should appeal. However, it is important to know why you were denied so that your appeal addresses those issues. Simply appealing because you believe the SSA was wrong will not result in benefits. Often, cases are denied for nonmedical reasons. That is why it is so important to read the denial letter.

The following examples are based on actual cases. In every case, the claimant eventually was awarded Social Security Disability benefits.

Case #1

Reason for denial: Sherry did not have enough work credits.

Facts: Sherry, age 42, was denied benefits because she did not have enough work credits. She had worked since she was 18. She continued to appeal her case and was at the hearing stage when she contacted our office. We reviewed her earnings statement, which showed no reported income for three of the last five years before she stopped working due to her rheumatoid arthritis. When questioned, Sherry informed us that she had divorced and remarried. She had never informed the SSA of her new name and filed her tax returns with her husband using his last name. Unfortunately, her wages were not credited against her Social Security number. Once the report was corrected, she was granted benefits.

Sherry's mistake: Though Sherry's denial letter cited that she did not have enough work credits, she continued to appeal her case on the wrong assumption that the denial was based on her medical condition. As stated in Chapter 3, regardless of how serious your medical condition is, you must also meet the nonmedical requirements to be awarded benefits. Had she read the denial letter correctly, she may have been awarded benefits earlier in the appeal process.

Case #2

Reason for denial: Mae did not submit reports from her treating doctors.

Facts: Mae was 56 years old and had worked for twenty years as a book binder. She was diagnosed with multiple sclerosis (MS) in 1998 but continued working until 2005. She stopped working due to fatigue. She filed her claim, citing fatigue and providing the name of her surgeon, who operated on her herniated disk, as well as her neurologist, who diagnosed the MS. The SSA sent her for a consultative examination. In her denial letter the SSA cited that she could sit and stand for more than six hours per day and could lift up to twenty pounds on a regular basis. She appealed but was denied again. Upon our review of her denial letters, both the surgeon and the neurologist were not listed as medical providers.

Mae's mistake: When Mae received her first denial letter, she failed to realize that the decision was made based on the consultative examination alone. Had she realized this when she was first denied, she could have gone directly to her medical providers and obtained the medical records to provide to the SSA. When we reviewed the records, Mae had had several brain scans that documented the MS. Her doctor's notes also cited fatigue both when active as well as at rest with muscle weakness. The chart notes and findings clearly met the medical listings of 11.00 (E) for MS. Never assume that the SSA has received all of your records.

Case #3

Reason for denial: Ernie did not have recent doctor records.

Facts: Ernie had back surgery in the early 1990s. He was able to return to work as an estimator, but in 2005, the pain in his legs became so bad that he had to quit. He filed for SSDI in the summer of 2006 and provided the names of his surgeons. On the disability report, when asked when he last saw his doctor, he answered that it had been over a year. He gave no further explanation. Ernie was denied twice. When he consulted with our office, we learned that Ernie no longer had insurance. Furthermore, a friend was obtaining pain medication for him from Mexico, as he had no money to see a doctor.

Ernie's mistake: Though Ernie had a severe impairment, he had not seen his doctor for over a year. This raises a presumption that the condition may not be as disabling as the claimant presents. Arguably, if his pain was so great, he would have sought emergency medical care. It is a bad strategy to file a claim unless you are under current medical care. If you cannot pay for medical care, you can always go to a county facility.

Case #4

Reason for denial: Jason did not inform the SSA of a change in his medical condition.

Facts: Jason worked as a car salesman and was 45 when he suffered a stroke. After collecting state disability for one year, he applied for SSDI and was denied. Shortly after he filed his Request for Reconsideration, he suffered a second stroke, which resulted in paralysis of his left arm. He was denied again and his wife, on his behalf, filed a Request for Hearing. Prior to the hearing date, she retained our office to represent her husband at the hearing. In the denial letter the SSA cited that Jason had made improvements in the year following his first stroke and could sit and stand for six out of eight hours per day. In developing the case, we obtained all the records concerning the second stroke and submitted them to the judge assigned to the case along with a completed questionnaire from his doctor. We also asked the court to grant an on-the-record decision considering the seriousness of the second stroke. The court granted our request and awarded Jason benefits.

Jason's mistake: Jason and his wife wrongly presumed that the SSA received the medical records concerning the second stroke. It is important to advise the SSA as soon as possible about any change in your medical condition. This may include subsequent surgeries or an aggravation of your condition. Had the SSA been made aware of the second stroke, Jason would have been granted benefits at the Request for Reconsideration stage.

OBTAINING FIRST-TIME BENEFITS FOR CHILDREN AND ADULTS WITH CHILDHOOD DISABILITIES

22

SSI benefits may be available for disabled children under age 18 as well as people who have reached their eighteenth birthday and have a childhood disability.

Obtaining Benefits if the Child is Under 18

A child under 18 years old may be eligible to receive Supplemental Security Income child benefits if he or she is found to be disabled and his or her parents' income and resources qualify. That is, regardless of the severity of the impairment, if the child's parents do not meet the nonmedical requirements for allowable assets and income, the child cannot receive benefits.

Nonmedical Requirements for Children Under Age 18

Children are classified as dependents of their parents. As a result, the SSA will consider the income and assets of the parents to determine eligibility. If the assets exceed $2,000 (or $3,000 for both parents) or if the income exceeds what is established by the state where the child resides, the child is not qualified to receive benefits regardless of the severity of his or her disability. Note that each state has established a maximum income level. To determine the maximum amount allowed by your state, contact the SSA at 800–772–1213. A state-by-state chart is also available on its website at **www.ssa.gov/regions/regional.html**.

Defining Childhood Disabilities

According to the Social Security regulations, a child under age 18 will be considered disabled if he or she has a "medically determinable physical or mental impairment or combination of impairments that causes marked and severe functional limitations, and that can be expected to cause death or that has lasted or can be expected to last for a continuous period of not less than twelve months."

The sequential evaluation for a finding of childhood disability is similar to what the SSA uses to evaluate adults, as the SSA applies a three-step process to determine if a child is disabled.

Step One: Is the child working at substantial gainful activity (SGA) level?

If the child is working, the claim for the child's SSI will be denied. If the child is not working, the SSA will then move to Step 2.

Step Two: Does the child claimant have a severe impairment?

If not, the child will be denied. If the child has a severe impairment, the SSA will then move to Step 3.

Step Three: Does the child's impairment meet, medically equal, or functionally equal one of the listed impairments?

Childhood listings are categorized as follows:

100.00 Growth Impairment

101.00 Musculoskeletal System

102.00 Special Senses and Speech

103.00 Respiratory System

104.00 Cardiovascular System

105.00 Digestive System

106.00 Genitourinary System

107.00 Hematological Disorders

108.00 Skin Disorders

109.00 Endocrine System

110.00 Impairments that Affect Multiple Body Systems

111.00 Neurological

112.00 Mental Disorders

113.00 Malignant Neoplastic Diseases

114.00 Immune System

The childhood listings can be found on the SSA's website at **www.ssa.gov/ disability/professionals/bluebook/ChildhoodListings.htm**.

Functionality

Note that at Step 3 of the sequential evaluation for adults, if a claimant meets or equals a listing, he or she is found to be disabled, but for children, there is the added element of *functionality*. Most childhood cases are ultimately decided on whether the child functionally equals or meets one of the listed impairments. For a child to *functionally* meet or equal a listed impairment, the impairment must cause what the SSA has termed a *marked limitation* in two of six domains or an *extreme limitation* in one.

The six domains are:

- acquiring and using information;

- attending and completing tasks;

- interacting and relating with others;

- moving about and manipulating objects;

- caring for yourself; and,

- health and physical well-being.

Practical Point

Similar to developing a residual functional capacity for adults as required by Step 5 of the sequential evaluation and discussed in Chapter 7, these terms are subjective. What may be considered by one doctor to be marked may not be viewed the same way by another doctor. That is why, in proving childhood disabilities, it is so important when filing to have collected all of your child's medical records as well as to obtain current written opinions from the child's treating doctors.

In each of these domains the child is compared to other children his or her age. The SSA will look at each of these domains and determine if the child's limitations from the impairment in each domain are severe enough to be marked or extreme. If a child is found to have a marked limitation of two domains or an extreme limitation of one domain, then the impairment is functionally equivalent to a listed impairment. If the child functionally equals a listed impairment, he or she will be found disabled. According to the Social Security regulations:

A "marked" limitation in a domain [exists] when your impairment(s) interferes seriously with your ability to independently initiate, sustain, or complete activities. Your day-to-day functioning may be seriously limited when your impairment(s) limits only one activity or when the interactive and cumulative effects of your impairment(s) limit several activities. "Marked" limitation also means a limitation that is "more than moderate" but "less than extreme."

Children with Severe Disabilities

In most cases, it takes a long time for claims to be evaluated, and it is difficult to speed up the process. However, the SSA does recognize certain childhood disabilities as so severe that the claimants are *presumed* to be disabled. In these cases, SSI benefits will begin immediately and will be paid for a six-month period while the SSA completes its evaluation.

Childhood claims that involve a presumption of disability include the following impairments:

- mental retardation;

- cancer;

- diseases affecting the central nervous system resulting in paralysis;

- kidney and other endocrine diseases that are not reversible; and,

- AIDS and HIV infections.

If, after evaluation, it is the opinion of the SSA that the claimant is not disabled, it will not ask for the money to be returned. The claimant, however, may still appeal the decision by filing a Request for Reconsideration (discussed in Chapter 12).

Tips for Winning Children's Cases

- Provide the SSA with all of your child's medical records. Do not be concerned about how old the records may be, as they will assist in establishing the date of diagnosis.

LEGALLY SPEAKING

A finding of a presumption of disability is based on an evaluation of the medical impairment only. Accordingly, in the case of a claim for SSI, if the claimant has assets that exceed $2,000 or a monthly income in excess of the limitation as set by the state where he or she resides, he or she will be denied benefits regardless of the severity of his or her disability.

- Obtain all school attendance and academic records.

- Submit any school evaluation that was done for your child.

- Submit all records from your child's school pertaining to behavioral issues. An example would be detentions, suspensions, or notes sent home about behavior.

- Make sure the child's file includes teacher questionnaires filled out by the child's teachers.

- If asthma is one of the child's disabilities, get documentation of all emergency room visits at hospitals and any emergency visits to doctors.

- Try to get your child's doctor to fill out an RFC form or to give an opinion on whether your child meets a listed impairment. (see Chapter 11.)

- Keep a journal of the child's behavior so you will be able to give good examples of how the child's condition affects him or her.

Top Five Misconceptions about Childhood Disabilities

As a law firm that provides services for persons seeking representation for Social Security, we feel it is our responsibility to educate as well as provide services. One of the areas of disability that causes the most confusion concerns benefits for children. As with all claims for benefits, the SSA's definition of disability is very restrictive. The following list dispels some of the most common misconceptions about childhood disabilities and how the SSA views the impairments.

1. If a child is in special education classes, he or she is disabled.

WRONG. Being in special education is not enough. Independent and credible testing is required to prove the level of functionality the child is working at.

2. If a child's doctor diagnoses the child as disabled, the child can get SSI.

WRONG. Doctors treat their patients but are not experts on Social Security law. A child must meet or equal the medical listings to qualify for benefits.

3. A parent can provide financial support for a child, including room and board, and the child can still qualify for SSI benefits.

MAYBE. Each state has established the maximum amount a child can receive and still qualify to receive SSI.

4. Autism is a disability.

MAYBE. If the child is diagnosed as autistic, he or she will still be evaluated as to his or her ability to function.

5. Once a child qualifies for disability benefits, those benefits will continue for the child's lifetime.

WRONG. If a child receives benefits before his or her eighteenth birthday, he or she will be reevaluated when he or she turns 18 to determine if he or she is still qualified to receive benefits.

Obtaining Benefits for Adults with Childhood Disabilities

When a child turns 18 and is disabled, he or she may be qualified to receive Supplemental Security Income (SSI). As previously stated, the definition of disability is very specific. That is, it must be proven that the disability is severe and that the disability has lasted or will last twelve months or longer. In addition, the disability must be documented prior to age 18, although the disability will be evaluated by using the adult medical listings as discussed in Chapter 5.

Furthermore, for adults with childhood disabilities, if the claimant owns certain types of property with a value in excess of $2,000, that person is not qualified to

> ### Practical Point
>
> An adult with childhood disabilities applies for SSI benefits and not SSDI. This is because the adult child has not worked and therefore has not paid any money into his or her Social Security retirement account.

receive benefits despite being disabled. There are many exceptions to the $2,000 limitation, as discussed later.

The Application Process

The process to apply for first-time benefits for an adult with a childhood disability is the same as making an initial application as discussed in Chapter 9. In general, you must produce the following documents:

- original birth certificate;

- Social Security card or Social Security number of the claimant;

- names, addresses, and phone numbers of all medical providers;

- school records; and,

- any medical records that are available.

If the claimant does not have a Social Security number, you should apply for one as soon as possible, because the SSA cannot start the application without it. You will also be required to complete an initial application and a disability report. These forms are discussed in Chapter 9.

When to Apply

Obtaining Social Security benefits may take several months. Since it may take time to gather all of this information, it is recommended that you begin gathering this information a few weeks or a month prior to the child's eighteenth birthday. This way, when you apply, your application will be complete and the SSA will be able to begin the evaluation process.

The application can be made by phone or in person by visiting the Social Security office closest to where you and the child reside. To locate the closest office, you can call the SSA at 800–772–1213. The SSA does not allow online filings for SSI.

Once your application has been completed, the SSA will have the medical records reviewed by your state's DDS. Often, however, an adult with a childhood disability may not be under current medical care. If this is the case, the DDS will schedule the claimant to be examined by a physician to evaluate the disability.

To illustrate, a child may be born with Down's syndrome that has resulted in a severely limited mental acuity. The claimant may be functioning at the level of a 4-year-old even though he is now 18. However, other than normal annual checkups with his physician, he has not been seen by a doctor in several years to evaluate his mental abilities. In such cases, the DDS would require an examination to document the claimant's impairment. Such an examination will be at no expense to you.

Highest Grade in School Completed

The SSA's definition of disability includes the requirement that the impairment be severe enough to prevent the person from being gainfully employed. It is not uncommon for a child to have graduated high school but still have severe mental limitations. For example, the child may have been in special education but still graduated. In such cases, it is very important that you make it clear to the SSA that the claimant was not in a regular school setting. Otherwise, the SSA often considers a child who is able to complete the twelfth grade as someone who can be gainfully employed and therefore is not disabled.

> **Practical Point**
>
> In Chapter 10, I recommend that a claimant have a family member or friend go into the examination room with him or her. In childhood claims, this is especially important if the child has a mental impairment and is unable to effectively communicate with the examining doctor.

Satisfying the Nonmedical Requirements

As with all SSI claims, the claimant must satisfy both the medical and nonmedical requirements for SSI. That is, you must have assets and resources below the allowed limit for your state as previously discussed in this chapter and in Chapter 3. Accordingly, you may have to produce income and expense information for your child. Furthermore, if your child is living with you, you will also have to provide income and asset information about yourself. Be prepared to provide the following documents.

- If the child is living with you:

  - copies of recent pay stubs;

  - copies of recent tax returns; and,

  - an itemization of assets.

- If the child is living on his or her own:

  - a copy of any lease or rental agreements;

  - an itemization of monthly expenses including rent, food, and utilities;

  - copies of utility bills (if any); and,

  - a copy of checking and/or savings account statements for the most current month.

Upon review, the SSA may require additional information to determine the child's financial eligibility.

Nonfinancial Requirements to Receive Benefits

If a claimant has assets in excess of $2,000, he or she is not eligible to receive benefits regardless of his or her disability. In determining what assets are, the SSA excludes the following that the child might have:

- an interest in real estate used as his or her primary residence, regardless of value;

- a vehicle, provided it is used for necessary transportation, and if not used for that purpose, then it cannot exceed a value of $4,500; and,

- all other property, provided the total amount does not exceed $2,000.

The claimant can own a beachfront home with no mortgage and still be eligible to receive SSI benefits. Though at first blush this may appear absurd, as SSI is considered a federal and state welfare program, Congress has rationalized that it is of paramount interest that a claimant should have shelter, and it is not the role of Congress to define what proper shelter for a claimant is.

Interest in Trusts

Money received through an inheritance is included in the assets that cannot exceed $2,000. To illustrate, if a claimant's father passed away and the child was left $25,000, which was deposited in a savings account, he would be ineligible to receive SSI benefits until the total value of his assets was below $2,000. If the claimant used the $25,000 for living expenses, once the balance of the account was below $2,000, he could apply for benefits.

Special Needs Trusts

In determining whether a claimant has an interest in the asset, the deciding factor is whether the claimant has direct access and can control the asset. In the case of money on deposit in a bank, if the claimant's name is on the account then he or she has access to the money. However, if the money was left to the claimant as part of a trust and the language of the trust specifically states that the claimant cannot withdraw the money but it is instead deposited for the claimant's needs, the SSA views such *special needs trusts* as an exception to the $2,000 limitation.

SARAH'S STORY

Derek and Donna Able have one daughter, Sarah, who is severely autistic. They also have an older son, Brian. Sarah is about to turn 18. The Ables set up a trust and title it "Revocable Trust of Derek and Donna Able." The trust includes the following terms.

A. Distribution After Death of Derek and Donna Able:

One-half of the trust estate shall be distributed free of the trust to Brian Able.

One-half of the trust estate shall be held in trust for the benefit of Sarah Able for the remainder of her natural life pursuant to the terms of the Sarah Able Trust below.

B. Sarah Able Trust

Sarah Able shall have no right to withdraw or invade the corpus of the Sarah Able Trust.

In addition to setting up a trust, any account must also be in the name of the trust, such as:

"The June Gellis Trust

Steven Gellis, Trustee"

In this trust, if June Gellis went to her bank to withdraw money from her account, the bank would advise her that only the trustee, Steve, would have the authority to do so. This would satisfy the SSA requirement that the trustee did not have direct access.

Assets that Have Been Invested for Your Child

If financially able to do so, parents often invest money for their children's future needs. The money can be designated for a specific purpose such as college expenses, or it can simply be deposited into an account that bears both the parents' and child's name. When applying for SSI, however, the SSA will consider such assets as assets of the child and therefore benefits can be denied if the total asset value exceeds $2,000.

Prior to filing an application for SSI, you should consult with an attorney who is experienced in both estate planning and Social Security law to explore how to set up a special needs trust that would be able to protect the asset and still allow your child to qualify for benefits.

LORI'S STORY

Lori was 14 years old when she was involved in a very serious automobile accident that resulted in brain trauma. After months of rehabilitation, she was able to return to school but was placed in special education classes, as her mental capacity was greatly diminished. When Lori was born, her grandparents had set up an investment account and deposited $75,000 for her future education. Lori's parents had not considered the money as an asset when they applied for SSI when Lori turned 18. Though she was granted SSI benefits upon making the initial application, her benefits were suspended a year later when the SSA learned of the account. Fortunately, the SSA viewed the failure to report the asset as an oversight instead of filing a fraud complaint against her parents. Regardless, the one year of benefits had to be repaid. Furthermore, she was not qualified to receive any further benefits until the $75,000 was exhausted. Had her parents consulted with an attorney to set up a special needs trust, the entire matter may have been avoided.

Calculating the Amount of Benefits

As previously discussed, SSI benefits are jointly contributed from both the federal government and the state where you reside. As the cost of living varies from state to state, the total amount of monthly benefits will also differ. For example, in California, the maximum amount a person can receive for SSI is $836.

Practical Point

Unless a disabled child qualified to receive benefits as a dependent or to receive survivor benefits, often disabled children do not qualify if their parents have assets beyond the legal limit set by the SSA. However, once the child turns 18, the SSA only considers assets in the name of the claimant. Therefore, if the child was not eligible before to receive benefits, an application for SSI should be filed when the child turns 18.

However, not everyone receives the maximum amount of benefits, since the SSA will make an inquiry as to what support the claimant receives in calculating benefits. For example, if the claimant lives at home and all of his or her shelter and food are provided, the SSA will apply standards that it has determined to apply for food and shelter. As a result, the maximum monthly award for SSI benefits will be reduced by one-third. If the claimant was in California, instead of receiving $836 he or she would receive approximately $557. However, if the same claimant lived independently, with no support from his or her parents, he or she would be entitled to receive the maximum amount. The latter example, however, is not realistic unless the claimant was receiving income from a special needs trust, as he or she would not have sufficient income to pay expenses like rent and food while he or she was applying for SSI benefits.

There are obvious benefits to establishing a special needs trust. However, prior to doing so, you should consult with an estate planning attorney who is knowledgeable in the areas of both trust and Social Security Disability law.

The Representative Payee

If an adult with a childhood disability does not have the mental ability to understand and complete the process and is not financially responsible, a parent or some other representative

> ## LEGALLY SPEAKING
>
> The representative payee is different from the authorized representative. An authorized representative is the person whom you appoint to represent you in your claim for Social Security Disability benefits. This person, most commonly your attorney, must file Form SSA-1696 before the SSA will discuss your claim with him or her.

can make the application. In addition, that person may ask that he or she be appointed as the *representative payee* for the claimant. Similar to a power of attorney to make financial decisions, a representative payee will be recognized by the SSA as the claimant's spokesperson. In addition, when benefits are awarded, payments will be sent in the name of the representative in care of the claimant. To be appointed the representative payee, you must complete SSA Form SSA-11-BK.

Divorced Parents

If the parents of an adult child with disabilities are divorced, the SSA will only recognize one parent as the representative payee. That is typically the parent who has custody of the child. In situations where parents cannot decide, such issues are best resolved by having the matter heard in the family court that originally issued the custody order.

Do I Need an Attorney? | 23

The purpose of writing this book is to provide you with all the information you will need to win your Social Security Disability case. Furthermore, if your case is scheduled for a hearing, Chapter 16 walks you through the hearing process as if an attorney were sitting next to you. However, you may eventually decide you would like representation, and this chapter will help you make that determination.

Do Not Be Discouraged By Statistics

As you begin the initial application, it is important that you pay very close detail to all the information that is requested, with the understanding that over 75% of cases of initial claims are denied even if the claimant is represented. In fact, only a very small percentage of claims are initially filed with attorney assistance.

Do not get frustrated. If you are disabled and meet the definition of disability, you must continue the appeals process. However, even at the first appeal step, the Request for Reconsideration, the majority of cases are denied again.

As you continue to appeal your claim it is expected that you will become frustrated, angry, and irritated, because even though you see your claim one way, the SSA has a completely different opinion. After filing out form after form, and submitting medical report after medical report, most claimants report that they have jumped through too many hoops and need help.

LEGALLY SPEAKING

As we discussed in Chapter 1, the SSA has invented its own language, which includes the title given to persons who represent claimants. Whether you are an attorney or not, the SSA defines you as an *authorized representative*. However, the government's failure to make a distinction between those who are licensed to practice law and those who are not has never been embraced by attorneys. As a result, attorneys who specialize in this area of the law rarely promote their practice by including the phrase *authorized representative*.

Claimants who are represented typically seek representation after their claim has been denied a second time and they are applying for a hearing. It is at this point that a claimant may no longer want to deal directly with the SSA or fears the unknown of walking into a courtroom without representation.

When it Is Advisable to Seek Legal Representation

Chapter 14 discusses the hearing letter, which outlines how a hearing is conducted and states whether any experts will be appearing on behalf of the SSA.

If a medical expert has been scheduled, that is because the judge needs more information in explaining your disability and about whether or not the medical expert believes that you meet or equal the listings as discussed in Chapter 5. Even if the SSA, in its prior evaluation, did not conclude that you met or equaled the listings, the ALJ will make an independent decision and will seek the assistance of the medical expert. Accordingly, after you have reviewed the medical listings, and conclude that the way your impairments affect your ability to do daily activities does not match up with how the listings read, you may wish to at least consult with an attorney so that you will have a better understanding of the questions to ask the expert or what additional information you should provide.

HECTOR'S STORY

Hector was 49 years old and worked in a warehouse. He was having severe abdominal pain and his doctor diagnosed his problem as colonic inertia, which meant that his digestive process was very slow. As a result, he avoided eating so that he would not have pain. Hector became weaker and weaker and eventually quit his job. Unfortunately, Hector's medical condition was not part of the listings. Fearing that the medical expert would testify at the hearing that Hector was not disabled, he retained an attorney who was able to compare Hector's symptoms with other medical conditions that are listed. As a result, the court made a favorable decision ruling that Hector "equaled the listings."

If a vocational expert (VE) is scheduled to appear, that is because the ALJ needs more information about how you performed your previous work, and more importantly, whether there is any other work that you are capable of performing. Accordingly, you will also need to be prepared to cross-examine the VE in the event that the VE states that you are capable of working. It is not enough to say that you are hurt. Instead, you must argue your position by citing from the *Dictionary of Occupational Titles* published by the Department of Transportation. When you do this, you will need the knowledge to describe how different jobs are performed by their exertional requirements and the time it takes to learn the job.

This information is beyond the scope of this book. In fact, attorneys attend classes each year just to keep up with this information. Accordingly, as winning your case is your goal, you would be better represented by an attorney who is knowledgeable in this area of the law.

Finding an Attorney

In seeking representation, it is very important that you find an attorney who is experienced in Social Security Disability law. Unlike many other types of the law, there are not a lot of attorneys who practice in this area. This is because it is not taught in law school, and most attorneys do not even know that it exists. Even among lawyers, most attorneys think of Social Security law as something that has to do with applying for retirement when you are 65. So, how do you find an attorney who practices Social Security Disability law?

NOSSCR

The best referral source is the *National Organization of Social Security Claimants' Representatives* (NOSSCR). This organization is the voice of Social Security Disability attorneys and acts as their lobbyist in Washington. As new procedures are proposed by the SSA, NOSSCR is the first to challenge any changes that may prove detrimental to claimants. NOSSCR also maintains a lawyer referral service. Upon contacting NOSSCR, you will be provided with the name of an attorney who has an office close to where you reside. You can then make an appointment with that attorney, who will provide a free consultation. Even if you decide to continue representing yourself, the attorney will answer any of your questions. NOSSCR's phone number is 800–431–2804. You can also email NOSSCR with a question by visiting its website at **www.NOSSCR.org**.

Phone Book Advertising

Phone book advertising lists attorneys by their specialty. In the attorney or lawyer section, look for the specialty heading "Social Security Disability" or "Disablity Law."

Online Referral Sources

When searching for an attorney online, begin by entering the following phrases in a search engine:

Social Security Disability Lawyers

Social Security Disability Attorneys

Social Security Disability Representation

Social Security Disability Law

The search engine will show you many lawyer directories. At that point, you can narrow your search by your state and city. Many law directory sites are also linked to the attorneys' profiles and websites. Some attorneys also have a form where you can provide information about your case. Specifically, you will be asked to provide the

> **Practical Point**
>
> When contacting an attorney through the phone book or online, make sure that Social Security Disability law represents a major part of the attorney's practice.

nature of your disability, the last day you worked, and what type of doctors you are seeking treatment with. The attorney will evaluate the information and then advise you if he or she can assist you.

A Word about Nonattorneys

The SSA allows nonattorneys to represent claimants from the initial application to the hearing stage, appearing before an administrative judge. It is probably the only type of law where a nonattorney can appear in court representing someone else.

As a result, there are claimant representatives who do provide legal representation. Even though these representatives cannot be listed in the attorney section of a phone book, many representatives do advertise on the Internet. If you are seeking the advice of a nonattorney, you should inquire as to his or her experience in taking cases to hearing before a judge. If, however, the representative's role is to only complete the paperwork, you should seek other assistance.

Note that the SSA will award the nonattorney the same fee as if he or she were an attorney.

A Word about Multistate Law Firms

Unlike other areas of the law where an attorney must be a member of that state bar to practice in a state court, Social Security Disability law is federal law. As a result, there are no restrictions for an attorney to accept a case in any state, regardless of whether he or she is admitted to practice in that state. So long as the attorney is in good standing with the bar where he or she is admitted (his or her license to practice law is active) and he or she has not been disciplined or disbarred, the attorney can accept your case. This allows attorneys to advertise on television and the Internet, offering their services.

For many cases, this does not create a problem so long as you are all right knowing that you may never meet the attorney directly but will be communicating with his or her office by phone, mail, email, and fax. The problem, however, occurs when a hearing is required and the attorney advises you that for practical reasons he or she cannot appear and is making arrangements with a local attorney to make the appearance.

As a claimant who is already stressed out by the appeal process, you may only feel more anxiety upon hearing such news. Immediately you will have concerns that the new attorney may not be familiar enough with your case and will not do a good job. For this reason alone, it is best to retain an attorney who practices in your community and who is familiar with the court process in your community.

The Fee Agreement

By rules set forth by the SSA, an attorney's agreement must be approved by the SSA before fees are awarded. Furthermore, there are two types of agreements used by attorneys who represent claimants seeking Social Security benefits—the fee agreement and the fee petition.

Fee Agreement

The fee agreement is the most common agreement used by attorneys. It expressly states that the attorney is accepting representation based on a contingency—that is, the attorney will be awarded a fee only if he or she is successful. Furthermore, all contingency fee agreements must state that the fee will be the lesser of 25% of all past-due benefits with a maximum recovery capped at what has been dictated by the SSA. At the time this book was written, the capped fee is $5,300, but that amount is subject to being revised by the SSA.

To illustrate, if you receive back benefits of $20,000, the attorney fee is 25% of that, or $5,000. Likewise, if you receive back benefits of $30,000, the attorney fee is $5,300, as $5,300 is less than 25% of 30,000.

The language of the contingency fee agreement must be approved by the SSA and all attorneys who regularly practice Social Security Disability law are well-aware of the requirements. The following is a typical contingency fee agreement.

LAW OFFICES OF BENJAMIN H. BERKLEY, A PLC
1440 NORTH HARBOR BLVD, STE 250
FULLERTON, CALIFORNIA 92835
TEL: 714.871.6440 FAX: 714.871.9714
E-mail: ben.berkley@berkleylaw.net

1. ATTORNEY'S FEES: I employ **Benjamin H. Berkley, a PLC,** to represent me before the Social Security Administration (SSA) in my disability case. If I win at any administrative level through the first administrative law judge (ALJ) decision after the date of this agreement, I agree that the attorney fee will be the lesser of twenty-five percent (25%) of all past-due benefits awarded to my family and me, or the dollar amount established pursuant to 42 U.S.C. §406(a)(2)(A), which is currently $5,300, but may be increased from time to time by the Commissioner of Social Security. I understand that my attorney has the right to seek administrative review to increase the amount of the fee set under the preceding sentence of this agreement; but if that happens, my attorney will not ask for a fee of more than 25% of total back benefits awarded in my case. If the first ALJ decision after the date of this agreement is a denial and my attorney agrees to appeal and I win my case later, the fee will be 25% of all back benefits awarded in my case. If I receive both Social Security Disability and SSI benefits, I understand that my total fee will not be more than 25% of all

past-due benefits, or no more than the limit set by 42 U.S.C. §406(a)(2)(A), if the limit applies. I understand that if I do not win benefits, then the attorney gets no fee.

2. SCOPE OF REPRESENTATION: I have employed my attorney to represent me in my Social Security Disability and/or SSI claim. I understand that my attorney does not represent me in any other public or private claim related to my disability, or with any other government agency or any insurance company unless separate arrangements, including a separate contract, have been made for representation on any other claim.

3. PAYMENT OF ATTORNEY'S FEES: I understand that the SSA will hold out 25% of past-due benefits and pay my attorney for his work on my case unless my attorney waives withholding and direct payment. If the attorney waives withholding and direct payment or if the SSA fails to withhold attorney's fees, I will pay my attorney promptly from the back benefits I receive.

4. I WILL PAY EXPENSES: In addition to fees, I agree to pay my attorney for reasonable expenses that he pays in my case. These may include medical records and reports, photocopying, travel expenses, transcript preparation, and the like. I will get a bill for expenses that show how and when my attorney spent the money. In a case in which I get benefits, I agree to pay my attorney back for these expenses as soon as I get a check for back benefits. I agree to pay expenses whether we win or lose.

5. I HAVE NOT BEEN PROMISED THAT I WILL WIN: My attorneys promised that he will do his best to help me. He did not promise me that I will win. I accept and approve this agreement.

Note that in the first paragraph, it states that the maximum fee is currently $5,300. Since the commissioner of the SSA has the authority to increase the fee, most attorneys include this language in the event that the attorney's fee is increased while your claim is pending.

Also, in paragraph 4, it states that the claimant is responsible for costs. Occasionally, a doctor will charge a fee to complete a report or a hospital will charge a copying fee for records. If this occurs, your attorney will bill you for these expenses. However, it is common practice to not require payment until you have received your first benefits check.

In addition to the contingency fee agreement, the SSA has developed Form SSA-1696, the Appointment of Representative, for you to complete when you are represented. This form, shown on page 252, must be signed by both you and the attorney.

Note that the form asks the attorney to state whether he or she has been disbarred or disciplined. This requires the attorney to state whether he or she is in good standing. Logically, however, I do not know why you would want this attorney to represent you if this box was checked.

LEGALLY SPEAKING

In the sample fee agreement, paragraph 3 states that the SSA will withhold the attorney's fee from your past benefits. As a result, once your benefits are approved, the attorney will receive his or her fee directly from the SSA. In most cases, this will occur. However, my colleagues and I can recite several cases in which the SSA failed to withhold the fee, sending the entire back benefits check directly to the claimant. If this does occur, it is your legal responsibility to pay your attorney directly. If you do not, the attorney will notify the SSA of the overpayment to you, which will cause your future benefits to be disrupted until the attorney is paid in full.

Practical Point

Before retaining an attorney, read the agreement very closely and compare it with the language in the agreement presented on page 249. If you have any questions about the agreement, ask the attorney before you sign it.

Social Security Administration
Please read the back of the last copy before you complete this form.

Form Approved
OMB No. 0960-0527

Name (Claimant) (Print or Type)	Social Security Number
Wage Earner (If Different)	Social Security Number

Part I　　　　　　　　**APPOINTMENT OF REPRESENTATIVE**

I appoint this person, _____ ,
(Name and Address)

to act as my representative in connection with my claim(s) or asserted right(s) under:

☐ Title II　☐ Title XVI　☐ Title XVIII　　☐ Title VIII
(RSDI)　　(SSI)　　(Medicare Coverage)　　(SVB)

This person may, entirely in my place, make any request or give any notice; give or draw out evidence or information; get information; and receive any notice in connection with my pending claim(s) or asserted right(s).

☐　I appoint, or I now have, more than one representative. My main representative
is _____ .
(Name of Principal Representative)

Signature (Claimant)	Address
Telephone Number (with Area Code)	Fax Number (with Area Code)	Date

Part II　　　　　　　　**ACCEPTANCE OF APPOINTMENT**

I, _____ , hereby accept the above appointment. I certify that I have not been suspended or prohibited from practice before the Social Security Administration; that I am not disqualified from representing the claimant as a current or former officer or employee of the United States; and that I will not charge or collect any fee for the representation, even if a third party will pay the fee, unless it has been approved in accordance with the laws and rules referred to on the reverse side of the representative's copy of this form. If I decide not to charge or collect a fee for the representation, I will notify the Social Security Administration. (Completion of Part III satisfies this requirement.)

Check one:　☐ I am an attorney.　☐ I am a non-attorney who is eligible to receive direct fee payment.

☐ I am not an attorney and I am ineligible to receive direct fee payment.

I have been disbarred or suspended from a court or bar to which I was previously admitted to practice as an attorney.　☐ YES　☐ NO

I have been disqualified from participating in or appearing before a Federal program or agency. ☐ YES ☐ NO

I declare under penalty of perjury that I have examined all the information on this form, and on any accompanying statements or forms, and it is true and correct to the best of my knowledge.

Signature (Representative)	Address
Telephone Number (with Area Code)	Fax Number (with Area Code)	Date

Part III (Optional)　　　　　　　　**WAIVER OF FEE**

I waive my right to charge and collect a fee under sections 206 and 1631(d)(2) of the Social Security Act. I release my client (the claimant) from any obligations, contractual or otherwise, which may be owed to me for services I have provided in connection with my client's claim(s) or asserted right(s).

Signature (Representative)	Date

Part IV (Optional)　　　　　　　　**WAIVER OF DIRECT PAYMENT**

by Attorney or Non-Attorney Eligible to Receive Direct Payment

I waive only my right to direct payment of a fee from the withheld past-due retirement, survivors, disability insurance or supplemental security income benefits of my client (the claimant). I do not waive my right to request fee approval and to collect a fee directly from my client or a third party.

Signature (Attorney or Eligible Non-Attorney (for Direct Payment) Representative)	Date

Form SSA-1696-U4 (1-2005) EF (1-2005)　　(See Important Information on Reverse)　　　　　　　**FILE COPY**
Destroy Prior Editions

The Fee Petition

The fee petition is not used as often as the fee agreement, as most attorneys are comfortable working on a contingency bases. However, if your case is very complicated, and the attorney feels that the fee that would be awarded if taken on a contingency would not be sufficient to compensate him or her for his or her time, your attorney may ask that you agree to representation with a fee being awarded based on the number of hours of work that he or she performs times an hourly rate. Under such an agreement, the attorney's fee could well exceed $5,300. In fee petition arrangements, the attorney must submit an itemization of all the time that he or she performed work and the hourly rate that he or she charges must be reasonable in comparison to what other attorneys charge in your community.

> ### LEGALLY SPEAKING
>
> Hourly rates that attorneys may charge differ from one part of the country to another. Therefore, it may be common for an attorney to charge $300 per hour in Boston, but a typical hourly rate for legal work is $200 in Tulsa. The SSA is aware of this and will adjust the attorney's bill based on what is common practice for the attorney's community.

SANDY'S STORY

Sandy, age 45, was diagnosed with multiple sclerosis. Her symptoms did not meet or equal the listings. She filed for benefits, was denied twice, and appeared before a judge, where she was denied again. She filed a new claim for benefits but retained an attorney when her initial application was denied. As she had not worked for the past four years, she no longer had enough work credits to qualify for SSDI. (See Chapter 3 for an explanation of work credits.) Her attorney told her that he would need to reopen the first case, as she had enough work credits when she made her first application. Because of the complexity of the issues and the additional work required, the attorney accepted representation based on a fee petition agreement.

Negotiating Attorney's Fees

Occasionally I am asked by a prospective client if I would agree to modify my fee and perhaps work on less than a 25% contingency. I will not say that I have never agreed to do so. There are always extenuating circumstances where I have to weigh a business decision against my client's financial circumstances.

However, the reasoning behind contingency fees was to allow someone who could not afford to pay an attorney an hourly rate the same access to the legal system as those people who could afford the hourly rate. Because the attorney was investing his or her time and office expenses to provide representation in consideration of taking a case where there were no guarantees, attorneys were willing to assume the risk in return for a percentage of the recovery.

In the practice of Social Security Disability law, an attorney's expenses must be covered each month regardless of whether he or she has won two cases or ten in the last month. Even though the fee is a contingency, not every case results in an attorney's fee of $5,300. In fact, if a case is won at the Request for Reconsideration, the fee is usually only a couple hundred dollars. Therefore, as the attorney cannot gauge with certainty where in the appeal process you will be awarded benefits, it is very unlikely that he or she would agree to a negotiation of the fee. Unless you are prepared to hear a polite but philosophical explanation of why the attorney cannot agree to your request, it is best to accept the agreement as proposed.

GLOSSARY OF ACRONYMS

The Social Security Administration uses abbreviations for almost every part of the application and appeals process. So that you know what SSA representatives are saying, the following are the most common acronyms used by the SSA:

AC	Appeals Council
ACE	average current earnings—factor used in workers' compensation offset calculations
ADL	activities of daily living
ALJ	administrative law judge
AME	average monthly earnings—benefit calculation factor
AOD	alleged onset of disability or alleged onset date
CE	consultative examination or examiner
COLA	cost of living adjustment
DAA	drug addiction and/or alcoholism
DED	Disability Evaluation division—the state agency
DDS	Disability Determination service—the state agency
DI	disabled individual—Title XVI

DIB   disability insurance benefits—Title II

DLI   date last insured—Title II disability insured status

DO   district office—local SSA field office

DOB   date of birth

DOE   date of entitlement—Title II

DOT   *Dictionary of Occupational Titles*

EOD   established onset of disability

ER   earnings record

FBM   first benefit month

FBR   federal benefit rate—Title XVI

HA   hearing assistant

ID   initial determination

LMER   last met earnings requirement—same as DLI

LSDP   lump-sum death payment

ME   medical expert—designated physician at OHA level

MRFC   mental residual functional capacity

OASDI   Old-Age, Survivor, & Disability Insurance—Title II

ODAR   Office of Disability, Adjudication, and Review (formerly OHA)

OHA   Office of Hearings and Appeals—former name of ODAR

OTR   on-the-record decision

PRW   past relevant work

RFC   residual functional capacity

RFH	Request for Hearing
RFR	Request for Reconsideration
SGA	substantial gainful activity
SSA	Social Security Administration
SSDI	Social Security Disability Insurance—Title II
SSI	Supplemental Security Income—Title XVI
SSID	Supplemental Security Income Disability
TWP	trial work period—Title II
UWA	unsuccessful work attempt
VE	vocational expert
WC	workers' compensation
WE	wage earner—Title II

Frequently Asked Questions

The following are some of the most common questions asked by claimants applying for Social Security Disability benefits.

1. What is the definition of disability used by Social Security?

Under the *Social Security Act*, *disability* means "inability to engage in any substantial gainful activity by reason of any medically determinable physical or mental impairment, which can be expected to result in death or has lasted or can be expected to last for a continuous period of not less than twelve months."

2. How many different types of Social Security Disability benefits are there?

There are five major types of Social Security Disability benefits:

1. Disability Insurance Benefits are the most important type of Social Security Disability benefits. It goes to individuals who have worked in recent years (five out of the last ten years in most cases) who are now disabled.

2. Disabled Widow's and Widower's Benefits are paid to individuals who are at least age 50 and become disabled within a certain amount of time after the death of their husband or wife. The late husband or wife must have worked enough under Social Security to be insured.

3. Disabled Adult Child Benefits go to the children of persons who are deceased or who are drawing Social Security Disability or retirement benefits. The child must have become disabled before age 22. For Disability Insurance Benefits, Disabled Widow's or Widower's Benefits, and Disabled Adult Child benefits, it does not matter whether the disabled individual is rich or poor. Benefits are paid based upon a Social Security earnings record.

4. Supplemental Security Income Benefits are paid to individuals who are poor and disabled. It does not matter for SSI whether an individual has worked in the past or not.

5. SSI Child's Disability Benefits are a variety of SSI benefits paid to children under the age of 18 who are disabled. The way in which disability is determined is a bit different for children.

3. How do I apply for Social Security Disability benefits?

The best way to file a Social Security Disability claim is to go to the nearest Social Security office in person and wait (often for a few hours) to see someone to file the claim in person. In the alternative, you may contact Social Security by telephone and arrange for a telephone interview to file the claim or file online at **www.socialsecurity.gov**.

4. I am disabled, but I have plenty of money in the bank. Do I have to wait until this money is gone before I apply for Social Security Disability benefits?

No. If you have worked in recent years or if you are applying for Disabled Widow's or Widower's benefits or Disabled Adult Child benefits, it does not matter how much money you have in the bank.

5. I used to work but now I cannot. I have now become sick. Can I get Social Security Disability benefits?

Possibly. If you have worked five out of the past ten years under Social Security before becoming disabled, you will have enough earnings to potentially qualify for Social Security Disability benefits. For individuals age 31 or less, the requirements are a little different, since such individuals have not had as long of a time to work.

6. How long do I have to wait after becoming disabled before I can file for Social Security Disability benefits?

Not even one day. You can file for Social Security Disability benefits on the very same day that you become disabled. Many individuals make the mistake of waiting months and even years after becoming disabled before filing a Social Security Disability claim. There is no reason to file a Social Security Disability claim if one has only a minor illness or one that is unlikely to last a year or more. However, an individual who suffers serious illness or injury and expects to be out of work for a year or more should not delay in filing a claim for Social Security Disability benefits.

7. I am still on sick leave from my employer. Can I file for Social Security Disability now or do I have to wait until the sick leave is exhausted?

No, you do not have to wait until the sick leave is exhausted. You should file for Social Security Disability benefits now, if you believe that you will be out of work for a year or more.

8. I got hurt on the job. I am drawing workers' compensation benefits. Can I file a claim for Social Security Disability benefits now or should I wait until the workers' compensation ends?

You do not have to wait until the workers' compensation ends and you should not wait that long. An individual can file a claim for Social Security Disability benefits while receiving workers' compensation benefits. It is best to file the Social Security Disability claim as soon as possible, because otherwise there may be a gap between the time the workers' compensation ends and the Social Security Disability benefits begin.

9. Can I get both workers' compensation and Social Security Disability benefits?

Yes. There is an offset, which reduces Social Security Disability benefits because of workers' compensation benefits paid, but in virtually all cases, there are still some Social Security Disability benefits to be paid. In a few states the offset works the other way—workers' compensation benefits are reduced because of Social Security Disability benefits.

10. How can I tell if I will be found disabled by Social Security?

Unless your disability is catastrophic (such as terminal cancer, a heart condition so bad that you are on a heart transplant waiting list, total paralysis of both legs, etc.), there is no easy way for you to tell whether you will be found disabled by Social Security. In the end, the decision of whether or not to apply for Social Security Disability benefits should not be based upon whether or not you feel that Social Security will find you disabled. Attorneys familiar with Social Security Disability can make predictions about who will win and who will lose, but even they can seldom be sure. You should decide whether or not to file for Social Security Disability based on your own belief about your condition. If you feel that you are disabled and are not going to be able to return to work in the near future, you should file for Social Security Disability benefits. If you are denied, you should consult with an attorney familiar with Social Security Disability to get an opinion as to the chances of success on appeal.

11. Can you receive Social Security Disability benefits for any disease if you cannot work?

In almost every case, no matter what the disease is, the answer is the same— "Maybe; it just depends on how badly you are affected by the disease." One example might be cancer. The word *cancer* is scary to anyone, but there are many cancers that can be treated and cured very quickly, with little or no lasting effect. On the other hand, of course, there are cancers that cause great suffering and ultimately death. The question in each individual case is, "How sick is this particular individual with cancer and how long is this person going to remain sick?" Almost without exception, the mere fact that an individual has a disease with a certain name does not guarantee that the individual either will or will not be found disabled. It all depends on how sick the person is.

12. Do you have to be permanently disabled to get Social Security Disability benefits?

No. You have to have been disabled for at least a year, be expected to be disabled for at least a year, or have a condition that can be expected to result in death within a year.

13. I have several health problems and although each problem by itself is not disabling, I am disabled by the combination of the problems. Can I get Social Security Disability benefits?

Social Security is supposed to consider the combination of impairments that an individual suffers in determining disability. Many, perhaps most, claimants for

Social Security Disability benefits have more than one health problem and the combined effects of all the health problems must be considered.

14. I got hurt in an automobile accident. I am disabled now, but I expect that I will be able to return to work after I recover. Should I file for Social Security Disability benefits?

If you expect to be out of work for a year or more on account of illness or injury, you should file for Social Security Disability benefits.

15. How does Social Security determine if I am disabled?

The Social Security Administration is supposed to gather your medical records and carefully consider all of your health problems, as well as your age, education, and work experience. In general, the SSA is supposed to decide whether you are able to do your past work. If the SSA decides that you are unable to do your past work, it is supposed to consider whether there is any other work you can do considering your health problems and your age, education, and work experience.

16. Who decides if I am disabled?

After you file a Social Security Disability claim, the case is sent to a disability examiner at the Disability Determination Services office in your state. This individual, working with a doctor, makes the initial decision on the claim. If the claim is denied and you request reconsideration, the case is then sent to another disability examiner at your state's office of Disability Determination Services, where it goes through much the same process. If a claim is denied at reconsideration, the claimant may then request a hearing. At this point, the case is sent to an administrative law judge who works for Social Security. The administrative law judge makes an independent decision upon the claim. This is the only level at which the claimant and the decision-maker get to see each other.

17. Why does Social Security consider my age in determining whether I am disabled?

Social Security has to consider age because that is what the *Social Security Act* requires. As people get older, they become less able to switch to different jobs to cope with health problems. A severe foot injury that might cause a 30-year-old person to switch to a job in which he or she can sit down most of the time might disable a 60-year-old person if he or she could not make the adjustment to a different type of work.

18. Is there a list of illnesses that Social Security considers disabling?

Not really. Because most types of illnesses can vary from minor to severe, there is no one simple list of illnesses that Social Security considers to be disabling. However, if an illness has reached a very severe level with certain medical hallmarks, Social Security will award benefits on the basis of medical considerations alone.

19. What can I do to improve my chances of winning my Social Security Disability claim?

Be honest and complete in giving information to Social Security about what is disabling you. Many claimants, for instance, fail to mention their psychiatric problems to Social Security because they are embarrassed about them. In almost all cases, individuals who were slow learners in school fail to mention this fact to Social Security, even though it can have a good deal to do with whether or not the Social Security Disability claim is approved. Beyond being honest and complete with Social Security, the most important thing that you can do is to just keep appealing and hire an experienced person to represent you. It is important to appeal because most claims are denied at the initial level but are approved at higher levels of review.

20. How do I find an attorney to represent me on my Social Security Disability claim?

The National Organization of Social Security Claimants' Representatives (NOSSCR) offers a referral service. You may call NOSSCR at 800–431–2804.

21. If I am approved for Social Security Disability benefits, how much will I get?

For disability insurance benefits, it all depends upon how much you have worked and earned in the past. For Disabled Widow's and Widower's Benefits, it depends upon how much the late husband or wife worked and earned. For Disabled Adult Child Benefits, it all depends upon how much the parent worked and earned. For all types of SSI benefits, there is a base amount that an individual with no other income receives. Other income that an individual has reduces the amount of SSI benefits that an individual can receive.

22. How far back will Social Security pay benefits if I am found disabled?

For Disability Insurance Benefits and for Disabled Widow's and Widower's Benefits, the benefits cannot begin until five months have passed after the person becomes disabled. In addition, benefits cannot be paid more than one year prior to the date of the claim. For a Disabled Adult Child, there is no five-month waiting period before benefits begin, but benefits cannot be paid more than six months prior to the date of the claim. SSI benefits cannot be paid prior to the start of the month following the date of the claim.

23. What do I do if Social Security denies my claim for Social Security Disability benefits?

First, do not be surprised. Only about 25% of Social Security Disability claims are approved at the initial level. If you are denied at the initial level, unless you have already returned to work or expect to return to work in the near future, you should appeal—that is, file a Request for Reconsideration.

24. Why does Social Security turn down so many claims for disability benefits?

There is no simple answer to this question. One reason is that there is no simple way to determine whether an individual is disabled. Most people who are disabled suffer from pain. There is no way of determining whether or not another individual is in pain, much less how much pain he or she is in. A second reason is that Social Security, over the years, has been more concerned with making sure that everyone who is receiving Social Security Disability benefits is "truly" disabled than with making sure that everyone who is disabled receives Social Security Disability benefits. An underlying reason is that Congress has always believed that, given a chance, many people will "fake" disability in order to get benefits.

25. I only want to get back the money I put into Social Security. Why do they make it so hard for me to get my own money back?

Actually, when you file a Social Security Disability claim, you are not trying to just get "your own money" back. The money that an individual may have paid into Social Security over the years would not last very long if that was all that an individual could draw from Social Security.

26. How long does it take to get a hearing on a Social Security Disability claim?

There is much variation around the country. However, the average wait is now more than a year.

27. What is the Social Security hearing like?

The hearings are fairly informal. The only people likely to be there are the judge, the judge's assistant operating a tape recorder, the claimant, and anyone else the claimant has brought with him or her. In some cases, the administrative law judge has a medical doctor or vocational expert present to testify at the hearing. There is no jury nor are there any spectators at the hearing. There is no attorney representing Social Security and trying to get the judge to deny the disability claim.

32. What are my chances of winning at a hearing?

Statistically, over half the claimants who have a Social Security Disability hearing win.

33. If the administrative law judge denies my claim, can I appeal any more?

Yes. You can appeal to the Appeals Council, which is still within Social Security.

34. What is the Appeals Council?

The Appeals Council exists to review administrative law judge decisions. The Appeals Council is located in Falls Church, Virginia, and neither the claimant nor the attorney sees the people at the Appeals Council who are working on the case.

35. Can I appeal a case beyond Social Security to the federal courts?

Yes. After being denied by the Appeals Council, it is possible for a claimant to file a civil action in the United States District Court, requesting review of the SSA's decision. A Social Security Disability claim can go all the way to the Supreme Court. Perhaps once every year or two years, the United States Supreme Court actually hears an appeal about a Social Security Disability case.

36. If I get on Social Security Disability benefits and get to feeling better and want to return to work, can I return to work?

Certainly you can return to work. The Social Security Administration wants individuals drawing disability benefits to return to work and gives them every encouragement to do so. For persons receiving Disability Insurance Benefits, Disabled Widow's and Widower's Benefits, and Disabled Adult Child Benefits, full benefits may continue for a year after an individual returns to work. Even thereafter, an individual who has to stop work in the following three years can get back on Social Security Disability benefits immediately without having to file a new claim. In SSI cases, things work a bit differently, but there is still a strong encouragement to return to work.

37. I know someone who is on Social Security Disability and he does not look a bit disabled. Why do they put all of these freeloaders on benefits?

When it comes to disability, looks can be very deceiving. There are many people who look quite healthy but who are quite disabled by anyone's standard. For instance, many individuals who suffer from very severe psychiatric illnesses are physically healthy and able to do things such as mow their yards.

38. I am disabled, but I have never worked at public work. Can I get Social Security Disability benefits?

If you are poor enough, you can qualify for Supplemental Security Income (SSI) if you are disabled, even if you have never worked in the past. It is also possible to qualify for Disabled Adult Child Benefits on the account of a parent if you became disabled before age 22, or for Disabled Widow's or Widower's benefits on the account of a late husband or wife.

39. I am a widow. I have not worked in public work in many years. I am disabled. Can I get Social Security Disability benefits?

If you are over 50 and became disabled within seven years after your husband or wife died or within seven years after you last drew mother's or father's benefits from Social Security, you can get Disabled Widow's and Widower's Benefits. Perhaps more importantly, if you are poor, you can draw Supplemental Security Income benefits no matter what age you are or when you became disabled.

40. I have a daughter who has been disabled by cerebral palsy since birth and has never been able to work. Can she get disability benefits from Social Security?

Very possibly. If the child is under 18 and you are poor enough, the child may be able to qualify for SSI child's disability benefits. If the child is over 18, she may be able to qualify for SSI disability benefits without regard to the income of her parents. If her father or mother is drawing Social Security benefits of some type or is deceased, the child may be eligible for Disabled Adult Child Benefits.

41. I am already on Social Security Disability benefits, but I am worried that my benefits will be stopped in the future. What are the chances of this happening?

Social Security is not supposed to cut off disability benefits for an individual unless his or her medical condition has improved. When the Social Security Administration reviews a case of someone already on Social Security Disability benefits, it continues benefits in the vast majority of cases. In recent years, the SSA has been doing few reviews to determine whether or not individuals already on Social Security Disability benefits are still disabled. This is changing—the SSA should be doing far more reviews in the next few years. However, the vast majority of individuals who are reviewed will see their Social Security Disability benefits continued.

42. My doctor says I am disabled, so why is the Social Security Administration denying my Social Security Disability claim?

The Social Security Administration's position is that it is not up to your doctor to determine whether or not you are disabled. It is up to the SSA, and it will make its own decision regardless of what your doctor thinks.

43. The Veterans Administration (VA) says I am disabled, so why is the SSA denying my Social Security Disability claim?

It is the SSA's position that VA decisions are not binding upon them. Social Security and the VA have very different standards for approving disability claims.

44. I am 60% disabled. Do I get 60% of my Social Security Disability benefits?

No. There are no percentages of disability in Social Security Disability determination. For purposes of Social Security Disability benefits, you are either disabled or not disabled. There are no percentages of disability, nor any percentages of disability benefits.

45. I am disabled by mental illness. Can mental illness serve as the basis for a Social Security Disability claim?

Yes. Mental illness is a frequent basis for awarding Social Security Disability benefits.

46. Will it help if I ask my Congressional representative to help me get Social Security Disability benefits?

Many Social Security Disability claimants become frustrated with claim delays and eventually ask their U.S. representative or senator to help. The local Congressional office typically will have staff members who are experienced with Social Security procedures and personnel. A *Congressional inquiry*, as it is called at the Social Security Administration, may help to get a stalled process moving again. Note that the inquiry will have no impact on how Social Security decides the outcome of the case.

47. How long does it take before the Social Security Administration makes a decision once I file a claim for Social Security Disability benefits?

In most cases, the SSA makes the first decision within four months.

48. How long does it take for the SSA to make a reconsideration determination on my Social Security Disability claim?

In most cases, the SSA makes the reconsideration determination within four months.

49. How long does it take for the SSA to act upon a request for Appeals Council review?

In most cases, it takes the SSA about a year, sometimes longer.

50. I am disabled. I need help with medical bills even more than I need a cash income. How do I get help with medical bills?

Getting help with medical bills is usually tied up with getting cash benefits; that is, you do not start getting help with medical bills until after you start getting the cash benefits, so you have to keep going with the Social Security Disability claim in order to get help with medical bills.

MEDICAL QUESTIONNAIRES

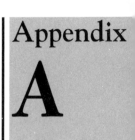

In developing your case, it is not enough that your doctor has provided you with copies of your treatment records and test results. In addition, you must develop the medical evidence so that it can be documented that you meet or equal the listings. Or, in the alternative, because of the demands of work, it must be substantiated that you would not be productive on the job.

Accordingly, medical questionnaires have been developed for both physical and mental impairments.

The physical questionnaire addresses your impairment and asks your doctor to comment about how long you can sit and stand, and whether there are work environments, such as those with dusty surroundings, that you should avoid exposure to.

The mental questionnaire addresses your ability to concentrate and follow instructions.

The questionnaires are presented here for your review and may be reproduced.

PHYSICAL RESIDUAL FUNCTIONAL CAPACITIES QUESTIONNAIRE

To: _____

Re: (Your Patient) _____

Date of Birth: _____

Social Security Number: _____

Dear Doctor _____,

As you are aware, I have applied for Social Security Disability benefits. Accordingly, I need your cooperation. Please answer the following questions concerning my impairments.

Please note that Part A of this form includes questions that relate to whether I have limitations in my ability to work. In Part B, you are asked to comment specifically on my diagnosis.

In addition to completing the form, I request that you attach all relevant treatment notes, radiologist reports, and laboratory and test results that assist in documenting my disability.

Thank you very much.

Part A: RESIDUAL FUNCTIONAL CAPACITY

1. Please indicate the date that you first saw this patient: _____

2. Please indicate the date that you last saw this patient: _____

3. Please indicate how often you see this patient: _____

4. What is the diagnosis?

_____

5. What is the prognosis?

_____

6. What are the symptoms?

_____

7. Are the symptoms severe enough that they would interfere with concentration?

_____

8. What are the clinical findings that support the diagnosis?

_____

9. What is the treatment?

_____

10. How long has this condition lasted?

_____

11. How does this condition affect daily activities?

_____

12. List of prescribed medications:

_____

_____

13. Please list any side effects the patient is experiencing and what implications any side effects would have on his or her ability to work.

_____

14. Is your patient a malingerer? Yes _____ No _____

15. Do emotional factors contribute to the severity of your patient's symptoms and functional limitations? Yes _____ No _____

16. How often during a typical workday is your patient's experience of pain or other symptoms severe enough to interfere with **attention and concentration** needed to perform even simple work tasks?

_____ Never _____ Rarely _____ Occasionally _____ Frequently _____ Constantly

(For this and other questions on this form, "rarely" means 1%–5% of an 8-hour working day; "occasionally" means 6%–33% of an 8-hour working day; and, "frequently" means 34%–66% of an 8-hour working day.)

17. To what degree can your patient tolerate work stress? Please circle:

Incapable of even low-stress jobs

Capable of low-stress jobs

Capable of moderate-stress jobs

Capable of high-stress jobs

18. As a result of your patient's impairments, estimate your patient's functional limitations if your patient were placed in a competitive work situation:

a. How many city blocks can your patient walk without rest or severe pain?

_____

b. Please circle the hours and/or minutes that your patient can sit at one time before the need to get up.

   Sit: 0 5 10 15 20 30 45 one hour two hours

c. Please circle the hours and/or minutes that your patient can stand at one time before needing to sit down, walk around, etc.

   Stand: 0 5 10 15 20 30 45 one hour two hours

d. Please indicate how long your patient can sit and stand/walk *total* in an 8-hour working day (with normal breaks).

   Sit/Stand/Walk

   less than 2 hours

   about 2 hours

   about 4 hours

   at least 6 hours

e. Does your patient need to include periods of walking around during an 8-hour working day? Yes _____ No _____

   1. If yes, approximately how *often* must your patient walk?

      Every: 1 5 10 15 20 30 45 60 90 minutes

   2. How *long* must your patient walk each time?

      1 2 3 4 5 6 7 8 9 10 11 12 13 14 15 minutes

f. Does your patient need a job that permits shifting positions *at will* from sitting, standing, or walking? Yes _____ No _____

g. Will your patient sometimes need to take unscheduled breaks during an 8-hour working day? Yes _____ No _____

If yes,1) how *often* do you think this will happen? _____

    2) how *long* (on average) will your patient have to rest before returning to work? _____

    3) on such a break will your patient need to lie down or sit quietly? Yes _____ No _____

h. With prolonged sitting, should your patient's leg(s) be elevated? Yes _____ No _____

If yes,1) how *high* should the leg(s) be elevated?

    2) if your patient had a sedentary job, *what percentage of time* during an 8-hour work day should the leg(s) be elevated? _____

i. While engaging in occasional standing/walking, must your patient use a cane or other assistive device? Yes _____ No _____

j. How many pounds can your patient lift and carry in a competitive work situation?

    less than 10 lbs: Never Rarely Occasionally Frequently

    10 lbs: Never Rarely Occasionally Frequently

    20 lbs: Never Rarely Occasionally Frequently

    50 lbs: Never Rarely Occasionally Frequently

k. Circle how often your patient can perform the following activities.

Stoop/Bend: Never Rarely Occasionally Frequently

Twist: Never Rarely Occasionally Frequently

Crouch: Never Rarely Occasionally Frequently

Squat: Never Rarely Occasionally Frequently

Climb: Never Rarely Occasionally Frequently

1. Does your patient have *significant limitations* in doing *repetitive* reaching, handling, or fingering? Yes _____ No _____

If yes, please indicate the percentage of time during an 8-hour workday at a competitive job that your patient can use hands/fingers/arms for the following repetitive activities:

Grasping/Turning/Twisting Objects _____%

Fingering and Fine Manipulations _____%

Reaching Overhead _____%

Please indicate if one hand or arm is more impaired in movement than the other.

_____

m. Circle the degree to which your patient should avoid the following:

Extreme Cold:
No Restrictions Avoid Concentrated Moderate All exposure

Extreme Heat:
No Restrictions Avoid Concentrated Moderate All exposure

High Humidity:

No Restrictions   Avoid Concentrated   Moderate   All exposure

Wetness:

No Restrictions   Avoid Concentrated   Moderate   All exposure

Dampness:

No Restrictions   Avoid Concentrated   Moderate   All exposure

Tobacco Smoke:

No Restrictions   Avoid Concentrated   Moderate   All exposure

Fragrances:

No Restrictions   Avoid Concentrated   Moderate   All exposure

Solvents/Cleaning Materials:

No Restrictions   Avoid Concentrated   Moderate   All exposure

Fumes/Odors:

No Restrictions   Avoid Concentrated   Moderate   All exposure

Dust:

No Restrictions   Avoid Concentrated   Moderate   All exposure

Chemicals:

No Restrictions   Avoid Concentrated   Moderate   All exposure

Other (insert) _____:

No Restrictions   Avoid Concentrated   Moderate   All exposure

n. Are your patient's impairments likely to produce "good days" and "bad days"? Yes _____ No _____

If yes, please circle, on the average, how many days per month your patient is likely to be absent from work as a result of the impairments or treatment:

Never

About one day per month

About three days per month

About four days per month

19. Please describe any other limitations (such as psychological limitations, limited vision, difficulty hearing, etc.) that would affect your patient's ability to work at a regular job on a sustained basis:

_____

_____

Dated _____

Name of Physician _____

Signature _____

Address _____

_____

PART B:

In addition to Part A, the following supplemental questionnaires direct your doctor to comment specifically about your diagnosis. Accordingly, if your disability includes impairments as a result of bladder incontinence, please have your doctor complete the following.

PART B: BLADDER INCONTINENCE

1. Diagnosis: _____

2. Prognosis: _____

3. List your patient's symptoms:

_____

_____

4. Identify the clinical findings and objective signs:

_____

5. Please estimate approximately how often your patient must urinate.

_____

6. Does your patient have urinary incontinence? Yes _____ No _____

If yes, a) please estimate approximately how often your patient is incontinent.

_____

    b) please estimate the volume of urine involved. _____

7. What makes your patient's urinary incontinence better?

_____

8. What makes your patient's urinary incontinence worse?

_____

PART B: LUPUS (SLE)

If your disability includes impairments as a result of systemic lupus, please have your doctor complete the following.

1. Does your patient fulfill the diagnostic criteria for systemic lupus erythematosus (SLE) identified by the American College of Rheumatology (namely, does the patient exhibit at any time at least four of the first eleven signs or symptoms listed in question #2 below)? Yes____ No____

2. Please circle any clinical findings, laboratory and test results, symptoms, and positive objective signs of your patient's impairment.

   1. Malar rash (over the cheeks)

   2. Discoid rash

   3. Photosensitivity

   4. Oral ulcers

   5. Nonerosive arthritis involving pain in two or more peripheral joints

   6. Cardiopulmonary involvement shown by pleurisy pericarditis

   7. Renal involvement shown by a) persistent proteinuria shown

      by: greater than 0.5 gm/day *or* 3+ on test sticks *or* cellular casts

   8. Central nervous system involvement shown by seizures and/or psychosis (in absence of drugs or metabolic disturbances known to cause such effects)

   9. Hemolytic anemia *or* leukopenia (white blood count below $4,000/mm^3$) *or* lymphopenia (below 1,500 lymphocytes/mm^3) *or* thrombocytopenia (below 100,000 platelets/mm^3)

10. Positive LE cell preparation *or* anti-DNA *or* anti-Sm anti-body *or* false positive serum test for syphilis known to be positive for at least six months.

11. Positive test for ANA at any point in time (in absence of drugs known to cause abnormality)

3. Please circle any of the following that apply:

Gastrointestinal complaints with:

Diarrhea or constipation
Abdominal cramping or pain
Nausea
Vomiting
Urinary urgency or incontinence
Severe fatigue
Severe weight loss
Severe fever
Severe malaise
Lupoid hepatomegaly
Muscle weakness
Episodes of paralysis due to central nervous system involvement
Easy bruising or changed blood clotting capacity
Lymph node enlargement
Frequent and persistent infections (including urinary tract)
Raynaud's phenomenon
Poor sleep
Sjogren's syndrome
Migraine headaches
Impaired muscle coordination
Avascular necrosis
Impaired vision
Dermal vasculititis
Peripheral neuropathy

Hair loss
Peritonitis

4. List any other signs or symptoms including any other renal or cardiopulmonary involvement:

_____

_____

PART B: CHRONIC FATIGUE SYNDROME

If your disability includes impairments as a result of chronic fatigue syndrome, please have your doctor complete the following.

1. Does your patient have chronic fatigue syndrome? Yes_____ No_____

2. Other diagnoses:

_____

3. Prognosis:

_____

4. Does your patient have unexplained persistent or relapsing chronic fatigue that is of new or definite onset (has not been lifelong), is not the result of ongoing exertion, and results in substantial reduction in previous levels of occupational, educational, social, or personal activities? Yes _____ No _____

If yes, please describe your patient's history of fatigue.

_____

_____

_____

_____

5. Have you been able to exclude any other impairments as a cause for your patient's fatigue such as HIV-AIDS, malignancy, parasitic disease (Lyme

Disease), psychiatric disease, rheumatoid arthritis, drug or alcohol addiction or abuse, side effects of medications, etc.? Yes _____ No _____

If yes, identify which impairments you have excluded and on what basis.

_____

_____

_____

_____

6. Does your patient have the *concurrent occurrence of four or more* of the following *symptoms*, all of which must have persisted or recurred during six or more consecutive months of illness and must not have predated the fatigue? Yes No

If yes, circle the symptoms:
   Self-reported impairment in short-term memory or concentration severe
      enough to cause substantial reduction in previous levels of occupational,
      educational, social or personal activities
   Sore throat
   Tender cervical or axillary lymph nodes
   Muscle pain
   Multiple joint pain without joint swelling or redness
   Headaches of a new type, pattern, or severity
   Unrefreshing sleep
   Postexertional malaise lasting more than 24 hours

7. Describe the treatment and response, including any side effects of medication that may have implications for working, e.g., drowsiness, dizziness, nausea, etc:

_____

_____

PART B: SPINAL NERVE ROOT COMPRESSION

If your disability includes impairments as a result of spinal nerve root compression, please have your doctor complete the following.

Please comment on whether your patient has the following impairment:

Disorders of the spine (e.g., herniated nucleus pulposus, spinal arachnoiditis, spinal stenosis, osteoarthritis, degenerative disc disease, facet arthritis, vertebral fracture), resulting in compromise of a nerve root (including the caudal equina) or the spinal cord. With:

A. Evidence of nerve root compression characterized by neuro-anatomic distribution of pain, limitation of motion of the spine, motor loss (muscle weakness or atrophy with associated muscle weakness) accompanied by sensory or reflex loss and, if there is involvement of the lower back, positive straight-leg raising test (sitting and supine).

   1. Does your patient have a disorder of the spine?
      Yes _____ No _____

If yes, please identify the disorder:

_____

_____

   2. Does your patient have evidence of nerve root compression?
      Yes _____ No _____

   3. Does your patient have neuro-anatomic distribution of pain?
      Yes _____ No _____

If yes, please describe:

_____

_____

4. Does your patient have any limitation of motion of the spine?
   Yes _____ No _____

If yes, indicate range of motion with the following movements:

   Flexion _____° Lateral bending—right _____°

   Extension _____° Lateral bending—left _____°

Other:

5. Does your patient have any muscle weakness?
   Yes _____ No _____

If yes, please identify the affected muscles and describe using the grading system 0 to 5:

_____

_____

Please circle any positive signs of motor loss:
   Inability to walk on heel   Inability to squat
   Inability to walk on toe   Inability to arise from squatting position

Atrophy: Indicate circumferential measurements of both thighs and lower legs or upper and lower arms as appropriate:

_____

6. Does your patient have sensory *or* reflex loss? Yes _____ No _____

If yes, please describe:

_____

_____

7. Is there involvement of the lower back? Yes _____ No _____

If yes, does your patient have a positive straight-leg raising test *both* sitting and supine? Yes _____ No _____

Please describe:

_____

8. If the clinical findings do not match *all* the findings required above, are your patient's combined impairments medically *equivalent* to the severity of conditions in the above listed impairment? Yes _____ No _____

If yes, please explain in detail how your patient's impairments are equivalent to the impairment listed above, with reference to *specific supporting clinical findings.*

_____

_____

PART B: LUMBAR SPINE

If your disability includes impairments as a result of a lumbar spine disorder, please have your doctor complete the following.

1. Diagnosis:

_____

_____

2. Prognosis:

_____

_____

3. Identify the *clinical findings* and laboratory and test results that show your patient's medical impairments:

_____

_____

4. Identify all of your patient's *symptoms,* including pain, insomnia, fatigue, etc.:

_____

_____

5. If your patient has pain:

    a. Characterize the nature, location, radiation, frequency, precipitating factors, and severity of your patient's pain:

    _____

    _____

    b. Identify any positive objective signs:

    _____ Reduced range of motion: _____

Description:

_____

_____

_____ Positive straight leg raising test: _____ Swelling

_____ Left at _____ ° Right at _____ ° _____ Muscle spasm

_____ Abnormal gait _____ Muscle atrophy

_____ Sensory loss _____ Muscle weakness

_____ Reflex changes _____ Impaired appetite or gastritis

_____ Tenderness _____ Weight change

_____ Crepitus _____ Impaired sleep

PART B: FIBROMYALGIA

If your disability includes impairments as a result of fibromyalgia, please have your doctor complete the following.

1. Does your patient meet the American College of Rheumatology criteria for fibromyalgia? Yes No

2. Other diagnoses:

_____

3. Prognosis:

_____

4. Identify the *clinical findings* and laboratory and test results that show your patient's medical impairments:

_____

5. Please circle all of your patient's symptoms:

Multiple tender points	Numbness and tingling
Nonrestorative sleep	Sicca symptoms
Chronic fatigue	Raynaud's phenomenon
Morning stiffness	Dysmenorrhea
Muscle weakness	Breathlessness
Subjective swelling	Anxiety
Irritable bowel syndrome	Panic attacks
Frequent, severe headaches	Depression
Female urethral syndrome	Mitral valve prolapse
Premenstrual syndrome (PMS)	Hypothyroidism
Vestibular dysfunction	Carpal tunnel syndrome
Temporomandibular joint	Chronic fatigue syndrome
dysfunction (TMJ)	

6. If your patient has pain:

Identify the location of pain including, where appropriate, an indication of right or left side or bilateral areas affected:

	RIGHT	LEFT	BILATERAL
_____ Lumbosacral spine	_____	_____	_____
_____ Cervical spine	_____	_____	_____
_____ Thoracic spine	_____	_____	_____

_____ Chest

_____ Shoulders

_____ Arms

_____ Hands/fingers

_____ Hips

_____ Legs

_____ Knees/ankles/feet

Describe the nature, frequency, and severity of your patient's pain.

_____

_____

7. Circle any factors that precipitate pain:

Changing weather
Fatigue
Movement/overuse
Cold
Stress
Hormonal changes
Static position

PART B: ARTHRITIS

If your disability includes impairments as a result of arthritis, please have your doctor complete the following.

1. Diagnoses:

_____

2. Prognosis:

_____

3. Identify all of your patient's symptoms, including pain, dizziness, fatigue, etc.:

_____

4. If your patient has pain, characterize the nature, location, frequency, precipitating factors, and severity of your patient's pain:

_____

_____

5. Identify any positive objective signs:

　　[ ] Reduced range of motion:　　　[ ] Trigger points

Joints affected: _____

　　[ ] Joint warmth　　　　　　　[ ] Redness
　　[ ] Joint deformity　　　　　　[ ] Swelling
　　[ ] Joint instability　　　　　　[ ] Muscle spasm
　　[ ] Reduced grip strength　　　[ ] Muscle weakness
　　[ ] Sensory changes　　　　　　[ ] Muscle atrophy
　　[ ] Reflex changes　　　　　　[ ] Abnormal gait
　　[ ] Impaired sleep　　　　　　[ ] Positive straight leg raising test
　　[ ] Weight change
　　[ ] Impaired appetite
　　[ ] Abnormal posture
　　[ ] Tenderness
　　[ ] Crepitus

Other clinical findings: _____

6. Do emotional factors contribute to the severity of your patient's symptoms and functional limitations? Yes _____ No _____

7. How often is your patient's experience of pain severe enough to interfere with attention and concentration?

_____ Never _____ Rarely _____ Occasionally _____ Frequently _____ Constantly

8. Identify any psychological conditions affecting pain:

_____ Depression   _____ Anxiety

_____ Somatoform disorder   _____ Personality disorder

_____ Psychological factors   Other: _____

PART B: MENIERE'S DISEASE

If your disability includes impairments as a result of Meniere's disease, please have your doctor complete the following.

1. Does your patient have Meniere's disease? Yes _____ No _____

2. Does your patient have:

   a) History of frequent attacks of balance disturbance?
      Yes _____ No _____

   b) Tinnitus?
      Yes _____ No _____

   c) Progressive hearing loss?
      Yes _____ No _____

If yes, is the hearing loss established by audiometry?
Yes _____ No _____

If no, explain how the hearing loss was established:

_____

_____

   d) Disturbed function of vestibular labyrinth demonstrated by caloric or
      other vestibular tests? Yes _____ No _____

If no, explain how the absence of vestibular tests or a negative vestibular test affects the diagnosis and assessment of severity of the impairment.

_____

_____

_____

_____

Please circle all symptoms associated with your patient's Meniere's attacks.

Vertigo   Visual disturbances

Nausea/vomiting   Mood changes

Malaise   Mental confusion/inability to concentrate

Photosensitivity   Fatigue/exhaustion

Sensitivity to noise

Other:

_____

4. What is the average frequency of your patient's Meniere's attacks?
   _____ per week _____ per month

5. How long does a typical attack last?_____

6. Does your patient always have a warning of an impending attack?
   Yes _____ No _____

If yes, how long is it between the warning and the onset of the attack?
   _____ minutes

Can your patient always take safety precautions when he/she feels an attack coming on? Yes _____ No _____

7. Do attacks occur at a particular time of the day?

Yes _____ No _____

If yes, explain when attack occurs:

_____

8. Are there precipitating factors such as stress, exertion, sudden movement, certain kinds of light, computer monitors, etc.?

Yes _____ No _____

If yes, explain:

_____

9. What makes your patient's attack worse?

Bright lights   Moving around

Noise   Other: _____

10.What makes your patient's attack better?

Lying in a dimly lit room   Cold/hot packs

Other: _____

11. What are the postattack manifestations? Circle those that apply.

Confusion   Severe headache

Exhaustion   Paranoia

Irritability   Other: _____

12. How long after an attack do these manifestations last?

_____

13. Describe the degree to which having an attack interferes with your patient's daily activities following an attack:

_____

14. Prognosis

_____

PART B: SLEEP DISORDERS

If your disability includes impairments as a result of sleep disorders, please have your doctor complete the following.

1. Diagnoses:

_____

2. Prognosis:

_____

3. Circle your patient's symptoms and signs:

Cataplexy	Sinus arrhythmia	Hypnogogic phenomenon
Insomnia	Extreme bradycardia	Ventricular tachycardia
Atrial flutter	Sleep paralysis	Obesity
Hypoxia	Cognitive problems	Hypercapnia
Automatic behavior	Sleep apnea	Pulmonary insufficiency
Excessive daytime sleepiness		

Other: _____

a. Does your patient exhibit recurrent daytime sleep attacks?
Yes _____ No _____

If yes,

1. Can these attacks occur suddenly and in hazardous conditions (e.g., driving, while exposed to heights, or while moving machinery)?
Yes _____ No _____

2. How often do these attacks typically occur:
_____ per day or _____ per week or _____ per month

3. How long does your patient typically sleep with each attack?_____

4. Identify situations that can precipitate attacks:

Quiet   Sleep disturbance   Exertion   Repetitive activity

Side effects of medications:

_____

5. If your patient is working and has a sleep attack, would the attack likely disrupt the work of coworkers or supervisors in your patient's vicinity?
Yes _____ No _____

4. Identify positive clinical findings and test results (e.g., multiple sleep latency test, MSLT, MWT, REM testing, EEG, polysomnographic studies, etc.):

_____

_____

5. If your patient experiences symptoms that interfere with the attention and concentration needed to perform even simple work tasks during a typical workday, please circle the frequency of interference:

Rarely   Occasionally   Frequently   Constantly

(For this and other questions on this form, "rarely" means 1% to 5% of an eight-hour working day; "occasionally" means 6% to 33% of an eight-hour working day; and, "frequently" means 34% to 66% of an eight-hour working day.)

6. If your patient was placed in a competitive job, identify those aspects of workplace stress that your patient would be unable to perform or be exposed to:

Public contact

Routine, repetitive tasks at a consistent pace

Detailed or complicated tasks

Strict deadlines

Close interaction with coworkers/supervisors

Fast-paced tasks (e.g., production line)

Exposure to work hazards (e.g., heights or moving machinery)

Other _____

7. Identify any side effects of medications that may have implications for working:

Drowsiness/sedation

Other _____

PART B: CARDIAC

If your disability includes impairments as a result of a cardiac disease, please have your doctor complete the following.

1. Diagnosis (with New York Heart Association functional classification)

_____

2. Identify any clinical findings and laboratory and test results.

_____

_____

3. Circle all of your patient's symptoms.

Chest pain   Edema

Anginal equivalent pain Nausea

Shortness of breath   Palpitations

Fatigue   Dizziness

Weakness   Sweatiness

Other _____

_____

4. If your patient has anginal pain, describe the frequency, nature, location, radiation, precipitating factors, and severity of this pain.

_____

_____

5. Does your patient have *marked limitation of physical activity,* as demonstrated by fatigue, palpitation, dyspnea, or anginal discomfort during ordinary physical activity, even though your patient is comfortable at rest?
Yes _____ No _____

6. What is the role of stress in bringing on your patient's symptoms?

_____

7. Do your patient's physical symptoms and limitations cause emotional difficulties such as depression or chronic anxiety? Yes _____ No _____

Please explain:

_____

_____

8. Do emotional factors contribute to the severity of your patient's subjective symptoms and functional limitations? Yes _____ No _____

9. How often is your patient's experience of cardiac symptoms (including psychological preoccupation with his/her cardiac condition, if any) severe enough to interfere with attention and concentration?

_____ Never _____ Rarely _____ Occasionally _____ Frequently _____ Constantly

10. Are your patient's impairments (physical impairments plus any emotional impairments) *reasonably consistent* with the symptoms and functional limitations described in this evaluation? Yes _____ No _____

If no, please explain:

_____

_____

11. Prognosis:

_____

PART B: CROHN'S & COLITIS

If your disability includes impairments as a result of Crohn's Disease or colitis, please have your doctor complete the following.

1. Diagnoses:

2. Prognosis:

_____

3. Identify your patient's symptoms:

[ ] chronic diarrhea   [ ] malaise
[ ] bloody diarrhea   [ ] fatigue
[ ] abdominal pain and cramping   [ ] mucus in stool
[ ] fever   [ ] ineffective straining at
[ ] stool (rectal tenesmus)   [ ] peripheral arthritis
[ ] weight loss   [ ] kidney problems
[ ] loss of appetite   [ ] _____

[ ] bowel obstruction   [ ] _____
[ ] vomiting   [ ] _____
[ ] abdominal distention   [ ] _____
[ ] fistulas
[ ] anal fissures

4. If your patient has pain, characterize the nature, location, frequency, precipitating factors, and severity of your patient's pain:

_____
_____

5. If aspects of your patient's impairment are episodic, describe the nature, precipitating factors, severity, frequency, and duration of the episodic aspects:

_____
_____
_____
_____

6. Identify the clinical findings and objective signs:

_____
_____
_____
_____

7. Describe the treatment and response including any side effects of medication that may have implications for working, e.g., drowsiness, dizziness, nausea, etc.:

_____
_____
_____

PART B: DIABETES

If your disability includes impairments as a result of diabetes, please have your doctor complete the following.

1. Diagnoses:

_____

2. Prognosis:

_____

3. Please circle all of your patient's *symptoms*:

fatigue	general malaise	nausea/vomiting
difficulty walking	muscle weakness	loss of manual dexterity
episodic vision blurriness	retinopathy	diarrhea
bladder infections	kidney problems	frequency of urination
bed wetting	hot flashes	sweating
infections/fevers	excessive thirst	psychological problems
abdominal pain	headaches	chronic skin infections

rapid heart beat/chest pain   swelling

dizziness/loss of balance   difficulty thinking/concentrating

insulin shock/coma   hyper/hypoglycemic attacks

sensitivity to light,   extremity pain and numbness
    heat, or cold

vascular disease/leg cramping

Other: _____   _____

4. Clinical findings:

_____

PART B: OBESITY

If your disability includes impairments as a result of obesity, please have your doctor complete the following.

1. Does your patient meet the criteria for the diagnosis of obesity as defined by the National Institutes of Health (a Body Mass Index* of 30.0 kg/m2)?

    Yes _____ No _____

BMI is the ratio of patient weight in kilograms to the square of the patient's height in meters.

2.   a. What is your patient's current weight? _____

    b. Current height? _____

3. Other Diagnoses:

    _____

4. Prognosis:

    _____

5. List your patient's symptoms, including pain, shortness of breath, fatigue, etc:

    _____

    _____

    _____

6. If your patient has pain, shortness of breath, fatigue, etc., characterize the nature, location, frequency, precipitating factors, and severity of your patient's symptoms:

    _____

    _____

7. Identify the clinical findings and objective signs:

    _____

8. Describe the treatment and response including any side effects of medication that may have implications for working, e.g., drowsiness, dizziness, nausea, etc:

_____

_____

PART B: SEIZURES

If your disability includes impairments as a result of seizures, please have your doctor complete the following.

1. Diagnoses:

_____

2. Does your patient have seizures? Yes _____ No _____

3. What type of seizures does your patient have?

_____

4. Are the seizures _____ generalized or _____ localized?

5. Is there loss of consciousness? Yes _____ No _____

6   a. What is the average frequency of your patient's seizures?
        _____ per week _____ per month

    b. What are the dates of the last three seizures?
        (1) _____ (2) _____ (3) _____

7. How long does a typical seizure last?

_____

8. Does your patient always have a warning of an impending seizure?
    Yes _____ No _____

    If yes, how long is it between the warning and the onset of the seizure?
    _____ minutes

Can your patient always take safety precautions when he/she feels a seizure coming on? Yes _____ No _____

9. Do seizures occur at a particular time of the day?
Yes _____ No _____

If yes, explain when seizures occur:
Other: _____

10. Are there precipitating factors such as stress or exertion?
Yes _____ No _____

If yes, explain:

_____

11. What sort of action must others take during and immediately after your patient's seizure?

Check all that apply.

_____ Put something soft under the head
_____ Remove glasses
_____ Loosen tight clothing
_____ Clear the area of hard or sharp objects
_____ After seizure, turn patient on side to allow saliva to drain from mouth
Other:_____

12. Please circle if any of the following result from the seizure.

Check those that apply.

Confusion   Severe headache
Exhaustion   Muscle strain
Irritability   Paranoia

Other: _____

13. How long after a seizure do any of the above last? _____

14. Describe the degree to which having a seizure interferes with your patient's daily activities following a seizure:

_____

_____

15. Does your patient have a history of injury during a seizure?
Yes _____ No _____

16. Does your patient have a history of fecal or urinary incontinence during a seizure? Yes _____ No _____

17. Is your patient compliant with taking medication?
Yes _____ No _____

If no, does it make a difference in the frequency of seizures?
Yes _____ No _____

18. Does your patient suffer any side effects of seizure medication?

Circle those that apply:

Dizziness	Double vision
Eye focusing problems	Coordination disturbance
Lethargy	Lack of alertness
Other: _____	

19. If your patient's blood levels of anticonvulsant medication have recently been at less than therapeutic levels, please explain why there has been difficulty controlling blood levels.

_____

_____

20. Does your patient suffer from ethanol-related seizures or ethanol/other drug abuse? Yes _____ No _____

21. Are your patient's seizures likely to disrupt the work of coworkers?
Yes _____ No _____

22. Will your patient need more supervision at work than an unimpaired worker?
Yes _____ No _____

23. Can your patient work at heights? Yes _____ No _____

24. Can your patient work with power machines that require an alert operator?
Yes _____ No _____

25. Can your patient operate a motor vehicle? Yes _____ No _____

26. Can your patient take a bus alone? Yes _____ No _____

27. Does your patient have any associated mental problems?

Circle those that apply:

Depression	Short attention span
Irritability	Memory problems
Social isolation	Behavior extremes
Poor self-esteem	
Other: _____	

28. Will your patient sometimes need to take unscheduled breaks during an 8-hour working day? Yes _____ No _____

If yes, 1)how often do you think this will happen?

_____

2) how long (on average) will your patient have to rest before returning to work?

_____

PART B: HEADACHES

If your disability includes impairments as a result of headaches, please have your doctor complete the following.

1. Diagnoses:

_____

2. Does your patient have headaches? Yes _____ No _____

   If yes, please characterize the nature, location, and intensity/severity (mild to severe) of your patient's headaches: _____

3. Please circle any other symptoms associated with your patient's headaches:

   Vertigo   Visual disturbances
   Nausea/vomiting   Mood changes
   Malaise   Mental confusion/inability to concentrate
   Photosensitivity
   Other:_____

4. What is the approximate frequency of headaches?

_____

5. What is the approximate duration of your patient's headaches?

_____

6. What triggers your patient's headaches?

   Alcohol   Lack of sleep
   Bright lights   Menstruation
   Hunger   Weather changes
   Vigorous exercise
   Food—identify: _____
   Noise _____
   Stress _____
   Strong odors _____
   Other: _____

7. What makes your patient's headaches worse?

Bright lights   Moving around
Coughing, straining/bowel   Noise
   movement

8. What makes your patient's headaches better?

Lying in a dark room
Finger pressure/massage
Cold/hot packs
Other: _____

9. Identify any positive test results and objective signs of your patient's headaches.

Weight loss   X-ray
Tenderness   MRI
Impaired sleep   CT scan
Impaired appetite or gastritis   EEG
Other: _____

10. Identify any impairment(s) that could reasonably be expected to explain your patient's headaches.

Anxiety/tension   Intracranial infection or tumor
Cerebral hypoxia   Migraine
Cervical disc disease   Seizure disorder
History of head injury   Sinusitis
Hypertension   Substance abuse
Other: _____

11. Describe the treatment and response:

_____

12. List your patient's current medications used for control/treatment of headaches.

_____

13. Identify side effects of these medications experienced by your patient.

_____

14. Prognosis:

_____

PART B: STROKE

If your disability includes impairments as a result of a stroke, please have your doctor complete the following.

1. Did your patient have a stroke? Yes _____ No _____

    If yes, type of stroke: _____

2. Other diagnoses:

_____

_____

3. Prognosis:

_____

4. Circle all of your patient's symptoms:

Balance problems	Vertigo/dizziness
Poor coordination	Headaches
Loss of manual dexterity	Difficulty remembering
Weakness	Confusion
Slight paralysis	Depression
Unstable walking	Emotional lability

Falling spells   Personality change
Difficulty solving problems   Pain
Problems with judgment   Nausea
Fatigue   Shaking tremor
Bladder problems
Speech/communication difficulties
Problems with judgement
Numbness, tingling, or other sensory distrubance problems
Double or blurred vision/partial or complete blindness
Other: _____

5. Clinical findings:

_____

_____

6. Does your patient have significant and persistent disorganization of motor function in two extremities resulting in sustained disturbance of gross and dexterous
movement or gait and station? Yes _____ No _____

7. Do emotional factors contribute to the severity of your patient's symptoms and
functional limitations? Yes _____ No _____

8. Are your patient's impairments (physical impairments plus any emotional
impairments) *reasonably consistent* with the symptoms and functional limitations described in this evaluation? Yes _____ No _____

9. How often is your patient's experience of pain, fatigue, or other symptoms
severe enough to interfere with attention and concentration?

PART B: MULTIPLE SCLEROSIS

If your disability includes impairments as a result of multiple sclerosis, please have your doctor complete the following.

1. Does your patient have multiple sclerosis? Yes _____ No _____

    If yes, how was this diagnosis made? _____

2. Prognosis:

    _____

3. Please circle all of your patient's symptoms:

    Fatigue   Pain
    Balance problems   Difficulty remembering
    Poor coordination   Depression
    Weakness   Emotional ability
    Paralysis   Difficulty solving problems
    Unstable walking   Problems with judgment
    Involuntary rapid eye movement   Shaking tremor
    Bladder problems   Sensitivity to heat
    Bowel problems
    Numbness, tingling, or other sensory disturbance
    Double or blurred vision/partial or complete blindness
    Increased muscle tension (spasticity)
    Speech/communication difficulties
    Other: _____

4. Does your patient have significant and persistent disorganization of motor function in two extremities resulting in sustained disturbance of gross and dexterous movement or gait and station? Yes _____ No _____

    If yes, please describe the degree of interference with locomotion and/or interference with the use of fingers, hands, and arms:

    _____

    _____

5. Does your patient have significant reproducible fatigue of motor function with substantial muscle weakness on repetitive activity, demonstrated on physical examination, resulting from neurological dysfunction in areas of the central nervous system known to be pathologically involved with the multiple sclerosis process? Yes _____ No _____

   If yes, describe the degree of exercise and the severity of the resulting muscle weakness:

   _____

   _____

6. a. During the past year what are the approximate dates of exacerbations of multiple sclerosis? _____

   b. Of these exacerbations, circle the ones that would prevent *any* work for *more than one month*.

7. Does your patient complain of a type of fatigue that is best described as lassitude rather than fatigue of motor function?
   Yes _____ No _____

   If yes, is this kind of fatigue complaint typical of MS patients?
   Yes _____ No _____

8. Do emotional factors contribute to the severity of your patient's symptoms and functional limitations? Yes _____ No _____

PART B: MYASTHENIA GRAVIS

If your disability includes impairments as a result of myasthenia gravis, please have your doctor complete the following.

1. Does your patient have myasthenia gravis? Yes _____ No _____

If yes, how was this diagnosis made?

_____

_____

2. Prognosis:

_____

3. Identify all of your patient's symptoms:

Fatigability of muscles	Difficulty swallowing
Limb weakness	Difficulty breathing
General fatigue	Diarrhea
Double vision	Stomach cramping
Drooping upper eyelid	Facial muscle weakness
Difficulty speaking	Nasal regurgitate of food
Alteration in voice	Choking

Other: _____

4. Do your patient's symptoms and signs fluctuate in intensity over the course of hours to days? Yes _____ No _____

5. Does your patient have significant difficulty with speaking, swallowing, or breathing *while on prescribed therapy?* Yes _____ No _____

If yes, please describe the degree of difficulty:

_____

6. Does your patient have significant motor weakness of muscles of extremities on repetitive activity against resistance *while on prescribed therapy?*
Yes _____ No _____

If yes, describe the repetitive activity and the severity of the resulting muscle weakness:

_____

_____

7. Do emotional factors contribute to the severity of your patient's symptoms and functional limitations? Yes _____ No _____

8. Are your patient's impairments (physical impairments plus any emotional impairments) *reasonably consistent* with the symptoms and functional limitations described in this evaluation? Yes _____ No _____

   If no, please explain:

   _____

9. How often is your patient's experience of fatigue or other symptoms severe enough to interfere with attention and concentration?

   Never   Rarely   Occasionally   Frequently   Constantly

10. To what degree can your patient tolerate work stress?

    Incapable of even low-stress jobs
    Capable of low-stress jobs
    Capable of moderate-stress jobs
    Capable of high-stress jobs

    Please explain the reasons for your conclusion:

    _____

11. Have your patient's impairments lasted or can they be expected to last at least twelve months? Yes _____ No _____

12. What is the earliest date that the description of *symptoms and limitations* in this questionnaire applies?

    _____

MENTAL RESIDUAL FUNCTIONAL CAPACITIES QUESTIONNAIRE

If your disability includes impairments as a result of a mental disability, please have your doctor complete the following.

1. DSM-IV Multiaxial Evaluation:

Axis I: _____   Axis IV: _____

Axis II: _____   Axis V: Current GAF: _____

Axis III: _____   Highest GAF past year: _____

2. Treatment and response:

_____

3. Describe the *clinical findings*, including results of the mental status examination, that demonstrate the severity of your patient's mental impairment and symptoms:

_____

_____

_____

4. Prognosis:

_____

5. Circle your patient's signs and symptoms:

Anhedonia or pervasive loss of interest in almost all activities

Intense and unstable interpersonal relationships and impulsive and damaging behavior

Appetite disturbance with weight change

Disorientation to time and place

Decreased energy	Perceptual or thinking disturbances
Thoughts of suicide	Hallucinations or delusions
Blunt, flat, or inappropriate affect	Hyperactivity
Feelings of guilt or worthlessness	Motor tension
Impairment in impulse control	Catatonic or other grossly disorganized behavior
Poverty of content of speech	Emotional lability
Generalized persistent anxiety	Flight of ideas
Somatization unexplained by organic disturbance	Manic syndrome
Mood disturbance	Deeply ingrained, maladaptive patterns of behavior
Difficulty thinking or concentrating	Inflated self-esteem
Recurrent and intrusive recollections of a traumatic experience, which are a source of marked distress	Unrealistic interpretation of physical signs or sensations associated with the preoccupation or belief that one has a serious disease or injury
Psychomotor agitation or retardation	Loosening of associations
Pathological dependence, passivity, or agressivity	Illogical thinking
Persistent disturbances of mood or affect	Vigilance and scanning

Persistent nonorganic disturbance of vision, speech, hearing, use of a limb, movement and its control, or sensation

Pathologically inappropriate suspiciousness or hostility

Change in personality

Pressures of speech

Apprehensive expectation

Easy distractibility

Paranoid thinking or inappropriate suspiciousness

Autonomic hyperactivity

Recurrent obsessions or compulsions that are a source of marked distress

Memory impairment—short, intermediate, or long-term

Seclusiveness or autistic thinking

Sleep disturbance

Substance dependence

Oddities of thought, perception, speech, or behavior

Incoherence

Decreased need for sleep

Emotional withdrawal or isolation

Loss of intellectual ability of 15 IQ points or more

Psychological or behavioral abnormalities associated with a dysfunction of the brain with a specific organic factor judged to be etiologically related to the abnormal mental state and loss of previously acquired functional abilities

Recurrent severe panic attacks manifested by a sudden unpredictable onset of intense apprehension, fear, terror, and a sense of impending doom occurring on the average of at least once a week

Bipolar syndrome with a history of episodic periods manifested by the full symptomatic picture of both manic and depressive syndromes (and currently characterized by either or both syndromes)

A history of multiple physical symptoms (for which there are no organic findings) of several years' duration beginning before age 30 that have caused the individual to take medicine frequently, see a physician often, and alter life patterns significantly

Persistent irrational fear of a specific object, activity, or situation that results in a compelling desire to avoid the dreaded object, activity, or situation

Involvement in activities that have a high probability of painful consequences that are not recognized

6. To determine your patient's ability to do *work-related activities on a day-to-day basis in a regular work setting*, please give us your opinion **based on your examination** of how your patient's mental/emotional capabilities are affected by the impairment(s). Consider the medical history, the chronicity of findings (or lack thereof), and the expected duration of any work-related limitations, but not your patient's age, sex, or work experience.

Seriously limited, but not precluded means the ability to function in this area is seriously limited and less than satisfactory, but not precluded in all circumstances.

Unable to meet competitive standards means your patient cannot satisfactorily perform this activity independently, appropriately, effectively, and on a sustained basis in a regular work setting.

No useful ability to function, an extreme limitation, means your patient cannot perform this activity in a regular work setting.

I.	MENTAL ABILITIES AND APTITUDES NEEDED TO DO UNSKILLED WORK	Unlimited or very good	Limited but satisfactory	**Seriously limited, but not precluded**	**Unable to meet competitive standards**	**No useful ability to function**
	Remember work-like procedures					
	Understand and remember very short and simple instructions					
	Carry out very short and simple instructions					
	Maintain attention for two-hour segment					
	Maintain regular attendance and be punctual within customary, usually strict tolerances					
	Sustain an ordinary routine without special supervision					
	Work in coordination with or proximity to others without being unduly distracted					
	Make simple work-related decisions					
	Complete a normal workday and workweek without interruptions from psychologically-based symptoms					
	Perform at a consistent pace without an unreasonable number and length of rest periods					
	Ask simple questions or request assistance					
	Accept instructions and respond appropriately to criticism from supervisors					
	Get along with coworkers or peers without unduly distracting them or exhibiting behavioral extremes					
	Respond appropriately to changes in a routine work setting					
	Deal with normal work stress					
	Be aware of normal hazards and take appropriate precautions					

Explain limitations falling in the three most limited categories (identified by **bold type**) and include the medical/clinical findings that support this assessment:

_____

_____

II.	MENTAL ABILITIES AND APTITUDES NEEDED TO DO SEMISKILLED AND SKILLED WORK	Unlimited or very good	Limited but satisfactory	Seriously limited, but not precluded	Unable to meet competitive standards	No useful ability to function
	Understand and remember detailed instructions					
	Carry out detailed instructions					
	Set realistic goals or make plans independently of others					
	Deal with stress of semiskilled and skilled work					

Explain limitations falling in the three most limited categories (identified by **bold type**) and include the medical/clinical findings that support this assessment:

III.	MENTAL ABILITIES AND APTITUDE NEEDED TO DO PARTICULAR TYPES OF JOBS	Unlimited or very good	Limited but satisfactory	Seriously limited, but not precluded	Unable to meet competitive standards	No useful ability to function
	Interact appropriately with the general public					
	Maintain socially appropriate behavior					
	Adhere to basic standards of neatness and cleanliness					
	Travel in unfamiliar places					
	Use public transportation					

Explain limitations falling in the three most limited categories (identified by **bold type**) and include the medical/clinical findings that support this assessment:

7. Does your patient have a low IQ or reduced intellectual functioning?

Yes _____ No _____

Please explain (with reference to specific test results):

_____

_____

8. Does the psychiatric condition exacerbate your patient's experience of pain or any other physical symptom? Yes _____ No _____